Analecta Gregoriana

Cura Pontificiae Universitatis Gregorianae edita

Vol. LXXV
SERIES FACULTATIS THEOLOGICAE
Sectio A (n. 13)

GRACE AND ORIGINAL JUSTICE

ACCORDING TO ST. THOMAS

by

William A. VAN ROO, S. J.

ROMAE
APUD AEDES UNIVERSITATIS GREGORIANAE
1955

IMPRIMI POTEST

Romae, die 4 Februarii 1955

P. PETRUS M. ABELLÁN, S. I.
Rector Universitatis

IMPRIMATUR

Ex Vicariatu Urbis, die 7 Maii 1955

† ALOYSIUS TRAGLIA
Archiep. Caesarien., Vic. gerens

TYPIS PONTIFICIAE UNIVERSITATIS GREGORIANAE - ROMAE

TABLE OF CONTENTS

INTRODUCTION

This study was presented originally as a doctoral dissertation entitled *Formal and Efficient Causality in Saint Thomas' Teaching on Original Justice*. That title, which seems a bit too unwieldy, had the merit of indicating exactly the problem to be solved. I have attempted to find a definitive answer to a highly controversial question concerning St. Thomas' theology of original justice, the question regarding the relation of sanctifying grace to that justice.

Though there was some conflict of interpretations among the earlier followers of St. Thomas [1], the controversy was sharply focussed three decades ago on the occasion of the works of Martin, Bittremieux, and Kors [2].

According to the interpretations elaborated especially by the latter two authors, original justice was completely distinct from sanctifying grace. Grace is strictly a personal gift, supernatural, the efficient cause of original justice. The rectitude of original justice was a gift to the whole of human nature, a rectitude *in linea naturae*, a disposition for grace in the state of innocence. Against this interpretation, many theologians maintained that grace was a part of original justice, its formal cause,

---

[1] Cf. A. MICHEL, « Justice originelle», *Dictionnaire de Théologie Catholique,* vol. VIII[2], cols. 2038-2042.

[2] RAYMOND M. MARTIN, O. P., «La Doctrina sobre el Pecado Original en la *Summa contra Gentiles* », *La Ciencia Tomista* 10 (1914-1915) 389-400. Cf. also his notes in « Bulletin de théologie spéculative», *Revue des sciences phil. et théol.* 10 (1921) 646; 11 (1922) 705.

J. BITTREMIEUX, «La Distinction entre la justice originelle et la grâce sanctifiante d'après saint Thomas d'Aquin », *Revue Thomiste* 26 (1921) 121-150; « Het geestelijk leven en de oorspronkelijke gerechtigheid », *Ons Geloof* 8 (1922) 112-121.

J. B. KORS, O. P., *La Justice primitive et le péché originel d'après S. Thomas,* Le Saulchoir, Kain, 1922.

and that according to St. Thomas grace was both a personal gift and a gift to the nature. Grace and original justice, therefore, were distinct as part from whole, with the distinction now commonly called an inadequate real distinction [3].

Several years of controversy did not settle the issue. Dom Lottin, in his study of the theology of original sin according to Albert the Great, Bonaventure, and St. Thomas, published in nineteen hundred forty, regarded Kors' work as the classic on the question, and followed his interpretation of St. Thomas' theology of original justice [4]. The following year, Father Cyril O. Vollert, S. J. balanced the arguments of both sides and de-

---

[3] A. MICHEL, « La Grâce sanctifiante et la justice originelle », *Revue Thomiste* 26 (1921) 424-430. J. VAN DER MEERSCH, « De distinctione inter justitiam originalem et gratiam sanctificantem », *Collationes Brugenses* 22 (1922) 424-431 ; 506-517 ; « Het geestelijk leven en de oorspronkelijke gerechtigheid », *Ons Geloof* 8 (1922) 455-466. J. NAULAERTS, « Quid est justitia originalis? », *Vie diocésaine* 12 (1923) 550-554. J. STUFLER, S. J., « La justice primitive et le péché originel d'après S. Thomas ... Par J. B. Kors, O. P. » (review) *Zeitschrift für katholische Theologie* 47 (1923) 77-82. G. HUARTE, S. J., « De distinctione inter justitiam originalem et gratiam sanctificantem », *Gregorianum* 5 (1924) 183-207. R. GARRIGOU-LAGRANGE, O. P., « Utrum gratia sanctificans fuerit in Adamo dos naturae an donum personae tantum », *Angelicum* 2 (1925) 133-144 ; cf. *De Deo Trino et Creatore* (Turin-Rome, 1944) pp. 421-428. E. HUGON, O. P., « De gratia primi hominis », *Angelicum* 4 (1927) 361-381. L. TEIXIDOR, S. J., « Una cuestión lexicográfica : El uso de la palabra JUSTICIA ORIGINAL, en Santo Tomás de Aquino », *Estudios eclesiásticos* 6 (1927) 337-376 ; 8 (1929) 23-41. A. FERNÁNDEZ, O. P., « Justitia originalis et gratia sanctificans juxta D. Thomam et Cajetanum », *Divus Thomas* (Piacenza) 34 (1931) 129-146 ; 241-260. TH. DEMAN, O.P., (review of Gaudel's article « Péché originel » in DTC) *Bulletin Thomiste* (1936) 625-632, esp. 631-632.
Among the early supporters of the Martin-Bittremieux-Kors interpretation are the following: A. D'ALÈS, S. J., « Justice primitive et péché originel, d'après un livre récent », (a summary and favorable judgment of Kors' book) *Nouvelle Revue Théologique* 50 (1923) 416-427. N. SANDERS, O. F. M., « De oorspronkelijke gerechtigheid en de erfzonde volgens S. Thomas », *De Katholiek* (1923) 400-410. J. COPPENS, « Une controverse récente sur la nature du péché originel », *Ephemerides Theologicae Lovanienses* 1 (1924) 185-191. A. VAN HOVE, « Heiligmakene gratie en oorspronkelijke gerechtigheid », *Collectanea Mechliniensia* 4 (1930) 423-435 ; *De Erfzonde* (Brussels, 1936) 140-147. A. GAUDEL, « Péché originel », *Dictionnaire de Théologie Catholique* XII[1], cols. 275-606.
[4] O. LOTTIN, O. S. B., « Le péché originel chez Albert le Grand, Bonaventure, et Thomas d'Aquin », *Recherches de Théologie Ancienne et Médiévale* 12 (1940) 295, note 49 ; 304-305 ; 318.

cided that the opponents of Martin, Bittremieux, and Kors had prevailed[5]. A few years later Canon Van Hove reiterated his support of the Martin-Bittremieux-Kors interpretation[6]. Finally, after a few more refutations of that theory had been registered[7], Dom Lottin has re-published his study without any change in his position[8].

Nor does it seem that the refutations which have been made are likely to end the appeal of this interpretation. Thanks especially to Kors' book in the *Bibliothèque Thomiste*, Bishop Gaudel's impressive article on original sin in the *Dictionnaire de Théologie Catholique*, and Lottin's scholarly studies, the theory is firmly established in theological literature. Moreover, the refutations have been based on particular texts, and the clash has been between two sets of texts apparently clearly opposed. Nowhere does this clash seem more striking than in a single article of the *De Malo*[9]. The body of the article has supplied one side with its strongest text. The answer to an objection has provided one of the clearest texts for the opposite side.

Since there is this apparent clash of particular texts, it seems impossible to settle the controversy on the basis of selec-

---

[5] C. O. VOLLERT, S. J., « Saint Thomas on Sanctifying Grace and Original Justice », *Theological Studies* 2 (1941) 369-387. Cf. also, « The Two Senses of Original Justice in Medieval Theology », *Theological Studies* 5 (1944) 3-23; *The Doctrine of Hervaeus Natalis on Primitive Justice and Original Sin* (*Analecta Gregoriana* 42, series Fac. Theol. B, n. 18) Rome, 1947, pp. 11-44.

[6] A. VAN HOVE, *Tractatus de Deo Creante et Elevante* (Mechliniae, 1944), 256-261.

[7] MELCHIOR DE SE. MARIE, O. C. D., « La justice originelle selon les Salmanticenses et saint Thomas d'Aquin », *Ephemerides Carmeliticae* 2 (1948) 265-304. E. J. FITZPATRICK, *The Sin of Adam in the Writings of St. Thomas Aquinas*, (dissertation: Mundelein, St. Mary of the Lake Seminary, U.S.A., 1950) pp. 21 ff. C. BOYER, S. J., *De Deo Creante et Elevante*[4] (Romae, 1948) pp. 300-308. Cf. also the simple exposition of the more common interpretation in M.-M. LABOURDETTE, O. P., *Le péché originel et les origines de l'homme* (Paris, 1953) pp. 67-69.

[8] O. LOTTIN, O. S. B., *Psychologie et morale aux XIIe et XIIIe siècles*. Tome V, Problèmes de morale, troisième partie, I (Louvain, 1954) esp. pp. 254-257; 271. Neither here nor in the original article does Dom Lottin mention the controversy over the Kors interpretation. He cites only Kors, Gaudel, Martin, Bittremieux, and R. BERNARD, O. P., *S. Thomas d'Aquin. Somme théologique*, Le péché, t. II, 1931, éd. de la Revue des Jeunes, pp. 321-352 (p. 245, note 1).

[9] *De Malo* q. 5, a. 1 resp. et ad 13.

ted texts, or even of all the texts directly concerned with original justice and original sin. Both Bittremieux and Kors have
urged the necessity of interpreting the texts in the light of the
clear principles of the theology of St. Thomas. For Bittremieux
this means above all interpreting texts to agree with the general
teaching on the distinction between grace as a gift to the person
and original justice as a gift to the whole nature. Kors devotes
a long chapter to developing his interpretation of St. Thomas'
teaching on nature and grace, as a preparation for the proper
understanding of the definitive doctrine on original justice. Both
efforts, however, fail to explain many of the texts, and as the
matter stands now no one has given a satisfactory account of
all the texts involved.

In the present study I shall endeavor to determine as exactly as possible St. Thomas' position. Though the task may seem
hopeless after so many efforts have failed to resolve the controversy, I believe that a wider study of the texts of St. Thomas
does provide the basis for a definite answer. This conviction
is not a matter of principle, rejecting *a priori* the possibility
of an inconsistency in the theology of St. Thomas. Rather
it is the result of an effort not only to find and consider all the
texts which directly bear on original justice, but also to follow
the many hints which St. Thomas gives to relate the problem
to the rest of his theology. When there is a question of rectitude, of the role of grace and the virtues, of formal and efficient causality, it is necessary to consider the analogies which
St. Thomas himself suggests, to deal with the theology of original justice not as an isolated, utterly unique theory, but as
a part of his whole theology, in which his general principles
regarding potencies and virtues, and formal and efficient causality are functioning. Where a phase of the doctrine is not
developed explicitly, we may find more details in his treatment
of an analogous case. Thus we can determine whether original justice was a rectitude constituted principally by grace
and the virtues by considering the comparisons which St. Thomas makes between original justice and gratuitous justice, together with the texts merely concerned with the former. If the
two justices are essentially alike, the question of the causality

of grace must be answered in view not only of St. Thomas' general teaching on grace and the virtues, but also of the analogy with the human soul and its potencies, according to the proportion which he frequently cites.

In principle, therefore, I am in entire agreement with Bittremieux's rule for interpreting St. Thomas — who could disagree? It is necessary to consider particular texts, especially those which are obscure or seem to clash with others, against the background of the whole teaching of St. Thomas [10]. I believe, however, that the application of this principle demands a much wider study of the texts than that which has been provided by either Bittremieux or Kors. This study, therefore, will involve a reconsideration of the principles set down by those authors as the constant teaching of St. Thomas, the norms for the interpretation of controverted texts.

The first part will be a survey of St. Thomas' teaching on the perfection of man in the state of innocence, following the development of several distinct elements in the texts. The purpose of this survey is not to present a synthesis of the theology of original justice. It is rather to make several distinct exploratory operations, to establish a number of conclusions whose connection for the moment may remain somewhat obscure, but which will be important in the later stages of our inquiry. Grace and the virtues will be considered, since they are obviously part of the perfection of the state of innocence. They will not be presumed to be part of original justice as such, since that is the issue in the controversy.

The second part will be devoted to the relation of sanctifying grace and the infused virtues to original justice. Without considering the kinds of causality involved, we shall attempt to determine whether original justice was a justice constituted principally by grace and the virtues, or rather a justice somehow caused by grace, yet completely distinct from it, not including grace and the virtues as intrinsic principles. In this regard it is necessary first to determine clearly the theory of the *donum naturae,* which is essential to St. Thomas' theol-

---

[10] BITTREMIEUX, *op. cit.,* pp. 123-124.

ogy of original justice and original sin. Secondly, we must consider the comparison between original justice and gratuitous justice, and determine the role of grace and the virtues in the subjection of the lower powers to reason and of reason to God.

Finally, in the third part, we shall consider the question of causality. Generally this has been treated as an obvious corollary of the thesis on the distinction of grace and original justice. If grace is really completely distinct from original justice, and is its cause, then it must be the efficient cause. If it is distinct only as part from whole, and is a cause, then it is the formal cause. As we shall see, the matter is somewhat more complicated.

This is not a treatise in dogmatic or speculative theology. It is meant to be an historical study in the sense that it is concerned with determining as a matter of fact what St. Thomas Aquinas held on the relation of sanctifying grace to original justice. I have attempted to find and consider all the texts bearing directly and indirectly on this question, and to observe any appreciable developments in his thought. I have examined the texts always in chronological order. Where I have sought further light from a more explicit treatment of some analogous case, I have tried to be faithful to the limits of the analogy as it is indicated by St. Thomas, and in drawing conclusions I have attempted to observe the distinction between the certain and the probable, the explicit and the implicit. Though this is a difficult labor and full of the danger of going beyond the theology as it was developed by St. Thomas himself, I believe that it is part of an historical study. For in the effort to determine a man's thought, there is a work of intelligence which goes beyond the establishment of the chronological order of texts. The best-ordered texts will not cry out in unison the answers to all our questions, even our reasonable questions, which with a penetration and insight into the principles which run through the texts can be answered.

PART ONE

MAN IN THE STATE OF INNOCENCE

CHAPTER ONE

THE THREEFOLD SUBJECTION

There is a long series of texts in which St. Thomas describes original justice, usually in terms of a threefold subjection of body to soul, lower powers to reason, and reason to God. The elements of this formula are familiar, and in such an obvious matter it might seem sufficient to cite only one or two clear texts. There is, however, a considerable variety in these formulae, not merely in order and terminology, but even in the number of elements indicated as constituting the justice. Depending on the context, St. Thomas includes one, two, or three subjections in the notion of original justice. Let us examine the significant variations. For an accurate comparison of the formulae, I shall quote the Latin text.

> 1. ... Sciendum est ergo quod duplex justitia primo homini poterat convenire. Una originalis, quae erat secundum debitum ordinem corporis sub anima, et inferiorum virium sub superiori, et superioris sub Deo ... (*In II Sent.* d. 20, q. 2, a. 3 sol.).

The first text is of little importance in determining the teaching of St. Thomas, for it occurs in the statement of the opinion of those who held that man was not created in grace. In terms of that opinion, original justice consisted in the threefold subjection, and was opposed to *justitia gratuita*.

> 2. ... Talis erat primi status rectitudo ut superior pars rationis Deo subjiceretur, cui subjicerentur inferiores vires, quibus subjiceretur corpus; ita quod prima subjectio erat

> causa secundae, et sic deinceps. Manente autem causa, ma-
> neret effectus; unde sicut quamdiu homo erat subditus Deo,
> nihil in corporis partibus contingere poterat contrarium ani-
> mae; ita etiam nihil in viribus animae contingere poterat quod
> superior ratio non ordinaret in Deum ... (*Ibid.* d. 21, q. 2,
> a. 3 sol.).

This text, occurring in a discussion of the impossibility
of venial sin in the state of innocence, clearly describes the rectitude of the first state as comprising the threefold subjection
of the higher part of the reason, the lower powers, and the body.
It is the first text which speaks of the causal relationship of
the three subjections, and in this connection one may note a
peculiarity of the text: St. Thomas says here that the higher
part of the reason was subject to God; to it in turn were subject the lower powers; and to *them* the body was subject; in
such a way that the first subjection was the cause of the second,
and so forth.   Later texts describe the body as subject to the
soul, and declare that the first subjection is the cause of the
second and third, without indicating a causal connection between the subjection of the lower powers and that of the body.
The difference may seem slight, but it is important for the
explanation of the causes of immortality in the state of innocence.

> 3. ... Unde oportuit naturam humanam taliter institui ut
> non solum haberet illud quod sibi ex principiis naturalibus
> debebatur, sed etiam aliquid ultra, per quod facile in finem
> perveniret. Et quia ultimo fini amore inhaerere non poterat,
> nec ad ipsum tenendum pervenire nisi per supremam partem
> suam, quae est mens et intellectus, seu ratio, in qua imago
> Dei insignita est; ideo, ut illa pars libere in Deum tenderet,
> subjectae sunt sibi vires inferiores, ut nihil in eis accidere
> posset quod mentem retineret et impediret ab itinere in Deum;
> pari ratione corpus hoc modo dispositum est ut nulla passio
> in eo accidere posset per quam mentis contemplatio impedi-
> retur ... (*Ibid.* d. 30, q. 1, a. 1 sol.).

In this text St. Thomas is explaining how the defects
which we suffer are a punishment for the sin of the first man.

They are punishments when considered not in relation to man's natural principles — for so they must be regarded as natural defects — but in relation to the condition in which human nature was created by God. Since man has been directed to an end beyond the power of a created nature, a beatitude consisting in the vision of God, it was necessary that human nature be so constituted that it have not only that which was due to it according to its natural principles, but also something further, by which it might easily reach its end. The gifts given in that state, therefore, were to prevent hindrance to contemplation and to the free movement of the highest part of the soul to God, by subjecting the lower powers to the higher and by keeping the body free from suffering. The aid given, therefore, was twofold, corresponding to the second and third subjections in the other formulae. The text is loose, and in a sense it may not seem to qualify as a formula of original justice. Still it is important as a rough prefiguring of the several texts which clearly give the two-member formula.

> 4. ... Ex hoc autem quod continue homo Deo [1] adhaerebat, haec virtus illi indita erat ut sub obedientia rationis continue subderentur inferiores vires, et sub obedientia animae corpus, propter hoc scilicet quod ratio suo superiori continue subdita fuerat (*Ibid.* d. 33, q. 1, a. 1 sol.).

Clearly the special *virtus* had a twofold effect, subjecting the lower powers and the body. Its cause was the continual adherence of man's reason to God.

> 5. ... Hoc Deus humanae naturae in sui principio supra conditionem suorum principiorum contulerat, ut esset in ratione rectitudo quaedam originalis justitiae quam sine aliqua resistentia inferioribus viribus imprimere posset ... (*Ibid.* d. 31, q. 1, a. 1 sol.).

In this brief description of original justice the emphasis is on the rectitude of reason. Again this rectitude is indicated

---

[1] The Mandonnet text reads *Dei.*

as the cause of the rectitude of the lower powers. Only the
first and second subjections appear here explicitly.

> 6. Sic igitur, secundum doctrinam fidei, ponimus homi-
> nem a principio taliter esse institutum quod, quandiu ratio
> hominis Deo esset subiecta, et inferiores vires ei sine im-
> pedimento deservirent, et corpus ab eius subiectione impediri
> non posset per aliquod impedimentum corporale, Deo et sua
> gratia supplente quod ad hoc perficiendum natura minus ha-
> bebat ... (*C. G.* IV, c. 52).

> 7. ... Ut enim supra dictum est, sic natura humana fuit
> instituta in sui primordio quod inferiores vires perfecte ra-
> tioni subiicerentur, ratio Deo, et animae corpus, Deo per gra-
> tiam supplente id quod ad hoc deerat per naturam. Huiusmo-
> di autem beneficium, quod a quibusdam originalis iustitia
> dicitur, sic primo homini collatum fuit ut ab eo simul cum
> natura humana propagaretur in posteros ... (*Ibid.* ad 1).

One may question whether the first of these texts is meant
to include two or three elements in the special condition in which
man was created. The interpretation depends on how *quandiu*
is understood. Should the *quandiu* clause be regarded as a loose
construction, meant to be parallel with the two independent
clauses which follow, so that the text would enumerate a threefold gift of grace? It is possible, especially considering the formula which occurs in the second text, in the answer to the first
objection. The context of the body of the article, however,
seems to indicate that *quandiu* should be taken strictly as temporal-conditional, and that there is question directly of a special twofold grace, dependent on the continued subjection of
the human reason to God.

In the context St. Thomas is seeking probable arguments
for the existence of original sin in mankind: *praemittendum
est quod peccati originalis in humano genere probabiliter quaedam signa apparent.* Since God rewards good actions and pun-
ishes evil, we can judge guilt from the nature of its punishment. Among the punishments which mankind suffers in common, the principal bodily suffering is death, to which all others
are dispositions. The principal spiritual punishment is the weak-

ness of reason, because of which man has difficulty in attaining knowledge of the truth, easily falls into error, and cannot completely overcome his animal appetites; frequently, on the contrary, his reason is clouded by them. Though one might protest that these are natural defects, yet, supposing a Divine Providence which adapts to every perfection a fitting subject to receive it, it is probable that God joined a higher nature to a lower so that it might have dominion over it, and that if through a defect of nature there should occur some hindrance to this dominion, it would be removed by his special supernatural gift. Thus, since the rational soul is of a higher nature than the body, one would believe that it had been joined to the body in such a condition that there could be nothing in the body opposed to the soul, by which the body lives. Likewise, if in man reason is joined with sense appetite and other sense powers, one would believe that reason would not be hindered by the sense powers, but would rather hold dominion over them. In this context, the special gift is clearly intended to remedy a twofold weakness and cause of disorder in man: the body and the sense powers. The weakness of reason is not intrinsic, and its remedy does not consist apparently in any special aid to the reason except the control over the senses and the body. Original justice, then, as it is described (without being named as such) in this text, would seem to be considered only as it included the second and third of the three subjections. The defects to be remedied lie in the lower powers and the body. There is no indication of a special rectitude of the will. In this text St. Thomas seems to be concerned with treating the doctrine of original justice only in so far as it corresponds to the probable arguments which can be drawn from the dignity of the human soul and reason.

> 8. ... Alio modo potest considerari natura hominis secundum quod per divinam providentiam fuit ei per justitiam originalem provisum: quae quidem justitia erat quaedam rectitudo, ut mens hominis esset sub Deo, et inferiores vires essent sub mente, et corpus sub anima, et omnia exteriora sub homine; ... Hoc autem providentia divina disposuit propter dignitatem animae rationalis, quae cum naturaliter sit incor-

ruptibilis, debebatur sibi incorruptibile corpus ... (*In Epist. ad Rom.*, c. 5, lect. 3).

Chronologically this text seems to belong here in spite of the fact that the revision of the Commentary seems to have been made in 1272. Lottin points out that the text is closely related to that of the *Contra Gentiles,* and that in the revisions of the Commentary this portion was left unchanged; consequently it dates from about the same period as the *Contra Gentiles*[2]. This text also explains the gift of original justice in terms of Divine Providence and the dignity of the soul. As in the *Contra Gentiles* the answer to the first objection gives the threefold formula, though the argument of the body of the article is concerned only with explaining a twofold gift; so here, though the full formula is given, and extended even to include the subjection of external things, still the argument is concerned only with one element of original justice: immortality. The question in the context is whether death is natural for man.

9. ... Haec autem fuit rectitudo hominis divinitus instituti, ut inferiora superioribus subderentur, et superiora ab inferioribus non impedirentur. Unde homo primus non impediebatur per res exteriores a clara et firma contemplatione

---

[2] LOTTIN, *Recherches de théol. anc. et méd.* 12 (1940) 307, note 76. I. TH. ESCHMANN, O. P., « Studies on the Notion of Society in St. Thomas Aquinas, II. Thomistic Social Philosophy and the Theology of Original Sin », *Mediaeval Studies* 9 (1947) 23-24, attempts to refute Lottin's proposal, without however representing it accurately. Eschmann's arguments indicate that the matter is by no means settled, but they do not destroy the solid probability of Lottin's position. P. GLORIEUX, « Essai sur les Commentaires scripturaires de saint Thomas et leur chronologie », *Recherches de théol. anc. et méd.* 17 (1950) 254-258, confirms Lottin's arguments: the commentary on the *Epistle to the Romans* seems to be St. Thomas' revision of Reginald's *reportatio*. In the commentary as we have it there are some marks of progress in doctrine over the parts of the commentaries on St. Paul which remain in the *reportatio (I Cor.* 11 - *Hebr.).* There are also some traces of terminology and doctrine which are closer to the *De Veritate, Contra Gentiles,* and the commentary on the *Sentences.* In his recent edition of his study Dom Lottin maintains his position, citing Glorieux. He does not, however, observe Eschmann's objection (*Psychologie et Morale* IV. I, 258).

I believe that the doctrine and formulae on original justice in the commentary on *Romans* confirm Lottin's claim: there is a marked similarity to the *Contra Gentiles* and a difference from the later works.

intelligibilium effectuum, quos ex irradiatione primae verita-
tis percipiebat, sive naturali cognitione, sive gratuita ... (*S.T.*
I, q. 94, a. 1 resp.).

10. Quod etiam ex ipsa rectitudine primi status apparet,
secundum quam, quandiu anima maneret Deo subdita, tandiu
in homine inferiora superioribus subderentur, nec superiora
per inferiora impedirentur ... (*Ibid.* a. 4 resp.).

In these texts, again, St. Thomas speaks of the special rectitude of the first man in a very restricted sense, limiting it to
the subjection of the lower powers to the higher, a special gift
which insured the perfection of human knowledge by freeing
man from the distraction and the deception which normally
would spring from the lower powers. St. Thomas is not excluding grace from the description of the state of the first man:
the gift of which he is speaking would facilitate contemplation,
whether natural or supernatural. However the rectitude which
is described consists merely in the subjection of the lower powers to the higher, and the freedom of the higher power from
any hindrance by the lower. This state is conditioned upon the
continued subjection of the soul to God: *quandiu anima mane-*
ret Deo subdita. The text states explicitly only a condition.
There is no evidence here that the rectitude involved any special
aid perfecting the reason in its own operation: on the contrary,
the intellect is always true with respect to its own object, and
the only need is to free it from the source of deception by controlling the phantasy and the other lower powers.

11. ... Erat enim haec rectitudo secundum hoc, quod ratio subdebatur Deo, rationi vero inferiores vires, et animae
corpus. Prima autem subiectio erat causa et secundae et ter-
tiae: quandiu enim ratio manebat Deo subiecta, inferiora
ei subdebantur, ut Augustinus dicit ... (*Ibid.* q. 95, a. 1 resp.).

The text occurs in the discussion of the important question
whether the first man was created in grace. Citing the opinion
of certain theologians that the first man was not created in grace,

---

[3] *S.T.* I, q. 94, a. 4 resp.

but that grace was given to him later before he sinned, St. Thomas indicates why they held that he received grace then: several passages in Scripture testify that man had grace in the state of innocence. But that he was also created in grace, as others say, seems to be required by the very rectitude of the first state, the rectitude in which God made man, according to the word of *Ecclesiastes,* vii, 30: « God made man right ». For this rectitude was such that reason was subject to God, the lower powers to reason, and the body to the soul. Moreover, the first subjection was the cause of the second and of the third: for as long as the reason remained subject to God, the lower parts were subject to it, as St. Augustine says. But it is clear that that subjection of the body to the soul, and of the lower powers to reason, was not natural: otherwise it would have remained after the sin. Therefore it is clear that the first subjection also, by which the reason was subject to God, was not only according to nature, but according to a supernatural gift of grace: for it is impossible that the effect exceed its cause [4].

Thus St. Thomas begins his treatment of what concerns the will of the first man. In this matter two things must be considered: first, the grace and justice of the first man; and secondly, his use of this justice in what regards dominion over others [5]. It seems significant that at this point St. Thomas restores the full formula. In some of the important texts preceding this in our series, attention was directed only to one or both of the lower elements in original justice: the subjection of the reason to God either was unmentioned in the formula [6] or seemed to be merely the condition on which the twofold gift depended [7]. Here the first subjection reappears, and the whole formula is fully operative. St. Thomas is not merely quoting the old words: every element in the threefold order is functional. The first subjection is the cause of the second and the third. It is a subjection whose principle is the supernatural gift of grace. Without any doubt in this context the

---

[4] *Ibid.*

[5] *Ibid.,* q. 95, prologue.

[6] *Ibid.* q. 94, a. 1 resp.

[7] *C.G.* IV, c. 52; *S.T.* I, q. 94, a. 4 resp.

grace is *gratia gratum faciens*. Though the subject of the whole discussion in this question is the will of the first man, and the occasion is most opportune for indicating whatever else there might have been to perfect the will and constitute the rectitude of the highest part of man, there is not a trace of any such principle other than grace.

> 12. Talis erat rectitudo primi status, quod ratio erat Deo subiecta, inferiores autem vires rationi (*Ibid.* q. 95, a. 3).

The short formula illustrates again St. Thomas' mention of only those elements of the original rectitude which are directly involved in the question. Since he is determining here whether Adam had virtues, he speaks only of the first and second subjections. As we shall see, the preservation of the body from suffering and death was not the effect of the virtues, and so the third subjection is irrelevant to the question in this text.

> 13. ... Originalis iustitia, per quam ratio subdebatur Deo, et inferiores vires rationi, et corpus animae ... (*De Malo* q. 4, a. 1 resp.).

> 14. ... Peccatum originale opponitur iustitiae originali, per quam superior pars animae et Deo coniungebatur, et inferioribus viribus imperabat, et etiam corpus absque corruptione poterat conservare ... (*Ibid.* q. 4, a. 6 ad 4).

> 15. ... Fuit autem in principio conditionis humanae quoddam donum gratuitum primo homini divinitus datum non ratione personae suae tantum, sed ratione totius naturae humanae ab eo derivandae, quod donum fuit originalis iustitia. Huius etiam doni virtus non solum residebat in superiori parte animae, quae est intellectiva, sed diffundebatur ad inferiores animae partes, quae continebantur virtute doni praedicti totaliter sub ratione; et ulterius usque ad corpus, in quo nihil poterat accidere, dono praedicto manente, quod contrariaretur unioni ipsius ad animam ... (*Ibid.* q. 4, a. 8 resp.).

These three texts, from the fourth question of the *De Malo* on original sin, preserve the full formula, with some noteworthy variations in the second and third texts. The second text introduces a nuance in the description of the three subjections : through original justice the soul is *united* with God, *commands* the lower powers, and *preserves* the body from corruption. The third text accentuates the causality of the first subjection : the gift of grace was not confined to the higher part of the soul, but was diffused to the lower parts of the soul and to the body; it was by the power of that gift that the lower parts were kept completely under the control of reason.

> 16. Sed circa hoc considerandum est, quod aliquod divinum auxilium necessarium est communiter omni creaturae rationali, scilicet auxilium gratiae gratum facientis, qua quaelibet creatura rationalis indiget, ut possit pervenire ad beatitudinem perfectam, secundum illud Apostoli, *Rom.* vi, 23 : *Gratia Dei vita aeterna.* Sed praeter hoc auxilium necessarium fuit homini aliud supernaturale auxilium, ratione suae compositionis. Est enim homo compositus ex anima et corpore, et ex natura intellectuali et sensibili ; quae quodammodo si suae naturae relinquantur, intellectum aggravant et impediunt, ne libere ad summum fastigium contemplationis pervenire possit. Hoc autem auxilium fuit originalis iustitia, per quam mens hominis si subderetur Deo, ei subderentur totaliter inferiores vires et ipsum corpus, neque ratio impediretur quo minus posset in Deum tendere. Et sicut corpus est propter animam, et sensus propter intellectum ; ita hoc auxilium, quo continetur corpus sub anima, et vires sensitivae sub mente intellectuali, est quasi dispositio quaedam ad illud auxilium quo mens humana ordinatur ad videndum Deum et ad fruendum ipso ... (*Ibid.* q. 5, a. 1 resp.).

This text has been of extreme importance in the controversy over the essence of original justice. Its sharp distinction between the *auxilium gratiae gratum facientis* and another aid consisting in original justice has been one of the chief rallying points of the defenders of the adequate distinction [8]. And yet, if we read this text correctly, that same sharp distinction leaves their theory of original justice neatly beheaded. For what is this special aid which is necessary for man alone

---

[8] Thus BITTREMIEUX concludes his article by citing this as a clear text, enough to remove all doubt (*op. cit.,* p. 144).

among rational creatures, and so is distinct from the supernatural aid consisting in sanctifying grace, which is necessary
for all alike to be able to attain perfect happiness? It is an aid
which remedies a twofold weakness in man, due to his being
composite.   « For man is composed of soul and body, and of
intellectual and sensible nature, *which* somehow if left to their
own nature burden the intellect and prevent its being able freely
to reach the summit of contemplation ».   St. Thomas' sentence
structure here is not the best, for the reference of the pronoun
« which » is obscure, but his meaning can hardly be mistaken :
the body and the sensible nature, if left to the course of their
own nature, are the burden and the hindrance.   It may seem
pedantic to labor a point of grammar and sentence-structure,
but it is of considerable importance to see clearly the meaning
of this text.   There is no weakness of the intellect or will as
such in question here.   The cause of man's weakness lies in
his bodily and sense nature, and the special gift of original
justice as it is here distinguished from grace was given to
remedy that twofold weakness.   The text parallels the other
important texts in which the limited formula has been used.
From the context here and in the other texts considered it is
clear, I believe, that St. Thomas is directly concerned only
with the second and third subjections.   The subjection of the
mind to God is not enumerated as one of the elements of original justice, but rather as the condition upon which the other
two depended.   Thus « *mens hominis si subderetur Deo* » is
merely a condition here, parallel with the temporal-conditional
quandiu clauses in the other texts.   The issue, of course, is
obvious.   If original justice *as distinguished from grace* in this
text is the full original justice in the definitive teaching of
St. Thomas, then original justice consisted in a twofold rectitude, a subjection of the body and of the lower powers of
the soul; it depended upon, but did not include, the subjection
of the higher part of the soul to God.   For there is no indication anywhere that this highest subjection is caused by anything but *gratia gratum faciens* (and the infused virtues, as we
shall see from other texts).   There is no trace of another « preternatural » rectitude of the will *in linea naturae,* a kind of

corrective of a natural defect, as the other gifts were correctives of the natural defects in the lower powers and in the body. If therefore the defenders of the complete distinction between grace and original justice stand upon this text, they have an original justice which lacks its most important part, the rectitude of the will: yet they hold that the rectitude of the will is the formal element in original justice, and the source of the perfect order of the lower powers and of the body.

> 17. ... Taliter homo erat in statu innocentiae institutus ... quod quamdiu pars superior hominis firmiter Deo inhaereret, omnia inferiora superiori parti subdebantur, non solum partes animae, sed etiam ipsum corpus et alia exteriora ... (*Ibid.* q. 7, a. 7 resp.).

This text is part of the proof that venial sin was impossible in the state of innocence. As long as that state lasted, man could in no way commit a venial sin; because as long as the higher part of man clung firmly to God, all the lower parts were subject to the higher, not only the parts of the soul, but also the body itself and other external things. Venial sin arising from the sense powers was impossible because the complete subjection rendered disorder impossible. This text goes one step farther, however, for under the general subordination of lower to higher St. Thomas here includes the unfailing order by which the *ratio inferior,* concerned with means, was subject to the *ratio superior,* concerned with the end.

> 18. Sciendum tamen est, quod in remedium horum defectuum Deus homini in sua institutione contulit auxilium iustitiae originalis, per quam corpus esset omnino subditum animae, quamdiu anima Deo subderetur; ita quod nec mors nec aliqua passio vel defectus homini accideret, nisi prius anima separaretur a Deo ... (*De Anima* q. un., a. 8 resp.).

Here St. Thomas attributes to original justice a single effect, conditioned as usual on the continued subjection of the soul to God: through this aid the body would be completely subject to the soul, so as to be free from death and all suffering and defects. The context explains the reason for the limited treatment of original justice: there is question of the proportion of matter to form, of the kind of body required by the human soul, of the dispositions which follow from the necessity of matter, and the remedy applied to these natural defects.

19. Sicut supra dictum est, homo in sui conditione taliter institutus fuit a Deo ut corpus omnino esset animae subiectum: rursumque inter partes animae, inferiores vires rationi absque repugnantia subiicerentur, et ipsa ratio hominis esset Deo subiecta. Ex hoc autem quod corpus erat animae subiectum, contingebat quod nulla passio in corpore posset accidere quae dominio animae super corpus repugnaret, unde nec mors nec infirmitas in homine locum habebat. Ex subiectione vero inferiorum virium ad rationem erat in homine omnimoda mentis tranquillitas, quia ratio humana nullis inordinatis passionibus turbabatur. Ex hoc vero quod voluntas hominis erat Deo subiecta, homo referebat omnia in Deum sicut in ultimum finem, in quo ejus iustitia et innocentia consistebat.

Horum autem trium ultimum erat causa aliorum. Non enim hoc erat ex natura corporis, si eius componentia considerentur, quod in eo dissolutio sive quaecumque passio vitae repugnans locum non haberet, cum esset ex contrariis elementis compositum. Similiter etiam non erat ex natura animae quod vires etiam sensibiles absque repugnantia rationi subiicerentur, cum vires sensibiles naturaliter moveantur in ea quae sunt delectabilia secundum sensum, quae multoties rectae rationi repugnant. Erat igitur hoc ex virtute superiori, scilicet Dei, qui sicut animam rationalem corpori coniunxit, omnem proportionem corporis et corporearum virtutum, cuiusmodi sunt vires sensibiles, transcendentem, ita dedit animae rationali virtutem ut supra conditionem corporis ipsum continere posset et vires sensibiles, secundum quod rationali animae competebat.

Ut igitur ratio inferiora sub se firmiter contineret, oportebat quod ipsa firmiter sub Deo contineretur, a quo virtutem praedictam habebat supra conditionem naturae. Fuit ergo homo sic institutus ut nisi ratio ejus subduceretur a Deo, neque corpus eius subduci poterat a nutu animae, neque vires sensibiles a rectitudine rationis: unde quaedam immortalis vi-

ta et impassibilis erat, quia scilicet nec mori nec pati poterat, si non peccaret ... (*Comp. Theol.* c. 186, ed. Marietti
n. 362).

This chapter of the *Compendium Theologiae* gives considerably more precision to the doctrine on original justice.
The formula is complete, the effects of the justice are detailed
at the three levels, and the causal relationship is explained.
A careful study of the text confirms some of the conclusions
already reached.   Especially it seems that from this text too
we must say that the subjection of the will to God is of a different order than that of the other two subjections. By it
man referred all to God as to his last end, and in this his justice and innocence consisted. It is the cause of the other subjections. In the case of each of the other two St. Thomas
explains that the complete subjection was not according to the
nature of the body or of the soul. It came from a higher
power : God gave the rational soul a special power to control
the body and the sense powers. In order to maintain a firm
control over the lower parts, it was necessary that reason itself
be firmly controlled by God, from whom it had that power
above the condition of nature. The subjection of the lower
powers and of the body, therefore, was effected by a special
aid remedying the defects of the lower nature. There is no
suggestion of such a rectification « *in linea naturae* », the cor-
rection of a natural defect, in the case of the will. There is
no indication here of what caused the subjection of the will,
in spite of the fact that this is clearly the crucial element in
original justice, the rectitude on which all else depends. The
continued silence on this point would seem to indicate that
for St. Thomas there was in fact no problem : the rectitude
of the will by which man directs all things to God as to his
last end, by which he clings to God, is so obviously the effect
of charity and grace.

20. ... Originalis iustitia, per quam non solum inferiores animae vires continebantur sub ratione absque omni deor-
dinatione, sed totum corpus continebatur sub anima absque
omni defectu ... (*S. T.* I-II, q. 85, a. 5 resp.).

21. ... Homini in prima sui institutione hoc beneficium fuit collatum divinitus, ut quandiu mens eius esset Deo subiecta, inferiores vires animae subiicerentur rationali menti, et corpus animae subiiceretur ... (*S.T.* II-II, q. 164, a. 1 resp.).

The last two texts in the series, both from the *Summa Theologiae,* are found in articles in which St. Thomas is proving that death is a punishment of the sin of the first parent. Both have the limited formula of the second and third subjections, one with the conditional « *quandiu mens eius esset Deo subiecta* ». Furthermore, in the first of the two texts St. Thomas implicitly distinguishes between original justice in this sense and grace: « *Subtractio autem originalis iustitiae habet rationem poenae, sicut etiam subtractio gratiae* ».

In studying this single series of parallel texts I have followed only one vein that runs through St. Thomas' treatment of original justice. Admittedly, designedly, I have by-passed momentarily many important texts which bring out other aspects of his teaching. We shall consider them soon. Let us pause, though, for a moment, to gather some of the results of this stage of our inquiry.

(1) The texts admit classification according to the number of elements of original justice which they treat. Depending on the requirements of the problem which he is discussing, St. Thomas considers all or only certain of the elements of original justice, and accordingly he uses the term *originalis iustitia* and its equivalent expressions variously.

(2) In some cases where St. Thomas gives the three-part formula he is merely citing the teaching of earlier theologians. This is the case in the first text. It seems also to explain how in the sixth text, *Contra Gentiles* IV. 52 in the answer to the first objection, he uses the three-part formula, citing other theologians; whereas the proof to which he refers, in the body of the article, has established only a twofold subjection.

(3) The most common restricted sense of « original justice » is that of a twofold aid given to remedy the natural defects caused in man by his body and the lower powers of the soul.

(4) When the cause of the first subjection is indicated, it is grace.

(5) Where original justice is clearly distinguished from sanctifying grace, it includes only the two lower subjections, only the gifts which remedy the defects of man's lower nature. There is no indication that original justice so distinguished from grace includes a similar « preternatural » rectitude of the will, as postulated by the advocates of the adequate distinction.

CHAPTER TWO

FORMAL AND MATERIAL ELEMENTS
IN ORIGINAL JUSTICE

One of the clear points in the texts which we have examined thus far is the relative importance of the subjection of the highest part of the soul to God in St. Thomas' explanation of original justice. This subjection, this rectitude of the highest part of the soul, is the cause of the other two subjections. St. Thomas' theory here coincides in part with the teaching found in another series of texts in which the rectitude of the will is said to be formal in original justice, whereas the rectitude impressed upon the lower powers is material. This formal-material terminology has its origins in St. Thomas in the discussion of original sin, and especially in the difficult questions concerning concupiscence. The terms formal and material have been taken over generally by those who have synthesized St. Thomas' doctrine, and have been imposed upon the more complete theory of original justice, as represented, for example, in the text cited from the *Compendium Theologiae,* chapter 186. This is a natural step in systematizing, but it should not be taken without noting that these two lines of thought, the causality of the first subjection with respect to the second and third, and the quasi formal-material relationship of the rectitude of the will and the rectitude of the lower powers, do not coincide perfectly, and that the general adoption of the formal-material terminology should not be made without some conscious adjustment. Keeping this in mind, let us examine the texts.

Both lines of thought appear early, in the Commentary on the *Sentences*. We have already noted a peculiarity of the

first text in which St. Thomas speaks of a causal relationship
between the elements of original justice: « Such was the rectitude of the first state that the higher part of the reason was
subject to God; to it were subject the lower powers; and to
them the body was subject; so that the first subjection was the
cause of the second, and so forth » [1].   The notion of a series
of essentially subordinated causes, with the implication that
immortality and freedom from suffering in the body could be
caused by acts commanded by the will, disappears after this
text.   Apart from this point, the doctrine of the Commentary
on the *Sentences* remains, receiving considerable development
and refinement in later texts.   While the cause remained, the
effect remained; as long as man was subject to God, nothing
could happen in the parts of the body which would be contrary
to the soul; so also nothing could happen in the powers of
the soul which the higher reason would not direct to God [2].
Thus the order of the higher part with respect to God was
the principle of original justice [3].   In what did this order consist?   In the speculative intellect the highest part is that which
holds to principles known *per se*.   In the practical reason the
highest part is that which holds to the end, since in what concerns operation the end is like the first indemonstrable principle [4].   The perfection of the whole man depended upon the
higher part of the mind, by which man clung to God through
the rectitude of justice [5].   In all of these texts, the role of
the will itself is only implicit: mention is made either of the
intellect or indeterminately of the highest part, the higher part
of the reason, the higher part of the mind.

The formal-material theory is applied to original justice
in the attempt to solve the question whether original sin is
concupiscence:

> ... In any sin it is possible to find something quasi for-
> mal and something quasi material.   For if we should con-

---

[1] *In II Sent.* d. 21, q. 2, a. 3 sol.   For the text, see pp. 15-16.
[2] *Ibid.*
[3] *Ibid.* ad 4.
[4] *Ibid.* ad 6.
[5] *Ibid.* d. 23, q. 2, a. 3 sol.

sider an actual sin, the very substance of the act which is out of order is *material* in the sin; but the lack of order with respect to the end is *formal* in the sin, because it is from this especially that it has the character of evil. Hence in this case it is said that turning to a commutable good is as it were material, and turning from the incommutable good is as it were formal. This happens because even in an act the perfection of virtue is from the order with respect to the end of the act. Moreover, as actual sin consists in the disorder of an act, so also original sin consists in the disorder of nature. Hence it is necessary that the disordered powers themselves, or the disorder of the powers, be *material* in original sin, and the very disorder with respect to the end be as it were *formal*. Moreover that part which is intended essentially to be joined to the end is the will itself, which has the power to impose upon the other parts the order with respect to the end. Consequently the defection of the will itself from that rectitude to the end which it had in the original disposition of nature is *formal* in original sin: and this is the privation of original justice. But the powers of the sense appetite are intended to receive the order toward the end from the will itself, according as they are subject to it; and therefore the withdrawal of that bond by which they were somehow held under the power of the upright (*rectae*) will is material in the sin. Moreover the result of this withdrawal is that every power tends inordinately to its object out of desire for it. Consequently the concupiscence by which we are disposed to evil desires is called original sin, being as it were the material element in original sin ... [6]

The text does not apply the formal-material terminology directly to original justice, but prepares the way for this step by identifying the formal element of original sin and the privation of original justice. Even the doctrine of formal and material elements in original sin is in a somewhat amorphous state here, as St. Thomas wavers between two analogies. The first analogy is based on the distinction in an actual sin between the substance of the act as material and lack of order

---

[6] *In II Sent.* d. 30, q. 1, a. 3 sol.

in the act as formal. Applying material-formal terminology to
original sin according to this analogy, St. Thomas says that
the powers of the soul in disorder are the material element,
and the lack of order is formal. The material-formal notion
is never applied to original justice according to this analogy:
if it were, all the powers of man in good order would be the
material element, whereas the very order or harmony would
be formal. The second analogy appears in the text unan-
nounced: when St. Thomas says that « the disordered powers
themselves *or* the disorder of the powers » is material in original sin, and the disorder with respect to the end is formal,
he seems to be blending his first analogy with a second. That
second analogy works in the remainder of the text: the defection of the will is formal; the withdrawal of the bond by
which the lower powers were held under the control of the
will is material. If the first analogy had prevailed throughout
the text, one would say that all the disordered powers, higher
and lower alike, taken concretely, were the material element
in original sin; and the privation of rectitude or order in all
of them, the formal element. But the second analogy does
not consider *malum-malitia,* concrete-abstract, substance of act
and lack of order, as the basis for the notions of material and
formal. Rather it takes the disordered will or the disorder
of the will as the formal element because of the priority and
pre-eminence of the will over the other powers. The withdrawal of the bond which kept the lower powers in order is material because it is consequent and dependent upon the defection of the will. The text is very obscure because the doctrine
itself is taking form. We have a hint of what is to come,
for St. Thomas identifies the formal element of original sin
according to the second analogy (defection of the will from
the rectitude it had) with the privation of original justice.
Implicitly then the rectitude of the will was the whole of original justice.

The doctrine is clearly formulated somewhat farther on
in the commentary on the same book of the *Sentences.* The
quasi formal element in original justice was the rectitude of
the will: with regard to this, original justice is opposed to the

deformity of guilt. The quasi material element was the right order impressed upon the lower powers: with regard to this, it is opposed to concupiscence and the tinder of sin [7].

In the *De Malo* St. Thomas resumes the discussion of the nature of original sin and once more identifies its formal element and the privation of original justice. For his solution of the problem concerning the nature of original sin, he presupposes two points already established: (1) original sin pertains to a person in so far as he is considered as a part of the multitude descended from Adam, as if he were a part of one man; (2) when a man sins, there is one sin in so far as the act is referred to the whole man and to the first principle of sin, though the execution of the sin be through different parts.

> Thus therefore original sin in this or that man is nothing but that which comes to him through his origin from the sin of the first parent, as sin in the hand or in the eye is nothing else than that which comes to the hand or to the eye from the motion of the first principle of sin, which is the will; though in the one case the motion occurs by way of natural origin, and in the other, through the command of the will. That which comes to the hand from the sin of an individual man is a certain effect and impression of the first inordinate movement, which was in the will: hence necessarily it bears its likeness. The inordinate movement of the will is a turning to some temporal good without right order to the proper end. This disorder is the turning from the incommutable good, and this is as it were formal, whereas the other is as it were material; for the formal nature of a moral act is understood by comparison with the end. Hence also that which pertains to the hand in the sin of one man is nothing else than its application to some effect without some order of justice. ...

Thus therefore in the sin of the first parent there was something formal, that is: the turning from the incommut-

---

[7] Ad primum ergo dicendum, quod in originali justitia erat aliquid quasi formale, scilicet ipsa rectitudo voluntatis, et secundum hoc sibi opponitur culpae deformitas. Erat in ea etiam aliquid quasi materiale, scilicet ordo rectitudinis impressus in inferioribus viribus; et quantum ad hoc opponitur sibi concupiscentia et fomes ... (*In II Sept.* d. 32, q. 1, a. 1 ad 1).

able good; and something material, that is: the turning to
a commutable good. Because he had turned from the incommutable good, he lost the gift of original justice. Because
he had turned inordinately to a commutable good, his lower
powers, which should have been raised toward his rational
nature, were lowered to the things beneath him. So also
in those who are born of his lineage, the higher part of
the soul lacks that orientation to God which existed through
original justice, and the lower powers are not subject to
reason, but turn according to their own inclination to the
things below, and the body too tends to corruption according
to the inclination of the contraries of which it is composed.

But the higher part of the soul, and also certain of the
lower powers, which are under the will and are intended
to obey it, receive the effect of this sin in the form of guilt;
for such parts can incur guilt ... Among the higher powers
which incur the defect passed on through origin in the form
of guilt, there is one which moves all the others: the will.
All the others are moved to their acts by the will. It is
always true that that which has the role of agent and mover
is as it were formal; and that which has the role of recipient and subject to motion is as it were material.

Accordingly, since in the will there is a lack of original
justice and in the lower powers moved by the will there is
an inclination to inordinate desire which can be called concupiscence, it follows that original sin in this or that man
is nothing else than concupiscence together with the lack of
original justice; in such wise, however, that the lack of original justice is quasi formal in original sin, and concupiscence
quasi material; just as in an actual sin the turning from
the incommutable good is quasi formal, and the turning to
a commutable good is quasi material. Thus in original sin
the soul is understood to be *aversa et conversa,* just as in
an actual sin the act is, so to speak, *aversus et conversus* [8].

This text is complicated by the blending of elements of
two analogies, involving two senses of « formal ». First, there
is the analogy of the actual sin of one man, involving the act
of the will and the acts of the lower powers moved by the will.

---

[8] *De Malo* q. 4, a. 2 resp.

According to the analysis which St. Thomas commonly makes, and which occurs toward the end of this article, the act of the will is formal since it moves the others; the acts of the lower powers dependent upon the will are material. If this analogy were applied simply to original sin considered as the sin of the whole race as somehow being one man, then the actual sin of Adam would be the formal element in original sin, and original sin as found in all the men descended from Adam would be material. Secondly, there is the analogy of actual sin, in which the formal element is aversion, or lack of order to the end, and the material element is the conversion or application to a perishable good. The two elements of aversion and conversion can be found either in the act of the will or in the act of the lower power or part of the body moved by the will. But when he applies this analogy to the soul as *aversa et conversa,* St. Thomas seeks to explain the whole disorder of original sin by locating the *aversio* in the will and the *conversio* in the lower powers moved by the will. At this point the two analogies are blended. In one, the formal-material elements are the will and the powers moved by the will; in the other, the formal-material elements are *aversio* and *conversio.*

From the fusion of analogies we have the theory elaborated in the text. In the actual sin of one man we can consider (A) the *act of the will,* in which there is a formal element, the turning from the incommutable good; and a material element, turning to some temporal good; and (B) the *act of the hand,* for example, which receives the motion from the will, and in which too there are the elements of aversion and conversion, formal and material. By analogy, in original sin considered as the sin of the human race forming as it were one man, we have the corresponding elements: (A) the *sin of the first parent,* in which there is a formal element, aversion from the incommutable good, resulting in the loss of the gift of original justice; and a material element, conversion to a commutable good, resulting in the depression of the lower powers; and (B) *original sin in those descended from Adam,* in which there is a formal element in the higher part of the soul, the lack of original justice; and a material element in the lower powers moved by the will, concupiscence. Thus original sin is concupiscence and the lack of original justice, the material and formal elements respectively. Since among the powers of the soul the will is formal with respect to the others which are subject to its motion, the formal element of original sin is found in the will; and the material element is in the powers moved by the will. Though the lack of original justice in the will and concupiscence in the lower powers are distinguished as formal and material in original sin, still *formal* here is taken in the sense of *movens* or *agens*. Consequently the causality seems to be really efficient, not formal[9]. We shall return to this question later.

For the present, let us fix the significance of this text for our question concerning the formal element in original justice. First of all, St. Thomas does not define original sin as the privation of original justice, and so we cannot simply take as formal and material in original justice the counterparts of the formal and material parts of the sin. St. Thomas seems anxious to preserve the Augustinian formula of original sin along with the Anselmian[10]. Perhaps it was this concern which motivated the highly complicated explanation from which he emerges with the definition of original sin as *concupiscentia cum carentia originalis justitiae*. The formal element is the lack of original justice, which is in the will. The material element is concupiscence, in the lower powers moved by the will. Directly, therefore, the formal-material terminology is not applied to original justice in this text. But original justice is the rectitude of the will, the privation of which is the formal element in original sin.

As we have seen, St. Thomas gave the most complete statement of the triple subjection in original justice in the *Compendium Theologiae*, chapter 186. With regard to the subjection of the reason to God, we have here a greater degree of precision. There is question primarily of the will: because

---

9 Cf. LOTTIN, *op. cit.*, pp. 313-315.
10 Cf. LOTTIN, *ibid.*, pp. 311-318.

man's will was subject to God, man directed all things to God as to his last end, and in this his justice and innocence consisted. This subjection of the will to God was the cause of the other subjections. Since the complete subjection of body to soul and of sense power to reason was not according to nature, it was caused by Divine power. Just as God joined to the body a rational soul transcending completely the proportion of the body and the bodily forces, such as the sense powers, so He gave to the rational soul a power (*virtus*) by which it might control both body and sense powers. To keep its firm control over the lower powers, reason itself had to be held firmly in subjection to God, from whom it had this power beyond the condition of nature.

It may be well to observe one subtle distinction in reading this text. Though the whole ordered integrity of this state was caused by the subjection of the will to God [11], the nature of the causality is not determined. In fact, as the explanation proceeds, it might seem that the continued subjection of the will to God was rather a condition or disposition necessary in order to keep the special power which God had given to keep the body and lower powers in subjection. It may seem that this is an excessive refinement. Yet, as we shall see later, it has a bearing on the principal object of this study concerning the kinds of causality in St. Thomas' theory of original justice.

Finally we have the treatment of the essence original sin in the second part of the *Summa Theologiae*. Original sin is a habit in the sense that it is a bad disposition which like sickness has become a kind of nature; for original sin is an inordinate disposition resulting from the dissolution of that harmony which constituted original justice, just as bodily sickness is a certain inordinate disposition of the body which destroys the balance which constituted health [12]. The species of such disorders is determined by their causes, as is clear in the case

---

[11] Quia igitur dicti status tam ordinata integritas tota causabatur ex subiectione humanae voluntatis ad Deum ... (*Comp. Theol.* c. 192).

[12] *S.T.* I-II, q. 82, a. 1 resp.

of diseases of the body [13]. Since a thing has its species from its form, and on the other hand the species of original sin, like any other inordinate disposition, is determined by the cause of original sin, the formal principle of original sin must be taken from its cause. Moreover, opposites have opposite causes. To discover the cause of original sin, therefore, we must consider the cause of its opposite, original justice.

> The whole order of original justice comes from this, that the will of man was subject to God. This subjection was first and foremost caused by the will, which has the power to move all other parts to the end ... Therefore from the will's turning away from God there followed disorder in all the other parts of the soul. Thus therefore the privation of original justice, through which the will was kept subject to God, is formal in original sin; and all other disorder of the soul's powers is as something material in original sin. The disorder of the other powers of the soul is principally observed in this, that they turn inordinately to a changeable good. This disorder can be called by the common name concupiscence. Consequently original sin materially is indeed concupiscence, but formally it is the lack of original justice [14].

In this discussion, which touches only indirectly the nature of original justice, we may observe first that though there is question of the formal element of original sin and the cause of that sin, and though St. Thomas uses the principle that opposites have opposite causes, still he does not say explicitly here that the subjection of the will to God is the *formal element* of original justice. It is the *cause* of original justice, and the privation of original justice is the formal element in original sin. Moreover in spite of the appeal to the principle of opposites, the definition of original sin again veers from a strict parallel between the two. Secondly, there is something strange in the fact that on the one hand the subjection of the will is the cause of original justice, and on the other hand it was through original justice that the will was kept subject to God [15]. In what sense,

---

[13] *Ibid.* a. 2 resp.
[14] *S.T.* I-II, q. 82, a. 3 resp.
[15] ... Est igitur attendenda causa originalis peccati ex causa originalis

then, is the subjection of the will the cause of original justice?
The will is said to be the cause of original justice because it
has the power to move all the other parts to the end. Considering original justice dynamically, if we may use the term in
this sense, there is a twofold sense in which the will is the cause
of original justice. First, it is a kind of *causa movens,* moving
the powers to their acts, and directing those acts to its own
end, the ultimate end. Thus it is the cause of the order and
harmony which reigns in the operations of the powers subject
to the will. Secondly, it seems to be a kind of cause of original justice in so far as its continued adherence to God the last
end is the condition or disposition required for the continued
possession of the supernatural gift of original justice. Since
man in that state was not confirmed in grace [16], the state of
original justice was contingent upon man's continued loyalty
to God. Consequently, the will was somehow a cause *per accidens* of the continuance of original justice in so far as it did
not turn from God, sever the bond which united man with the
source of this supernatural gift, and so destroy original justice.
This is a meagre type of causality, it is true, and it seems that
it has been emphasized rather because of the real importance
of its opposite. Its counterpart in original sin, the defection
of the will, is the all-important sole cause of original sin.

The analysis of these texts suggests the following reflec-
tions:

(1) Strictly, we do not have a series of texts on the formal and material elements in original justice. I have found
only one text in which the formal-material terminology is applied directly to original justice, and it is a brief answer to an
objection in the Commentary on the *Sentences* [17]. Rather we
have compared the principal texts indicating the causality of

---

iustitiae, quae ei opponitur. Tota autem ordinatio originalis iustitiae ex hoc
est, quod voluntas hominis erat Deo subiecta. Quae quidem subiectio primo
et principaliter erat per voluntatem, cuius est movere omnes alias partes in
finem... Sic ergo privatio originalis iustitiae, per quam voluntas subdebatur
Deo, est formale in peccato originali... (*Ibid.* a. 3 resp.).

[16] *Comp. Theol.* c. 186.
[17] *In II Sent.* d. 32, q. 1, a. 1 ad 1: cf. *supra,* note 7, p. 35.

the first subjection with the texts in which the analysis of formal and material principles in original sin points to the causality of the will in original justice and suggests that the rectitude of the will might be termed formal in original justice.

(2) The texts concerned directly with original justice and with the causal relationship of the three subjections are wider in scope than those which deal with the causality of the will in connection with the question of the nature of original sin. The first type of text deals with the three levels of subjection. The other is concerned only with the relation between the will and the powers moved by the will. This is natural because in all cases these texts are concerned with the nature of original sin, and especially with the role of concupiscence.

(3) « Formal » in the texts which deal with the causality of the will in original sin and original justice does not signify formal causality, but rather efficient : the *movens* or *agens* is « formal » with respect to the *mobilis* and *patiens*.

(4) There is a considerable tension in the texts on the nature of original sin. In part, perhaps entirely in the ultimate analysis, this seems to be due to St. Thomas' desire to preserve the Augustinian formula in the definition of original sin. In part it seems to be due to the attempt to blend two analogies, involving two different senses of « formal », one based on the relation of a moral act to its end, the other based on the relation of the act to its efficient cause.

(5) It may be clearer now that one cannot simply take over the « formal-material » relation between the will and the lower powers as developed in the texts on original sin and apply it to the whole causal relationship between the elements of original justice. First of all, this causality of the will corresponds to only one of the strata involved. It can explain the influence of the will upon the lower powers subject to the will. It cannot be expanded into a general theory of the causality of the lower subjection in original justice, because the complete subjection of body to soul, with the effects of immortality and freedom from suffering, cannot be explained in terms of voluntary acts. It is not by acts commanded by the will that these prerogatives of the body were caused, as we shall see pres-

ently.   Secondly, the « *formalis* » of these texts is not formal
in the strict sense, but rather somehow efficient.   We have not
here a means of explaining what constituted original justice
formally.   The causality of the will in original justice as revealed in these texts is (a) strictly efficient, in so far as the
will moved the other powers to the last end; (b) somehow efficient *per accidens* in the continuance of the whole of original
justice, in so far as at any time the will by turning from God
could have destroyed original justice.

(6) Finally, in the use of the term « original justice »
we may note a sharp contrast with the use observed in the formulae studied in the preceding chapter.   In those formulae,
when « original justice » is used in a restricted sense, it signifies only the two lower subjections: body to soul, and lower
powers of the soul to reason.   Here in the texts on the formal
and material elements of original sin there is a restricted sense
in which « original justice » means only the rectitude of the
will.   In the definition of original sin as *concupiscentia cum
carentia originalis iustitiae,* the formal element of original sin
is the privation of original justice, which was in the will.   The
other limited sense of original justice, however, persists in
these texts.   As we observed in the texts of the Second Part of
the *Summa Theologiae,* there is some obscurity in the paradox
that the subjection of the will was the cause of original justice, and was itself caused by original justice.   When the subjection of the will is said to be the cause of original justice by reason of its moving the other parts to the end, « original justice »
seems to be taken in the limited sense of the subjection of the
lower powers.

CHAPTER THREE

THE CAUSES OF IMMORTALITY AND FREEDOM FROM SUFFERING

We have seen how in general in the texts on the threefold subjection in original justice St. Thomas explains the reasons for the gift of immortality and freedom from suffering. Let us consider now what he says concerning the causes of these prerogatives. We shall examine first a group of texts from the Commentary on the *Sentences*.

> Hence this was given him beyond the condition of his nature, that the soul, which was directed to such a noble end, might communicate perpetual existence to matter according to its own power, beyond the general disposition of nature by which matter receives existence according to its own condition (*In II Sent*. d. 19, q. 1, a. 2 sol.).

> Man was preserved by several remedies against the many kinds and causes of corruption. For there are four ways in which the bodies of animals are corrupted. The first, which is found generally in all things subject to generation and corruption, is caused by the fact that material things have a limited power to exist; hence necessarily all are corrupted within a certain period ... The second is common to all composite bodies, caused by the inordinate excess of one of the contraries. Against both of these defects man was aided by a certain power given to the soul to perfect matter according to its own condition, in order that just as the soul has an unfailing existence, so it might give to the body an unfailing existence and a perpetual balance in its constitution. The third manner of corruption is proper to living bodies, just as they have their own manner of generation: it is caused by the fact that heat, which is the instrument of the soul, consumes the moisture in which there is life. Against this

defect he was aided by a twofold gift. By eating of the
other trees of paradise he restored the loss continually occurring in the body ... [The gradual weakening of the power
of nature through the mixture of foreign substances was
remedied by the] tree of life, through which by divine power
the food taken was perfectly assimilated ... The fourth manner of corruption is through violence of an external agent ...
and from this kind of corruption man was preserved free
from injury through Divine Providence ... (*Ibid.* d. 19, q. 1,
a. 4 sol.).

The tree of life was not the principal cause of immortality, but assisted in prolonging life in the manner already
determined. Therefore immortality should not be regarded
as natural because of the tree of life, but rather gratuitous
because of the power given to the soul beyond nature. This
was the principal cause of immortality ... (*l. c.* ad 5).

Though the human body in the state of innocence was
incorruptible by the grace of innocence, it was nevertheless
corruptible by nature (*Ibid.* d. 20, q. 1, a. 1 ad 2).

The body was so disposed that no suffering (*passio*) might
occur in it by which the mind's contemplation would be
hindered (*Ibid.* d. 30, q. 1, a. 1 sol.).

A form is received in matter according to the condition
of the matter itself ... accordingly, since the body is deprived
of that power (*virtus*) by which it was capable of perfect
subjection to the soul, it follows that the soul too lacks that
power by which it might rule the body in perfect subjection
(*Ibid.* d. 30, q. 1, a. 2 ad 5).

Because man adhered continually to God, this power was
given him, that his lower powers might be kept continually
subject in obedience to reason, and the body in obedience to
the soul (*Ibid.* d. 33, q. 1, a. 1 sol.).

Original justice, which was in the soul, kept the body
from death by the power of the soul which had the justice
(*Ibid.* d. 33, q. 1, a. 3 ad 4).

In the state of innocence the soul had a certain gift
freely given by God, so that beyond the manner of other
forms it might give the body an unfailing life, according to
the manner in which the soul itself is incorruptible, and not
according to the corruptible manner of the body. As long as
it remained subject to God, the body was completely subject

to it, and no disposition could occur in the body which might hinder the soul's communication of life (*In III Sent.* d. 16, q. 1, a. 1 sol.).

In these texts, besides the external cause in Divine Providence and the instrumental causality of the tree of life, we have these indications of the causes within man: (1) A *virtus*, a power was given to the soul enabling it to inform matter more completely than other forms, giving it an *esse* proportioned to the soul's own immortal existence, not to the conditions of matter. This power prevented all suffering which would interfere with the soul's contemplation or endanger its communication of life to the body (*vivificatio*); it preserved the balance of the contraries which constitute the body, and caused the body to be completely adapted to and subject to the soul. (2) There is a corresponding disposition or power in the body rendering it immune from suffering and capable of complete subjection to the soul. (3) Apart from the statements that this was a free gift, there is a possible reference to *gratia gratum faciens* where St. Thomas says that the body was incorruptible by the grace of innocence, but the text does not bear much weight. (4) The causality is clearly *formal*.

In the treatise on the state of innocence in the First Part of the *Summa Theologiae* we find some further developments and a somewhat different treatment of the causes of immortality. The principal text is the first article of question 97, « Whether man in the state of innocence was immortal ».

> ... Something can be called incorruptible in three ways. One way, because of *matter*: either it has no matter, or it has matter in potency to only one form, as in the case of a heavenly body. This is said to be incorruptible by nature. A second way, because of a *form*: that is, because a thing which is corruptible by nature has some inherent disposition by which it is completely preserved from corruption. This is said to be incorruptible in glory ... The third way, something is called incorruptible because of its *efficient cause*. In this way man in the state of innocence would have been incorruptible and immortal. For, as Augustine says in the book *De Quaestionibus Veteris et Novi Testamenti*; « God

made man, who, as long as he would not sin, would live immortally, so that he himself would be the cause of his life or death ». For the body was not imperishable through any immortal vigor in it, but there was in the soul a certain force supernaturally given by God, by which it could preserve the body from all corruption as long as the soul itself remained subject to God. This was reasonable. Since the rational soul exceeds the proportion of bodily matter, it was fitting that in the beginning it be given a power by which it could preserve the body beyond the nature of bodily matter [1].

In answering the third objection in the same article St. Thomas says that the power of preserving the body from corruption was given to the soul through the gift of grace. It seems clear that he means to indicate that this power was an effect of *gratia gratum faciens* in the state of innocence, for he certainly is speaking of this grace when he goes on to say that man recovered grace for the remission of guilt and to merit glory, but not for the effect of the lost immortality.

What is to be said of the causality indicated here? As we have seen, the texts of the Commentary on the *Sentences* attributed immortality to the soul's special power to inform matter and give it an *esse* proportioned to its own immortal existence. The causality, therefore, was a formal causality of the soul. Moreover, in the body there was a disposition or power corresponding to the power of the soul. Here in the *Summa Theologiae* there would seem to be a reversal of both positions : immortality is due to the efficient causality of the soul, and there is no form or disposition in the body. Consequently also, the text, combined with the reply to the third objection just cited, would seem to be a strong partial confirmation of the general interpretation that grace is the efficient, not

---

[1] *S.T.* I, q. 97, a. 1 resp. Cf. also : ... Dictum enim est supra quod immortalitas primi status erat secundum vim quandam supernaturalem in anima residentem; non autem secundum aliquam dispositionem corpori inhaerentem ... (a. 3, ad 1) and ... homo sic erat incorruptibilis et immortalis, non quia corpus eius dispositionem incorruptibilitatis haberet, sed quia inerat animae vis quaedam ad praeservandum corpus a corruptione ... (q. 102, a. 2 resp.).

the formal, cause of original justice. I do not think that such an interpretation can stand up under a careful analysis of the text.

First, in denying any form or disposition inherent in the body as a principle of immortality, St. Thomas is excluding the kind of disposition which is had in the glorified body, thus giving some clarification of the doctrine by contrasting the immortality of the state of innocence and that of the glorified body [2]. This contrast does not seem to involve necessarily a repudiation of the loosely-described power or disposition mentioned in the earlier texts. In any case, we shall see St. Thomas resuming this terminology in later texts.

What kind of causality is involved in this explanation of immortality, efficient or formal? Both, though the formal causality is not the same as that which figured in the texts of the Commentary. There is explicit mention of a power inherent in the soul, an effect of grace. In virtue of this power the soul is able to preserve the body from corruption. As for the efficient causality, the sense of the text is clear from the authority which is cited. Man is the cause of his own life or death, because his immortality depends on his continual subjection to God. Thus immortality depends on the operation of the soul, as we have already seen in the texts on the formal element in original justice that the whole of original justice depended upon the continued adherence of the will to God. Not only was the will the moving cause of the second subjection by directing the lower powers to the ultimate end, but also its own continued subjection to God was the condition, and in some sense the cause, on which the whole order depended. In the order of operation, *in actu secundo,* all depended on the will. Thus even immortality depended on the will as an efficient cause by reason of the constant contingency of the *posse non mori.* In this text, therefore, we have a different treatment of the cause of immortality. It does not oppose, but rather complements, the treatment of the formal causality given in earlier texts. We

---

[2] Thus, for example, the state of innocence differs from the state of glory in the necessity of food and in the use of the sex powers. Cfr. *S.T.* I, q. 97, a. 3 ad 1; q. 98, a. 1 resp. et ad obj.; a. 2.

shall return to discuss the two lines of causality in a later chapter.

The interpretation we have just given of the important text in the *Summa Theologiae* is confirmed by several other contemporary or later texts in which we find St. Thomas retaining and further developing the explanation of immortality in terms of the formal causality of the soul. Thus, in the fifth question of the *De Malo,* after explaining as usual how death and corruption are natural to man considering the necessity of matter, but how according to the nature of the form it would be fitting that he be immortal, and how moreover God gave man a special gift by which the necessity of matter would be prevented from passing into act [3], St. Thomas gives some further explanation of the causes of immortality.

> In reply to the thirteenth it must be said that matter is in potency to another form; yet it cannot be reduced to act by an external agent unless that agent have a power greater than the force which the form has through the influence of its cause. But the cause of this form which is the human soul is God alone, whose power infinitely surpasses all the power of another agent. Accordingly, as long as He willed to preserve man in being by His power, he could be corrupted by no agent exterior or interior ... [4].
>
> In reply to the fourteenth it must be said that it is of the nature of a potency to be reduced to act by an agent; but one act existing in a potency prevents the reduction of the potency to another act. Therefore, unless the agent is stronger than the power of the form which is in matter, whether it have the power of itself or from that which is conserving it, the matter will not be reduced to act by the external agent ... Hence it is not strange if by the divine influence the human soul was able in the state of innocence to resist every agent opposed to it [5].
>
> In reply to the sixteenth it must be said that the form itself is the effect of the agent. Therefore, what the agent

---

[3] *De Malo,* q. V, a. 5 resp.
[4] *De Malo,* l. c. ad 13.
[5] *L. c.* ad 14.

does by producing (*effective*) is the same as what the form does by informing (*formaliter*); as the painter and also the color color the wall. In this manner, therefore, only God causes immortality *effectively,* but the soul causes it *formally* through the gift infused by God, whether in the state of innocence or in the state of glory [6].

In connection with these texts from the *De Malo,* we may note a reply in which St. Thomas mentions that the power of not dying (*posse non mori*) came from grace: according to some this was not *gratia gratum faciens,* hence man in that state could not merit; according to others this gift of immortality proceeded from *gratia gratum faciens,* and man in that state could merit [7]. Though he does not commit himself here, seemingly his own final position on the question of creation in the state of grace would involve holding that immortality was an effect of sanctifying grace.

The emphasis upon formal causality, and especially upon a special disposition in the body adapting it to the soul, continues in the *Compendium Theologiae.*

> The rational soul beyond the manner of other forms exceeds the capacity of all bodily matter, as is shown by the intellectual operation which it has without the body. In order therefore that bodily matter be suitably adapted to the soul, it was necessary that some disposition be added to the body, through which it might become suitable matter for such a form. As this form comes into being from God alone through creation, so also that disposition exceeding the nature of a body was given by God alone to the human body, a disposition which would preserve the body itself incorrupt, so that thus it might match the unbroken existence of the soul. This disposition remained in man's body as long as man's soul clung to God; but when the soul of man turned from God by sin, fittingly also the human body lost that supernatural disposition through which it was immovably subject to the soul, and so man incurred the necessity of death. If therefore one regard the nature of the body, death is

---

[6] *L.c.* ad 16.
[7] *L.c.* ad 11.

natural ; but if one consider the nature of the soul and the
disposition which on the soul's account was in the beginning
added supernaturally to the human body, death is *per accidens*
and against nature, since it is natural for the soul to be
united to the body [8].

Finally, the analogy between immortality in the state of
innocence and that in the state of glory enables us to learn
something about the former from a clear text on the latter,
within the proper limits of the analogy. St. Thomas himself
has shown by his example in *De Malo* (q. V, a. 5, ad 16) that
the essential character of the formal causality involved does
come within the analogy. Consequently we may draw at least
a confirmation of a position already well-established from this
text of the *Compendium Theologiae,* in which St. Thomas explains the disposition of the glorified body :

> ... For the soul is the form and mover of the body. In
> so far as it is the form, it is the principle not only of the
> substantial being of the body, but also of the proper acci-
> dents which are caused in the subject from the union of
> form and matter. The stronger a form is, the less can the
> impression of the form in matter be hindered by any external
> agent ... Therefore, since the blessed soul is at the summit
> of excellence and power, being united with the first principle
> of things, it confers upon the body which God has united
> with it first a substantial being of the noblest kind, holding
> it entirely under its control, whence it will be subtle and
> spiritual ... etc. [9].

Though the degree of excellence in being, and the number
and degree of formal effects are different in the two states, yet
proportionally the same principles of formal causality hold for
both, as is evident from a comparison with the texts which we
have seen.

---

[8] *Comp. Theol.* c. 152. Other texts of the later period, more non-com-
mittal, yet giving some suggestion of the formal causality are the following :
In Epist. ad Rom. c. 5, lect. 3; *S.T.* I-II, q. 82, a. 6 resp.; II-II, q. 164,
a. 1 resp. et ad 1.

[9] *Comp. Theol.* c. 168; cf. c. 167.

As is evident from this series of texts, the predominant
element in St. Thomas' explanation of the causes of immortality is certainly the formal causality of the soul and a corresponding disposition in the body.   The text of the *Summa
Theologiae* is unique in its apparent rejection of the bodily
disposition and in its concern with efficient rather than formal
causality.   Not only does that text stand alone, but also it la-
bors under considerable obscurity.   It is not absolutely clear
whether by efficient cause here St. Thomas is referring directly to God or to the soul.   Supposing that he means the efficient
causality of the soul, what does he mean by the power given
to the soul?   Was it the power to cling to God and so preserve
the disposition of will required in order to keep immortality
and the other gifts of original justice?   Or was it a power enabling the soul somehow to act on the body or to act against
the forces which would corrupt the body?   One thing is clear:
St. Thomas has in mind the contingency of original justice,
which depended on the action of the soul in clinging to God.
It is this contingency which distinguishes the immortality of
the state of innocence from that of the state of glory, in which
there is a disposition completely and permanently preserving
the body from corruption.   Without attempting to minimize
the difficulties of the text, we may say fairly, I believe, that
it pursues rather obscurely another line of reasoning without
conflicting with the teaching of the many texts on formal causality.

This emphasis on strict formal causality in the explanation of immortality justifies the observation made in the preceding section of our study on the « formal » element of original justice.   No theory of « formal » element confined to the
causality of the will as moving the powers subject to it can
suffice to explain the causality of the whole of original justice.
At the level of the subjection of the lower powers to the reason it affords a partial explanation, but even there it is not
complete.   It explains the efficient causality but leaves strict
formal causality untouched.   Furthermore, it cannot be extended to explain the complete subjection of body to soul, with
the effects of immortality and freedom from suffering, for

here we have passed beyond the realm of the power of the will to move. Significantly here St. Thomas speaks almost exclusively of formal causality. We must seek further, therefore, to find an adequate theory of the causes of original justice.

CHAPTER FOUR

THE PERFECTION OF MAN'S INTELLECT

In our study of original justice to this point, we have been concerned largely with the general formulae describing man's perfection in the state of innocence, and with aspects of the subjection of the lower powers to the reason and the subjection of body to soul. To complete our summary of the principal features of St. Thomas' teaching we must consider first briefly the perfection of the intellect, then more at length the perfection of the will, involving the question concerning the role of grace and the virtues in the state of innocence.

St. Thomas has treated man's knowledge in the first state principally in three places, in the Commentary on the *Sentences,* the *De Veritate,* and the First Part of the *Summa Theologiae.* In general, the treatment falls under three headings: man's knowledge of God; his knowledge of other things; and his freedom from error and deception.

Man did not have the immediate vision of God ordinarily [1] in the state of innocence, but he had a knowledge midway between our knowledge (*cognitio viae*) and that of the saints in heaven (*cognitio patriae*) [2]. He knew God as the angels do, without demonstration, beholding God as in a mirror in His creatures, especially in His intelligible effects [3]. Adam was capable of this more perfect contemplation because the perfect rectitude of original justice freed him from the distraction of the things of sense [4]. Not only was his natural knowledge

---

[1] *S.T.* I, q. 94, a. 1 resp.
[2] *In II Sent.* d. 23, q. 2, a. 1 sol.
[3] *Ibid.; De Ver.* q. 18, a. 1 ad 1; *S.T.* I, q. 94, a. 1 resp. et ad 3.
[4] *S.T.,* l. c.

more perfect than ours, but also his knowledge by grace [5]; he received the truths of faith not by external revelation but through God's speaking within him [6].

Concerning the knowledge of other things in the state of innocence, St. Thomas follows this principle: it is necessary to attribute to man in the first state that knowledge without which he would have been imperfect, and no more. For his own actions he needed a knowledge of what he must do and what avoid: consequently he needed perfect prudence. Moreover he needed that perfect knowledge required to rule over other creatures. In this regard, one must distinguish between Adam, the first man, and his descendants who would have followed in the state of innocence. Adam had to be perfect as the principle of the human race, and so from the beginning had to have what he needed not only to beget his children, but also to instruct them [7]. Adam therefore had an habitual possession of all the natural knowledge which man could ever attain [8], all that is contained virtually in the first principles which are known *per se* [9]. In addition he had such supernatural knowledge as was required for management of human life in that state [10]. His descendants most probably would have had from the beginning the perfect prudence necessary for action, and would have attained only gradually the other perfect science [11].

Finally, the perfect subjection of the lower powers, which are normally the source of deception within us, would have preserved man from all deception, error, and false opinion [12]. In the *De Veritate,* St. Thomas goes so far as to hold that in the state of innocence there would have been no opinion: man would have had certain knowledge of everything he knew [13].

---

[5] *De Ver.* q. 18, aa. 2, 3; *S. T.,* l. c.
[6] *De Ver.* q. 18, a. 3.
[7] *In II Sent.* d. 23, q. 2, a. 2; *De Ver.* q. 18, a. 4 resp. et ad 3.
[8] *De Ver.* l. c.
[9] *S.T.* I, q. 94, a. 3.
[10] *Ibid.,* l. c.
[11] *In II Sent.,* l. c.; *De Ver.* l. c. et a. 7.
[12] *In II Sent.,* l. c., a. 3; *De Ver.* q. 18, a. 6; *S.T.* I, q. 94, a. 4.
[13] *De Ver.,* l. c.

CHAPTER FIVE

PERFECTION OF WILL: GRACE AND THE VIRTUES

A. CREATION IN GRACE.

The evolution of St. Thomas' thought on the question of Adam's creation in the state of grace is a matter of common knowledge. We must retrace it briefly, however, in this survey of the principal features of his teaching on the state of innocence.

In the first text in which he touches the question, in the Commentary on the *Sentences,* St. Thomas solves an objection in terms of both opinions. There is no indication of a preference except that he answers first in terms of the position of those who hold that Adam was created in grace. Then he gives the second solution: « ... but supposing also, according to the opinion ... » [1]. One might suspect that he favors less the opinion introduced thus: « Sed supposito etiam ... » — but one could prove nothing.

In a second text, treating directly the question whether man had grace before the sin, he gives three opinions. (1) Some say that man in the first state had neither grace nor gratuitous virtues. Thus all the opinions of the saints which the *Magister* introduces in the text to prove that man had virtues are interpreted as concerning natural virtues, which man had in a high degree because of the integrity of human nature. This however does not seem to agree with the authorities cited, who hold that Adam had charity, which cannot be without grace; and many other things are said which cannot be referred to

---

[1] *In II Sent.* d. 24, q. 1, a. 4 ad 2.

natural virtues except by a forced interpretation. (2) Others distinguish two states in the state of innocence. They say that man was created in the beginning with his natural gifts only, without grace; but afterwards grace was given, before the sin. Thus they try with this distinction to reconcile the various sayings of saints and doctors. Yet this does not seem to agree with the sayings of the saints and doctors, who speak of the state of innocence as one state without distinction. Therefore this position has not much authority. (3) Consequently others say that man was created in grace in the beginning; and this opinion seems to agree well enough with the opinion of Augustine, who holds that things were created and perfected at the same time, in matter and in form. The first opinion, however, seems to agree better with the opinions of other saints, who say that things were created and then perfected in the course of time. One cannot prove with a very compelling argument which of these opinions is truer — as in the case of all those things which depend only on God's will. Yet this is more probable: since man was created with his natural powers intact, and they could not be idle, he turned to God in the first instant of his creation and got grace [2]. Holding this opinion, St. Thomas replies to the objections. Without taking a definite position, therefore, he proceeds allowing two probable opinions: either man was created in grace, or he turned to God in the instant of his creation and received grace.

The next advance is marked in the *Summa Theologiae,* where St. Thomas handles the question in his treatise on the state of innocence. Mentioning two opinions, the second and third of the three given above, he holds that the first man was created in grace:

> Some say that the first man was not created in grace, but that afterwards grace was given to him before he sinned, for many statements of the saints attest that man had grace in the state of innocence. But that he was also created in grace, as others say, seems to be required by the very rec-

---

[2] *Ibid.* d. 29, q. 1, a. 2 sol.

titude of the first state in which God made man, according
to the word of *Ecclesiastes,* vii, « God made man right ».
The rectitude consisted in this, that reason was subject to
God, and the lower powers to reason, and the body to the
soul.   Moreover the first subjection was the cause of the
second and the third: for as long as the reason remained
subject to God, the lower powers were kept subject to it,
as Augustine says.   It is clear that this subjection of body
to soul, and of lower powers to reason, was not natural:
otherwise it would have remained after the sin, since even
in the demons natural gifts remained after their sin.   Hence
it is clear that that first subjection too, by which reason was
kept subject to God, was not only according to nature, but
according to the supernatural gift of grace; for it is impossible for an effect to be greater than its cause ... Thus it is
understandable that if through the loss of grace the obedience
of the flesh to the soul was destroyed, it was through grace
existing in the soul that the lower powers were kept subject to it [3].

This text obviously has an importance in the evolution of
St. Thomas' thought.   He is almost certain — or almost ready
to declare his certitude — that the very rectitude of the first
state is intelligible only if we say that Adam was created in
grace.   There are two signs of a lingering hesitancy: the
« *videtur* » with which he introduces his argument; and the
reply to the fifth objection, which may *possibly* be interpreted
as being given in terms of the position which he had regarded
as more probable in the preceding text from the Commentary:
that even if man were not created in grace, yet in the instant
of his creation he turned to God and received grace [4].

There is a further significance in the very substance of the
argument which St. Thomas uses here.   If we are aware of
his great care for proportion, for demonstrating from a given

---

[3] *S.T.* I, q. 95, a. 1 resp.

[4] It had been objected that the reception of grace requires the consent
of the recipient.   Since this implies a prior existence, man could not have
received grace *in primo instanti suae creationis.*   To this St. Thomas replies:
since the act of the will is not successive, there is nothing to prevent the
first man's having consented to grace in the first instant of his creation.

effect only that which is its cause *per se,* that which is strictly required to explain the existence of the effect, then this argument may seem at first to be defective. For there may seem to be a lack of proportion between effects which have come to be called by other theologians merely « preternatural » and a cause which is clearly *gratia gratum faciens.* St. Thomas here is proving the necessity of grace not from the supernatural end of man and the need of a principle proportioned to that end, but from the subjection of body to soul and of lower powers to reason. These subjections are not natural. Therefore the first subjection was not natural. Therefore it was caused by the supernatural gift of grace. It seems that where St. Thomas has sought to demonstrate the necessity of grace (*gratia gratum faciens*) he has proved only the necessity of *some* gratuitous gift, some supernatural or « preternatural » gift sufficient to explain the subjection of the reason to God. Yet I believe that the argument is perfectly sound, and that its full power can be perceived only if we realize a very important fact : there is no room in the theology of St. Thomas for a supernatural rectitude of will — of « reason », the highest part of the soul, etc. — other than that which is the effect of grace and charity. If there were a possibility of a so-called preternatural rectitude of will in his theology, then the present argument would not be sound. For the second and third subjections, both of them « preternatural », are the only reasons here for positing grace. A preternatural rectitude « *in linea naturae* » like the other two would suffice as their cause, if there were any such thing. Given the theology of St. Thomas, and especially his theory of the will and the virtues, the rectitude through grace and charity is the only possible supernatural rectitude of the will, and consequently the only possible supernatural cause at this level of the two lower subjections. Given these principles of his theology, the argument is sound. Concerning these principles, it must suffice for the present to affirm what will be demonstrated later.

Later in the same treatise St. Thomas reinforces his teaching concerning the necessity of grace, speaking however not of the creation of the first man, but of the birth of children in the state of innocence [5]. The problem is the same fundamentally. Others had held that children would have been born in original justice, but without the gratuitous justice which is the principle of merit. According to St. Thomas, *it is necessary* to say that if they had been born in original justice, they would have been born with grace. For the root of original justice consists in the supernatural subjection of reason to God, caused by *gratia gratum faciens,* as he has said before (in the article which we have just discussed). In this text there is no hesitation, no « *videtur* », but a firm *necesse est dicere.*

Finally, in the *De Malo,* St. Thomas says that original justice includes sanctifying grace (*gratum faciens*), declaring his belief that man was not created with only natural gifts (*in naturalibus puris*) [6]. Yet, having solved the objection on the basis of his own opinion, he indicates another solution which is good if original justice does not include grace. The « *credo* » and the alternative solution do not, however, reveal a weakening of his own position. As I have indicated in discussing the text of the *Summa Theologiae,* question 95, and as St. Thomas indicates by the « *necesse est dicere* » of question 100, there is a certitude, a necessity in his position that the first man was created in grace, and that original justice includes grace. These are certain, necessary conclusions, once given the facts of revelation *and* the principles which regulate the development of his theology. Yet St. Thomas can recognize that such conclusions are necessary only for one who shares his principles, and so can state his own belief in the matter, and also provide another line of reasoning to solve the objection in terms of principles acceptable to the objector. The alternative argument is properly dialectical.

These texts in which we find St. Thomas gradually clarifying and solidifying his position on creation in grace are based on the conviction that grace is necessary for the rectitude of original justice. One other text, not concerned directly with the question of creation in grace, holds similarly that grace

---

[5] Q. 100, a. 1 ad 2.
[6] *De Malo,* q. 4, a. 2 ad 1 in contr. (third series of objections).

is necessarily included in original justice : there can be no
original justice without grace [7].

In his definitive doctrine, therefore, St. Thomas clearly
holds that the first man was created in grace because grace is
necessary for original justice. It seems sufficiently clear, too,
that for him this was a necessary, certain conclusion; though
he allows for the opinion of others, expressing his position as
his belief, and proposing alternative solutions in terms of the
opposite opinion.

B. THE NECESSITY OF GRACE FOR MAN'S
SUPERNATURAL END.

The series of texts which we have just considered deals
with the necessity of grace from one point of view : the rectitude of original justice, the perfect subjection of body to soul
and of lower powers to reason, and also the presence of charity
and other supernatural virtues — all these supernatural effects
demand grace as their cause. There are other questions in
which the need of grace in the state of innocence is shown from
the supernatural end of man.

Two texts in the Commentary on the *Sentences* afford interesting examples of a loose sort of reasoning in which St. Thomas argues from the supernatural end of man and the principle of proportion to the end, and concludes not to the gift
of *gratia gratum faciens,* but to some gift beyond nature. Thus
the first text concerns immortality :

> Since man was made for an end which consists in a
> beatitude exceeding all the powers of human nature, it was

---

[7] *De Malo* q. 5, a. 1 ad 13. The objection is that since one could be in
original justice without grace, and therefore without title to the vision of
God, one cannot say that the lack of the vision of God is fitting punishment
for original sin. St. Thomas answers : ... dicendum, quod ratio illa procedit
secundum opinionem ponentium quod gratia gratum faciens non includatur in
ratione originalis iustitiae; quod tamen credo esse falsum, quia cum originalis
iustitia primordialiter consistat in subiectione humanae mentis ad Deum, quae
firma esse non potest nisi per gratiam, iustitia originalis sine gratia esse non
potuit. ... In the latter part of the reply, however, he gives an alternative
solution in terms of the other opinion.

necessary that in his very constitution something be given him beyond the powers of his natural principles. Through his natural principles he could not have a perpetual existence, because he is composed of contraries: that is a cause of corruption in things, since a form perfects matter according to its capacity. This, therefore, was given him beyond the condition of his nature, that his soul, which was destined to such a noble end, might communicate to matter a perpetual existence, beyond the general order of nature by which matter receives existence according to its own condition ... [8].

In the second text St. Thomas finds in the supernatural end to which man was destined the reason for the subjection of the lower powers to the highest part of the soul and the disposition of the body in such a way that it could not interfere with contemplation:

Those things which are directed to an end are disposed according to the necessity of the end. The end to which man has been directed is beyond the power of created nature, namely: a beatitude which consists in the vision of God; for to God alone is this natural. Therefore it was necessary that human nature be so constituted that it have not only that which was due to it according to its natural principles, but also something further, by which it might easily reach its end. And since it could not cling by love to its last end, nor arrive at its possession, except through the highest part, which is the mind and intellect or reason, which has been marked with the image of God; therefore, in order that that part might tend freely [9] to God, the lower powers were made subject to it, so that nothing might occur in them which would restrain and impede the mind in its journey to God. Likewise the body was so disposed that it could suffer nothing by which the mind's contemplation would be impeded. And since man had all these gifts because of his direction to an end, when by sin he turned from his end, human nature lost them all, and man was left with only those gifts which came to him from his natural principles [10].

---

[8] *In II Sent.* d. 19, q. 1, a. 2 sol.
[9] « *Libere* » here in Mandonnet's text is omitted in the Parma edition.
[10] *Ibid.* d. 30, q. 1, a. 1 sol.

We do find, however, another clear text in the Commentary on the same book of the *Sentences,* in which St. Thomas gives a more rigorous demonstration of the necessity of grace itself. Man in the state of innocence needed grace, not with the absolute necessity based on the causes which constitute his nature, but with a necessity conditioned upon his supernatural end. In this sense, then, man needed grace before the sin, because without grace he could in no way attain his end consisting in eternal life. It is impossible to attain an end except through actions proportioned to the end. Since eternal life is an end which exceeds completely the powers of human nature, necessarily also the actions by which one attains eternal life exceed the powers of human nature. Consequently, however perfect (*integra*) human nature is, man needs grace to attain eternal life [11].

As far as the essential need of grace is concerned, man needed it as much before original sin as after, since we speak of a need or exigency with respect to an end. The end to which man is directed through grace, namely glory, is beyond human power before or after sin. In this respect, then, the need is not greater after sin than before. As regards the accidental effect of grace, the removal of evil, man had greater need after sin than before. Grace, however, is measured in relation to glory, since with greater grace one merits greater glory; not in relation to the removal of sin or weakness, since the least grace suffices to destroy all sins. Consequently man did not need more grace after sin than before, but it is true that he needed grace for more numerous effects. Any amount of grace, however, could accomplish these effects [12].

The clearest statement of the necessity of grace in relation to man's supernatural end is given in the important text of *De Malo,* question five, which we have already examined in our study of the formulae with which St. Thomas has described original justice. The preeminence of a rational creature consists in this: it is capable of attaining the supreme good

---

[11] *Ibid.* d. 29, q. 1, a. 1 sol.
[12] *Ibid.* d. 29, q. 1, a. 3 ad 3. The same doctrine is repeated in the *Summa Theologiae* I, q. 95, a. 4 ad 1.

through the vision and enjoyment of God. To reach this perfect beatitude, man, in common with the angels, needs the aid of sanctifying grace (*gratia gratum faciens*). Besides this, however, man needs another supernatural help by reason of his composite nature. If the body and the sensible nature are left in their own natural condition, they are a burden and a hindrance to the intellect's contemplation. The special help by which they are perfectly subjected is called original justice. It is a kind of disposition to that help by which the human mind is directed to the vision and enjoyment of God [13]. Both gifts, sanctifying grace and original justice, are considered in relation to man's supernatural end. The text adds a refinement to the treatment of the purpose of original justice. Elsewhere it was explained as being proportioned to the natural dignity of the rational soul [14]. Here the true dignity and preeminence of the rational soul is more adequately expressed: it consists in the soul's capacity for the attainment of the supreme good through the vision and enjoyment of God.

Briefly, then, we may summarize the teaching of St. Thomas on the necessity of grace in the state of innocence. (1) Because man is destined to a supernatural beatitude, he needs the supernatural help of *gratia gratum faciens,* indispensable for the attainment of that end. This need is common to angel and man, to integral and corrupt human nature. It was as great before as after the first sin. (2) To dispose man properly for this grace, it was necessary to give another supernatural help, original justice, to remedy the twofold weakness in man which would burden and hinder him in his contemplation and his movement toward God. Retaining here the distinction between grace and original justice, we are using the latter term in its restricted sense, as including only the subjection of the lower powers to reason and of body to soul [15].

---

[13] *De Malo* q. 5, a. 1 resp.
[14] *C.G.* IV, c. 52.
[15] Cf. above, pp. 24-26, the commentary on the formula contained in the text of *De Malo,* q. 5, a. 1 resp.

C. Special Questions on the Necessity of Grace

Having considered the necessity of grace first as the cause of the subjection of the body and of the lower powers of the soul in original justice, and secondly as the indispensable means of attaining man's supernatural end, we must study a group of special questions in which St. Thomas tries to clarify the doctrine of the necessity of grace by determining in detail the limits of the power of pure nature. He has gathered these questions especially in the *Prima Secundae* of the *Summa Theologiae,* question 109. In almost every article he distinguishes between integral and corrupt nature, showing what each can and cannot do without grace. We shall examine those aspects of his teaching which present difficulties and contribute further precision to the theology of original justice.

The first of these questions is whether man can will and do good without grace. In his earlier treatment of the question St. Thomas made no distinction between integral and corrupt nature [16]. Here, however, he does. In both states of nature, the divine assistance is necessary as the first mover in any operation. But as far as the operative power is concerned, in the state of integral nature man was able by his natural powers to will and do all the good proportioned to his nature, such as the good of the acquired virtues; but not that which exceeds his nature, such as the good of the infused virtues. In the state of corrupt nature man can do particular good acts, but not the whole good which is natural for him. Thus, man needs a gratuitous power added to the power of nature for one thing in the state of integral nature: to will and perform supernatural good; but for two things in the state of corrupt nature: to be healed, and then further to perform a meritorious good work of supernatural virtue [17]. This text, then, deals with the general question of the natural power of the will, as the pre-

---

[16] *In II Sent.* d. 28, q. 1, a. 1; *De Ver.* q. 24, a. 14; *In II Epist. ad Cor.* c. 3, lect. 1.

[17] *S.T.* I-II, q. 109, a. 2 resp.

ceding article had handled the general question of the possibility of the knowledge of truth without grace.

The crucial question, most fascinating and most difficult,
is the next : can man love God above all things with his natural powers alone, without grace? [17a]. It is a question which
has an interesting history within the development of St. Thomas' thought, and its treatment suggests some of the really
profound difficulties and most delicate nuances of the theology
of original justice.

In the Commentary on the *Sentences* St. Thomas treats
the problem in connection with the love of God through charity. Distinguishing between the love of concupiscence and
the love of benevolence, he makes clear that there is question
here of the latter, and he lays down the principle that everyone
loves most that which is his own greatest good. As any part
is imperfect in itself and has its perfection in the whole, so
with a natural love the part tends toward the conservation
rather of the whole than of itself. Hence an animal naturally
puts out its foreleg to protect its head, on which the well-being
of the whole depends. Hence also individuals expose themselves to death to save the community of which they are a part.
Since our good is perfect in God as in the universal first and
perfect cause of good, the good in Him is more pleasing to
us naturally than the good in ourselves. Therefore even with
the love of friendship man loves God naturally more than
himself. Since charity perfects nature, by charity too man
loves God more than himself and all other particular goods [18].
In this first formulation of his doctrine St. Thomas draws no
distinction between integral and corrupt nature, and precisely

---

[17a] For a general treatment of the question of natural love of God, see
the excellent articles of Father M.-R. GAGNEBET, O. P., « L'amour naturel de
Dieu chez saint Thomas et ses contemporains », *Revue Thomiste* 48 (1948)
394-446; 49 (1949) 31-102. Cf. also L.-B. GILLON, O. P., « Primacia del apetito universal de Dios segun Santo Tomas », *Ciencia Tomista* 63 (1942) 328-
342; V. HÉRIS, O. P., « L'amour naturel de Dieu d'après saint Thomas »,
Mélanges Thomistes (Bibliothèque Thomiste III, Le Saulchoir, Kain, 1923)
289-310; P. ROUSSELOT, S. J., *Pour l'histoire du problème de l'amour au
moyen âge* (Paris, 1933; also published in *Beiträge zur Geschichte der Philosophie des Mittelalters*, B. VI. H. 6., Münster, 1908).

[18] *In III Sent.* d. 29, a. 3 resp.

because he fails to come to grips with the problem of nature in the state in which we know it, his argument has a hollow ring.

The question comes up again in the First Part of the *Summa Theologiae* when St. Thomas considers whether an angel loves God more than himself with a natural love. Some held that strictly speaking an angel loves himself more than God with a natural love. The falsity of this opinion is clear if we consider in things of nature what it is to which a thing is moved naturally. For the natural inclination in things which are without reason shows what is the natural inclination in the will of an intellectual nature. Every natural thing which pertains to another tends first and foremost to that to which it pertains, rather than to itself. Again we have the example of the part and the whole, and of the hand exposed to a blow to save the body. Since reason imitates nature, we find this kind of inclination in the virtue of the citizen: the good citizen exposes himself to the danger of death to save the whole state. If man were a natural part of this state, this inclination would be natural to him. Since, therefore, the universal good is God himself, and under this good are embraced angels and men and all creatures, since every creature naturally, in that which it is, belongs to God, it follows that angels and men too have a prior and greater love for God than for themselves. Otherwise, if naturally they loved themselves more than God, it would follow that natural love would be perverse, and that it would not be perfected by charity, but destroyed [19]. Here the argument is developed with greater care, but the discussion of natural love remains in the sphere of the absolute consideration of nature, apart from the problems of man's actual condition.

The first of the necessary distinctions is added in the reply to the fourth objection in the same article: God as the universal good on which all *natural* good depends is loved with a natural love by all; as the good which is the source of our supernatural beatitude, He is loved with the love of charity [20].

---

[19] *S.T.* I, q. 60, a. 5 resp.
[20] Ad quartum dicendum quod Deus, secundum quod est universale bonum, a quo dependet omne bonum naturale, diligitur naturali dilectione ab

With a change of formula the same distinction is given in the
Quaestio Disputata de Caritate[21]. In neither of these texts,
however, is there a distinction between integral and corrupt
nature; moreover, neither deals explicitly with a love of God
super omnia.

In his reply to an objection in the *Quaestio Disputata
de Spe* St. Thomas amplifies the formula of the *De Caritate*
with elements of the text in the *Summa Theologiae,* and adds
one important step. In the article of the *Summa* St. Thomas
had closed by saying that a natural love of self more than God
would be perverse[22]. Here in the *De Spe* he observes that
the natural love of God is perverted by sin, and consequently
it was in the state of integral nature that man was able to love
God above all in the manner described[23]. Thus for the first
time he qualifies his teaching on the natural love of God above
all by affirming its possibility in the state of integral nature,
which had not been perverted by sin. Its exclusion from the
state of corrupt nature is not explicit here.

With this development achieved in the earlier texts, St.
Thomas approaches the question in his treatise on the necessity
of grace in the *Prima Secundae*: « Whether man can love God
above all things with his natural powers alone, without grace ».
The objections are that such a love is proper to charity and
is beyond nature. It is interesting to note the *Sed Contra*:
the first man was created with only his natural powers, as certain theologians hold. Obviously he loved God somehow in

---

unoquoque. In quantum vero est bonum beatificans naturaliter omnes super-
naturali beatitudine, sic diligitur dilectione caritatis (*S.T.* I, q. 60, a. 5 ad 4).

[21] Ad decimum sextum dicendum, quod amor summi boni, prout est principium esse naturalis, inest nobis a natura; sed prout est obiectum illius bea-
titudinis quae totam capacitatem naturae creatae excedit, non inest nobis a
natura, sed est supra naturam (*De Car*. a. 2 ad 16).

[22] ... Sequitur quod naturali dilectione etiam angelus et homo plus et
principalius diligat Deum quam seipsum. Alioquin, si naturaliter plus seipsum
diligeret quam Deum, sequeretur quod naturalis dilectio esset perversa; et
quod non perficeretur per caritatem, sed destrueretur (*S.T.* I, q. 60, a. 5 resp.).

[23] ... Sed iste naturalis amor Dei pervertitur ab hominibus per peccatum;
unde in statu naturae integrae poterat homo Deum diligere super omnia secundum modum praedictum (*De Spe* a. 1 ad 9).

this state. He did not love God the same as himself, or less than himself, because thus he would have sinned. Therefore he loved God above himself. Therefore man with his natural powers alone can love God more than himself and above all things. St. Thomas' answer to the question is this:

As has been said above in the First Part [24], where also different opinions were set down concerning the natural love of angels, man in the state of integral nature could perform by virtue of his nature the good which is natural for him, without the addition of a gratuitous gift, though not without the aid of God moving him. To love God above all things is something natural to man, and also to any creature, not only rational, but irrational and even inanimate, in accordance with the kind of love which is proper to each creature. The reason for this is that it is natural for every thing to desire and love something according to its natural mode of being (*secundum quod aptum natum est esse*): for everything acts according to its nature, as is said in the second book of the *Physics*. Clearly the good of the part is directed to the good of the whole. Hence also with a natural desire or love every particular thing loves its own good because of the general good of the whole universe, which is God. Consequently Dionysius also says in the book *De Divinis Nominibus* that « God turns all things to a love of himself ». Hence man in the state of integral nature referred his love of himself to the love of God as to its end, and likewise the love of all other things. So he loved God more than himself and above all. In the state of corrupt nature, however, man falls short of this in the desire of his rational will, which because of the corruption of nature follows its individual good unless it is healed by God's grace. Accordingly we must say that in the state of integral nature man did not need the gift of grace added to his natural gifts in order to

---

[24] The reference to the first part is traced by the Leonine editors to question 60, article five, and this seems to be the place St. Thomas had in mind; yet that text makes no mention of integral nature or of the good proportioned to man's nature. It is only in I-II, q. 109, a. 2 that he has spoken of man's power to do the good proportioned to his nature in the state of integral nature.

love God above all; though he needed the help of God moving
him to this. But in the state of corrupt nature man needs
also for this the help of grace healing nature [25].

In this text St. Thomas has formulated clearly the necessary distinction between integral and corrupt nature. There
is an obscurity, however, and a serious difficulty in his position,
suggested in part by the *Sed Contra*. Is he dealing with the
state of integral nature according to the doctrine of those who
held that man was created in that state without grace, *in solis
naturalibus*? If so, how can we reconcile this teaching on the
natural love of God with the rest of his theology of original
justice? If, on the contrary, he is not granting that man was
created in a state of integral nature without grace, how can
he hold that man can perform this act without grace, yet only
in a state which necessarily depends on grace? We shall attempt to solve this difficulty after considering the remaining
texts.

The reply to the first objection distinguishes between this
natural love of God above all as the source and end of all
natural good, and charity, which loves God in a more excellent
way than nature. Charity loves God as the object of beatitude and as united spiritually with man. Another important
detail is added: charity also goes beyond natural love by add-
ing a certain promptness and delight, as any virtue adds something over and above the good act which is performed only
by the natural reason of a man who has not the virtue. This
is of some consequence for our study of original justice. One
reason why this natural love of God above all in the state of
integral nature could not suffice as the formal principle and
cause of the whole rectitude of original justice is that it is a
natural act, not an act of virtue, and so it lacks not only the
promptness and delight, but also the firmness and constancy
of a virtue, needed in the principle of original justice.

A later text in the *Summa Theologiae* presents a neat
synthesis of the doctrine developed in the texts which we have
examined. The natural love of God above all things as the

---

[25] *S.T.* I-II, q. 109, a. 3.

source of natural good is common to man in the state of integral nature and all other creatures, each according to its own kind of love : intellectual, rational, animal, or natural [26].

Finally, in the first *Quodlibetum* St. Thomas returns to the question whether man in the state of innocence loved God more than all things and above himself. By way of introduction to another synthesis of the elements of earlier texts he makes this observation on the question itself : « It must be said that if man was created in grace, as one can hold according to the words of Basil and Augustine, this question has no place. For it is evident that being in grace, he loved God more than himself through charity. But since it was possible for God to make man with only his natural powers, it is useful to consider the extent of the power of natural love » [27]. Note that the question here is *not* whether in the state of innocence man loved God above all *with his natural powers alone, without grace;* but simply whether he loved God above all and more than himself. It is this latter question, not the first, which has no place if man was created in grace. Holding that the first man was created in grace, and that obviously therefore he loved God above all with charity, one can still ask whether he could also love God above all with a natural love which does not require grace. The question which we have been considering all along, then, is relevant regardless of what is held on creation in grace.

The evolution of St. Thomas' teaching on the natural love of God has an important bearing on his theology of original justice. Ironically, what served to clarify and perfect the first seems to have obscured the second. As we have seen, it was the distinction between integral and corrupt nature which ena-

---

[26] ... Super communicatione autem bonorum naturalium nobis a Deo facta fundatur amor naturalis, quo non solum homo in suae integritate naturae super omnia diligit Deum et plus quam seipsum, sed etiam quaelibet creatura suo modo, idest vel intellectuali vel rationali vel animali, vel saltem naturali amore, sicut lapides et alia quae cognitione carent : quia unaquaeque pars naturaliter plus amat commune bonum totius quam particulare bonum proprium... (*S.T.* II-II, q. 26, a. 3 resp.).

[27] *Quodl.* I, q. 4, a. 3 resp.

bled St. Thomas to determine clearly man's power to love God
above all things without grace.   This same distinction, and the
notion of a natural love without grace in the state of integral
nature raises difficulties against what seems certainly to be his
definitive teaching on original justice.   Briefly the difficulties
are these : (1) At first sight, it seems that St. Thomas has aban-
doned his position on creation in grace and the necessity of
grace as the very root of original justice, the source of the
perfect rectitude of integral nature.   Since perfect natural love
of God is possible in integral nature without grace, it would
seem that the integrity of nature and original justice itself is
merely a natural perfection. (2) If we hold that St. Thomas certainly must be regarded as holding to his definitive position on
creation in grace, then we find an apparent contradiction in his
teaching: the natural love of God does and does not require
grace.   It does not require grace, because for man in the state
of integral nature this act is natural, within the powers of pure
nature, as it is for all other creatures.   It does require grace,
because it is possible only in this state of integral nature, which
in turn is caused by grace and possible only through grace.

First of all we may observe that St. Thomas is seeking
to determine clearly the necessity of grace by marking clearly
the limits of the power of pure nature.   Thus the early texts,
in which St. Thomas bases his argument on human nature considered absolutely, apart from any qualifications due to its
concrete historical condition, demonstrate a natural love which
is common proportionately to angels and men, animals and
stones.   It is a purely philosophical theory, and it does not
suffice.   Only when as a theologian St. Thomas makes the necessary distinction between integral and corrupt nature, does
he give a satisfactory account of man as we know him.

Man in the state of corrupt nature is unique in the universe.   With the powers of his nature unaided by grace he is
unable to make the act of love of God above all things which
is natural for him as for all creatures, each according to its
own kind of love.   All of them (the lost angels, of course,
excepted) can make this act, because their natures are sound
and well-ordered with respect to their end.   Man is incapable

of the perfect natural love of God because by original sin his nature has lost its orientation to God. His nature has been perverted by sin, and he seeks by preference his own individual good, setting the love of self above the love of God. The love of God above all things and more than himself is possible for him only through grace and charity, since only by grace can he be restored to right order and given the inclination to cling to God as his last end. Thus in corrupt nature grace is necessary not only to perform meritorious supernatural works, but also to heal a nature perverted and disordered by sin. The impossibility of a purely natural love of God above all things is universal in corrupt human nature, for there is no « natural » reconciliation and restoration possible for man born in original sin, much less for one who is in mortal sin. Moreover, in St. Thomas' theology, there is no adult to be found who is only in original sin without grace : as soon as one reaches the use of reason, he is offered the grace to turn to God, and thereafter he is in grace if he cooperates, or in mortal sin if he refuses [28].

So much is clear. Moreover, I believe it is obvious that we cannot suppose that in solving the problem of the natural love of God St. Thomas casually reverses his mature thought on creation in grace and the necessity of grace as the cause of original justice. The first alternative of the dilemma indicated above, then, is not at all probable, and our problem is to solve the apparent contradiction of an act performed without grace, yet only in a state of integral nature which depends necessarily on grace.

The analogies of natural love in angels and animals and inanimate things, together with the observation made in the first *Quodlibetum* [29] that there is question of the power of pure nature, indicate the way to a solution of the difficulty. Essentially we are concerned with what human nature can do when it has not been corrupted by sin. Consequently, had St. Thomas asked whether man in a state of pure nature (as it

[28] Cf. *In II Sent.* d. 42, q. 1, a. 5 ad 7 ; *De Ver.* q. 24, a. 12 ad 2 ; q. 28, a. 3 ad 4 ; *De Malo* q. 5, a. 2 ad 8 ; q. 7, a. 10 ad 8 ; *S.T.* I-II, q. 89, a. 6.
[29] *Quodl.* I, q. 4, a. 3 resp.

is discussed by later theologians) could have made the act of love of God above all things without grace, it seems that he would have answered affirmatively. In any state in which human nature could be found not corrupted by sin such an act would be possible, for it is a purely natural act. It is impossible now without grace only because human nature has been perverted by sin.

Why, then, the difficulty? Because in fact St. Thomas discusses the problem only in terms of two concrete historical states of human nature — the only two historical states which we know in this life. Historically the natural love of God above all things was possible without grace only in the state of integral nature, because as a matter of fact only in that state was the nature sound and well-ordered. It is the confusion of what is due to nature and what to grace in the state of integral nature which causes the obscurity and apparent contradiction here. Though historically the act was possible only in the state of integral nature, or original justice, caused by grace and directed to a supernatural end, yet the natural love of God did not depend essentially upon grace. Grace was its cause *per accidens,* since grace was the cause of original justice, of the perfect integrity of nature. Grace was the cause *per se* of charity and the supernatural rectitude of the higher part of the soul; it was the cause *per se* of the perfect subjection of the lower powers and of the body. But the natural love of God above all things does not depend essentially on the supernatural rectitude of the will, nor on the perfect supernatural subjection of the lower powers. It does not require, that is, the perfect integrity of original justice. It requires only a will with the natural rectitude of a nature uncorrupted by sin. It would be possible in a state of pure nature, prior to sin. There is no contradiction, then, in holding that this perfect love of God without grace was possible in the state of integral nature caused by grace. The act was not caused by grace, and if we say that it was possible only in the state of integral nature, the « only » is true historically, not absolutely: another state of pure nature remains possible.

Thus the principal difficulty raised by the treatment of

the natural love of God is solved, I believe. There remain
two observations to be made : first, the significance of this teaching for the understanding of the wound left in nature by original sin; and secondly, the relation of this natural love of God
to original justice.

The subtle and very difficult elaboration of the teaching
on man's natural love of God illumines the obscure doctrine
of the wound inflicted upon nature through Adam's first sin.
Original sin has left the human will in disorder [30], turned from
God, its last end and true good, and incapable of that love of
God which is proportioned to its nature. Though the will always
seeks the good naturally and necessarily, and though as *nature*
it is always right, even in the state of corrupt nature, yet as
reason, as rational appetite seeking happiness in this or that
good determinately, it can be perverted [31]. Thus St. Thomas
says that in the state of corrupt nature man falls short of loving
God more than himself and above all things « in the desire of
his rational will, which because of the corruption of nature
follows its own individual good, unless it is healed by grace » [32].

What is the relation of the natural love of God above all
things to original justice? We have here an act which is possible because of the natural rectitude of a will not perverted
by sin. Does this natural rectitude of the will suffice as the
formal element of original justice, the cause of the perfect rectitude of the lower parts? That seems impossible. First, St.
Thomas has mentioned that this act of natural love is an act
which proceeds not from a virtue, but merely from the faculty :
consequently it lacks the qualities which a virtue would contribute : promptness, delight, constancy. In itself, therefore,
this natural rectitude of the will and the act which it can pro-

----

[30] Respondeo dicendum quod per iustitiam originalem perfecte ratio continebat inferiores animae vires, et ipsa ratio a Deo perficiebatur ei subiecta.
Haec autem originalis iustitia subtracta est per peccatum primi parentis,
sicut iam dictum est. Et ideo omnes vires animae remanent quodammodo
destitutae proprio ordine, quo naturaliter ordinantur ad virtutem : et ipsa
destitutio vulneratio naturae dicitur. ... inquantum vero voluntas destituitur
ordine ad bonum, est vulnus malitiae ... (*S.T.* I-II, q. 85, a. 3 resp.).

[31] Cf. *In IV Sent.* d. 49, q. 1, a. 3 sol. 3.

[32] *S.T.* I-II, q. 109, a. 3 resp.

duce do not suffice to explain the firm, continual clinging to God
which has been indicated as the principal element of original
justice.   Secondly, since original justice is given in view of a
supernatural end, and involves not only charity and other infused virtues, but also a supernatural subjection of the body
and the lower powers of the soul, it cannot be caused by a
purely natural rectitude of the will, whose most perfect act is
the love of God as the source of natural good.   Rather we must
say that this natural rectitude is merely one of the natural
perfections of man in the state of original justice, a state which
included the fulness of grace and supernatural gifts together
with the full natural perfection of a human nature unspoiled
by sin.   As Adam was capable of natural and supernatural contemplation, so too he had the power of natural and supernatural
love of God.   Thus we cannot find here in the natural rectitude
of will and the natural love of God in the state of integral
nature the principal element and formal cause of original justice.
In our search for the formal element of original justice, therefore, we may eliminate another possibility.   As we have seen
in the description of original justice, there is no trace of a
preternatural aid to remedy the weakness of the will and serve
as the formal principle of the whole rectitude of original justice.
Actually, there was no need of such a preternatural gift to
rectify the will « in linea naturae », for the will was naturally
right before the sin.   We cannot, therefore, seek the formal
cause of original justice either in a preternatural rectitude of
will, which is unnecessary and nowhere described by St. Thomas;
or in the natural rectitude prior to sin, which as we have just
seen cannot suffice.

Two other questions concerning the necessity of grace have
a special bearing upon our study of original justice.   They are
closely related to the problem of the natural love of God, and
they present a similar difficulty.   The first of these questions is
whether man without grace can fulfill the precepts of the law
by his natural powers [33];   the second, whether without grace

---

[33] *S.T.* I-II, q. 109, a. 4.

man can avoid sin [34]. Really these questions present two aspects of the same problem [35]. The first need not detain us long, for it does not present any difficulty beyond that already considered in that case of natural love. Moreover, in the earlier treatment of the question of fulfilling the precepts of the law, as far as I can discover, St. Thomas does not distinguish between integral and corrupt nature [36]. He is content with the distinction between the substance of the law and the quality (*modus*) which the act receives from charity and which elevates it above nature.

The question concerning the avoidance of sin without grace presents one difficulty which goes beyond the problem posed by the act of natural love. It is this: apparently when St. Thomas says that in the state of integral nature man could avoid mortal and venial sin without grace [37] he means to include the perfect avoidance of both. If he includes the perfect avoidance of venial sin within the power of integral nature without grace, there seems to be a contradiction which cannot be resolved as easily as the apparent contradiction of the act of natural love without grace. In the latter case we are able to show that the act is purely natural, not caused *per se* by grace. This does not seem to be the case with the perfect avoidance of venial sin, which is possible only through the supernatural integrity, the complete subjection of the lower powers, which was the effect of grace. Let us examine the texts.

In the Commentary on the *Sentences* St. Thomas does not call attention to the distinction between the powers of integral and corrupt nature to avoid sin, though in fact he treats the

---

[34] *S.T.* I-II, q. 109, a. 8.

[35] Cf. *In I Epist. ad Corinth.* c. XII, lect. 1: to hold that a man in mortal sin can avoid all mortal sin without grace is to hold equivalently that a man could observe all the precepts of the law without grace, and that is Pelagianism.

[36] Cf. *In II Sent.* d. 28, q. 1, a. 3; *De Ver.* q. 24, a. 14 ad 1, ad 2; cf. also *In Epist. ad Rom.* c. 2, lect. 3.

[37] ... Secundum statum quidem naturae integrae, etiam sine gratia habituali, poterat homo non peccare nec mortaliter nec venialiter: quia peccare nihil aliud est quam recedere ab eo quod est secundum naturam, quod vitare homo poterat in integritate naturae. Non tamen hoc poterat sine auxilio Dei in bono conservantis: quo subtracto, etiam ipsa natura in nihilum decideret... (*S.T.* I-II, q. 109, a. 8 resp.).

cases separately.   Adam in his first state could avoid sin by his free will (*liberum arbitrium*).   There is no question of violence, which is entirely contrary to freedom of will, but rather of a habit or passion to which free will might succumb.   Neither could be said in the case of the first man, because he had a true, sound free will: consequently he had neither passions to urge him to evil, nor a perverse habit corrupting nature.   All these are the results of sin.   Hence not only could he resist sin, but he could do it easily [38].   At this point, as we have seen, St. Thomas has not yet taken a position on the question whether Adam was created in grace [39].

With regard to man in the present state of nature, St. Thomas holds here a position which he will later repudiate. Man in the state of mortal sin cannot avoid without grace a sin already committed: that is, he cannot absolve himself from a past sin unless he is freed by grace; in this Pelagius erred, thinking that a man making satisfaction by his own works without grace could absolve himself from past sins.   But man can avoid sin still to be committed, even without grace, however much he be in mortal sin [40].   The effect of sin on man's free will is such that, with regard to the avoidance of mortal sin, what formerly he could do easily (in the state of innocence) now he can do only with a difficult struggle.   He cannot avoid all venial sins, because of the rebellion of the flesh against the spirit [41].

Treating the problem several times in the *De Veritate,* St. Thomas clarifies and modifies his position.   At first, merely replying to objections, he gives the two conflicting opinions as to whether man can or cannot avoid mortal sin without grace [42].   Then, dealing with the power of free will, he treats the question whether free will without grace in the state of mortal sin can avoid mortal sin [43].   We may anticipate the answer to an ob-

[38] *In II Sent.* d. 24, q. 1, a. 4 sol.
[39] *In II Sent.* d. 24, q. 1, a. 4 ad 2.
[40] *Ibid.* d. 28, q. 1, a. 2 sol.
[41] *Ibid.* ad 2.
[42] *De Ver.* q. 22, a. 5 ad 7; q. 24, a. 1 ad 10, ad 12.
[43] *De Ver.* q. 24, a. 12.

jection in order to clarify the question: why does St. Thomas speak of man in the state of mortal sin? The reason is that if we are asking about the power of free will in the state of corrupt nature without grace, necessarily there is question of the state of mortal sin, because an adult cannot be merely in original sin without grace. As soon as he receives the use of free will, if he prepares himself for grace, he will have grace; otherwise he will be guilty of a mortal sin of negligence [44].

After reviewing the heresies which destroyed free will or exalted it excessively, St. Thomas explains how a sin or its avoidance can exceed the power of free will by the suddenness with which it occurs, escaping the choice made by free will, though the free will would have the power to commit or avoid the sin if it would direct its attention or effort to it. This sudden action can take place in two ways. First, through the impulse of passion, since the movements of anger and concupiscence sometimes anticipate the deliberation of reason. This movement tending to a forbidden act because of the corruption of nature is a venial sin.

> Accordingly, in the state of corrupt nature, it is not in the power of free will to avoid all such sins, because they elude its act, though it could stop any one of these movements if it struggled against it. It is not possible, however, for a man to struggle continually to avoid such movements because of the various occupations of the human mind and the need for rest. This happens because the lower powers are not wholly subject to reason, as they were in the state of innocence, when the avoidance of all such sins and each singly through free will was very easy for man, since no movement could begin in the lower powers except according to the command of reason. In the present state, generally speaking, man is not restored by grace to this rectitude, but we look forward to it in the state of glory. Consequently, in this state of misery, after his restoration by grace, man cannot avoid all venial sins, though this in no way prejudices his free will.

----

[44] *Ibid.* ad 2.

The second manner in which something occurs in us suddenly is from the inclination of a habit, for the less there is of premeditation, the more an act proceeds from habit. The act is not entirely without deliberation, since a virtue is a habit of choice; yet for one who has a habit, the end is already determined, and when something occurs which suits that end, it is chosen immediately, unless it is prevented by a greater and more attentive deliberation. A man in mortal sin clings to sin habitually. Though he may not always have a vicious habit, his will clings to a perishable good, and this inclination and adherence remain until he adheres again to the unchangeable good. The deliberation in these acts is enough to make him guilty of mortal sin, but not enough to withdraw him from sin. To resist sin he needs a greater deliberation, adequate to present the perishable good as evil. Consequently, supposing that the will clings to mortal sin, or to a wrong end, it is not in its power to avoid all mortal sins, though it can avoid each one if it struggles against it; for the constant vigilance necessary to make the required deliberation is impossible because of the many things which occupy a man's mind. One is not removed from this disposition except by grace, through which alone the human mind is brought to cling by charity to the unchangeable good as to its end [45].

One who is in grace can avoid mortal sin, because he has no habitual inclination to evil; on the contrary, he has an habitual inclination to avoid sin. However, since he cannot prevent some movements of concupiscence which anticipate completely the act of free will, he cannot avoid all venial sins [46].

The impossibility of avoiding all mortal sin without grace in the state of mortal sin is demonstrated also in the *Contra Gentiles,* where St. Thomas brands the opposite opinion as Pelagianism. Referring to his statement in the previous chapter that man is free to impede or not impede the reception of grace, he qualifies it by saying that it is true of those in whom the natural power was integral. After sin, however, it is not altogether in man's power to place no impediment to grace.

---

[45] *Ibid.* a. 12 resp.
[46] *Ibid.* a. 13 resp.

Though at a given moment he can refrain from a particular sinful act by his own power, still if he is left to himself for long, he will fall into sin and thus place an impediment to grace. There are three reasons why he will fall. First, when a man's mind has left the state of rectitude, clearly it has withdrawn from its order with respect to its proper end. What should be the principal object of its love as the ultimate end becomes less loved than that to which the mind is inordinately turned as to its last end. When anything occurs which suits the inordinate end but is contrary to the proper end, it will be chosen, unless the man is brought back to right order, to prefer his proper end to all things. This is the effect of grace. After sin, then, a man cannot avoid all sin until by grace he is brought back to right order. Secondly, in sudden actions a man will be led to act according to his habitual inclination to sin. Finally, the impulse of bodily passions, the things which attract the sense appetite, and the many occasions of sin easily provoke a man to sin unless he is held back by a firm adherence to his last end, which is the effect of grace [47].

A reply to an objection in the *De Malo* draws the distinction between the state in which human nature was created and the state of corrupt nature. In the former state man had nothing impelling him to evil, though his natural goodness (*bonum naturae*) did not suffice to attain glory. Accordingly he needed the help of grace to merit, but did not need it to avoid sins, because with what he had received naturally he could stand. But in the state of corrupt nature he has something impelling him to evil, and so he needs the help of grace not to fall [48].

Against the background of these earlier texts we may consider the problem presented by St. Thomas' teaching in the *Summa Theologiae*. The question here is simply whether man can avoid sin without grace, and in his reply St. Thomas gives a synthesis of the whole subject. In the state of integral nature,

[47] *C.G.* III, c. 160. Cf. *In Epist. I ad Corinth.* c. 12, lect. 1; *In Epist. ad Heb.* c. 10, lect. 3.
[48] *De Malo*, q. 3, a. 1 ad 9.

even without habitual grace, man could avoid mortal and venial sin: for to sin is nothing else than to withdraw from that which is according to nature. Man could avoid this in the integrity of nature. He could not, however, do this without the help of God preserving him in good: for if this were withdrawn, even nature itself would sink into nothingness. In the state of corrupt nature, however, man needs habitual grace healing nature in order to refrain completely from sin. In this life he is healed in mind, but his carnal appetite is not yet entirely repaired. Consequently man can avoid mortal sin, which is in the reason, but he cannot refrain from all venial sin, because of the corruption of the lower sensual appetite. Man in mortal sin, before he is restored by justifying grace, can avoid individual mortal sins for some time, for it is not necessary that he sin in act continually. But he cannot remain long without mortal sin [49]. The reasons are those already given in the earlier discussions of the question.

We may summarize St. Thomas' teaching on the possibility of avoiding sin without grace as follows. There are two states of human nature which are involved: integral nature and corrupt nature. In the latter case we are concerned immediately with man in mortal sin, since no adult with the use of free will can be without grace and merely in original sin. There are two principal causes of the impossibility of avoiding all sin: the impulse of disordered passions, whose movements anticipate the deliberation of reason and the act of free will; and perverse habits, which incline inordinately to some created good as the last end. In the state of corrupt nature grace is necessary to avoid all mortal sin, for only grace can heal nature and restore its orientation toward God as its last end. Even with grace, it is impossible to avoid all venial sin, since in the present life grace does not ordinarily cause the complete subjection of the lower powers to reason. In the state of integral nature, since the nature had its proper orientation toward God as its last end, man could avoid all mortal sin without grace, with the powers of unspoiled nature alone. There was no

---

[49] *S.T.* I-II, q. 109, a. 8 resp.

inclination to evil in the nature, no bad habits, which are the principal causes of the impossibility of avoiding all mortal sin in the state of sin. With regard to the avoidance of mortal sin, therefore, there is no difficulty in saying that it could be done in the state of integral nature without grace. Like the natural love of God above all, it seems to be within the power of nature unspoiled by sin.

There is some difficulty, however, in explaining the avoidance of all venial sin in the state of integral nature without grace. It seems that when St. Thomas treats the question of avoiding sin without grace, he has in mind the healing function of grace, by which the will is turned again to God as its last end. Certainly there is no need of grace to accomplish this orientation of the will in the state of integral nature, for as we have seen in the question of the natural love of God, the will naturally is *right,* naturally seeks God as the ultimate end prior to sin. For this reason it can fulfill the substance of all the precepts of the law without grace, and can avoid all mortal sin. It is free from the evil inclinations and the adherence to a wrong end which make the avoidance of all mortal sin without grace impossible in the state of mortal sin. But the problem is different in the case of venial sin. Adam was free from all venial sin because of the perfect subjection of his lower powers to reason. This, as we have seen in the texts on original justice, is not a condition due to nature, even before sin. It is supernatural, above the powers of nature, requiring a supernatural cause, *gratia gratum faciens* [50]. Consequently, though the right order with respect to the last end and the freedom from evil inclinations which make the avoidance of all mortal sin possible may be had *either* naturally in a nature unspoiled by sin *or* supernaturally in a corrupt nature healed by grace, yet the perfect subjection of the lower powers to reason which is required for the complete avoidance of venial sin is *always* the effect of grace, and can never be attributed to the power even of uncorrupted nature.

If, therefore, St. Thomas means to include the complete

---

[50] Cf. *S.T.* I, q. 95, a. 1 resp.

avoidance of venial sin within the power of integral nature without grace, it would seem that for a moment here he overlooked a difficulty. One may, of course, attempt to explain the text otherwise by saying that he does not mean that absolute freedom from venial sin, or that he is excluding formally only the need of grace to heal fallen nature. It seems better, however, to admit that more probably he nodded here momentarily.

We may review briefly, then, the results of our examination of these special questions concerning the necessity of grace. They seemed to involve an inconsistency because they spoke of acts possible without grace, yet only in a state caused by grace. As we have seen, there is no difficulty with regard to doing the whole good proportioned to nature, loving God naturally above all things, fulfilling the substance of all the precepts of the law, and avoiding all mortal sin in the state of integral nature without grace: for these acts are proportioned to nature and are within the power of a human nature uncorrupted by sin, in whatever state it might be found. They are not caused *per se* by grace. On the contrary, there remains one difficulty in the matter of avoiding all venial sin without grace: for this depends necessarily on a subjection of the lower powers which is beyond the power of nature, and is caused *per se* by grace.

Finally, one word on the nature of this whole excursus into the difficulties caused by the special questions on the necessity of grace. It should be clear that in attempting to solve these difficulties we are not holding a brief for either party in the controversy concerning the relation of grace to original justice in the theology of St. Thomas. The difficulties rather are basic, common to both parties. For whether one hold that grace is the formal cause of original justice or that it is the efficient cause or condition *sine qua non,* the problem suggested by these texts is equally difficult, and its solution equally urgent.

D. Kind and Degree of Grace in the State of Innocence.

Having considered the various aspects of the necessity of grace in the state of innocence, we may summarize briefly St. Thomas' teaching on the kind and degree of grace given to man in that first state.

Man did not have in the state of innocence those graces which are intended to remedy the defects of others, such as the gift of miracles, tongues, etc., because in that state there were no such defects to be remedied. He did have, however, all those graces which are intended to perfect the one who receives them, such as *gratia gratum faciens,* the virtues, the gifts of knowledge and wisdom, etc. [51]. He had all the virtues in one form or other, for they were required by the rectitude of the first state, in which reason was subject to God, and the lower powers to reason. For the virtues are nothing else than certain perfections by which reason is directed to God and the lower powers are disposed according to the rule of reason. Consequently he had both in habit and in act those virtues which involve no imperfection, such as charity and justice; and also those virtues which by their very nature involve some imperfection, but are not inconsistent with the perfection of the first state, such as faith and hope. The virtues which involve an imperfection inconsistent with his state were had in habit, but not in act, for example: penance and mercy, which suppose sin and misery [52]. Generally speaking, man in the state of innocence had these gifts of grace more abundantly than in the present state [53] because then there was no obstacle to grace in human nature [54]. Because of the abundance of his grace the first man was like an angel [55]. Though the children

---

[51] *In II Sent.* d. 29, q. 1, a. 3 sol.
[52] *S.T.* I, q. 95, a. 3 resp.
[53] *Ibid.* a. 4; *In II Sent.,* l. c.
[54] *S.T.* I, q. 95, a. 4.
[55] *De Ver.* q. 18, a. 7 ad 5.

of Adam in the state of innocence would not have had perfect
knowledge from the beginning [56], they would have had all virtues, since these are required for the perfect union with God
demanded by the state of innocence [57].

---

[56] *Ibid.* resp.
[57] *Ibid.* ad 2.

CHAPTER SIX

JUSTICE, HARMONY, INTEGRITY

Original justice, involving the perfect order of human nature, the complete subjection of body and lower powers of the soul to reason, and of reason to God, is *justice* in a very special sense. St. Thomas identifies it with the metaphorical justice described by Aristotle, a justice which is not the special cardinal virtue concerned with right order between individuals in the affairs of exchange and sharing of the things necessary for life: nor the general justice, legal justice, which is identified with all the virtues in so far as they direct their acts to the common good; but a state of right order prevailing within the man whose highest powers are subject to God, and lower powers subject to reason. Obviously there is some adaptation of the Aristotelian metaphorical justice here [1]. First, in Aristotle there is question merely of the mutual relations of the higher and lower powers in man, rational and irrational,

---

[1] Ostendit qualis sit metaphorica iustitia. Et dicit quod secundum quamdam metaphoram et similitudinem contingit, non quidem quod sit iustum vel iniustum totius hominis ad seipsum, sed quod sit quaedam species iusti inter aliquas partes hominis ad invicem. Non tamen inter eas est omne iustum, sed solum iustum dominativum vel dispensativum, scilicet oeconomicum: quia secundum has rationes dominii vel dispensationis videtur distare rationalis pars animae ab irrationali, quae dividitur in irascibilem et concupiscibilem. Nam ratio dominatur irascibili et concupiscibili et gubernat eas.

Et ad ista respiciunt aliqui, quibus videtur quod sit iustitia hominis ad seipsum, propter hoc quod in talibus contingit aliquem pati propter proprios appetitus. Puta cum ex ira vel concupiscentia aliquis facit contra rationem. Sic igitur in his est quoddam iustum et iniustum, sicut inter imperantem et eum cui imperatur. Non autem est verum iustum, quia non est inter duos; sed est similitudinarium iustum, inquantum diversitas animae assimilatur diversitati personarum (*In Ethic.* V, c. 15, lect. 17, nn. 1106-1107).

Cf. *In IV Sent.* d. 17, q. 1, a. 1 sol. 1; *De Ver.* q. 28, a. 1 resp.; *S.T.* I-II, q. 113, a. 1 resp.; q. 46, a. 7 ad 2; II-II, q. 58, a. 2 resp. et ad 1.

commanding and obeying. Faced first with the problems of
terminology in questions on the justification of the sinner, St.
Thomas extends the right order to include the subjection of
the higher part to God [2] and even right order with regard to
one's neighbor [3]. Moreover, in these texts obviously he is
dealing with a supernatural justice, the effect of grace and
charity, and he is concerned with explaining why justification
derives its name from *iustitia,* rather than from *gratia* or *caritas.* As far as I have been able to observe, it is only in the
Summa Theologiae that he applies this notion of metaphorical
justice explicitly to original justice.

One aspect of the earlier texts is noteworthy. St. Thomas is trying to explain how, considered from the point of
view of the *terminus a quo,* justification is the remission of sins.
Since he must answer objections which claim that this effect
should be named rather from grace, or faith, or charity, St.
Thomas emphasizes here not only the fact that this justice or
rectitude is universal, opposed to all sin, and thus different from
the special virtues of faith and charity; but also that it is properly in the faculties rather than in the essence of the soul, and
thus it is not the effect of grace as proximate cause [4]. Grace
is rather the cause of the proximate cause of justification (understood here as corresponding to *justificatum esse,* not to
justificari). The proximate cause is the very rectitude of the
potencies. In the later text in the *Summa* he does not mention
this argument, which does not harmonize either with his general thesis that justification is the formal effect of grace, or
with his teaching that original justice is first of all in the essence of the soul.

---

[2] *In IV Sent. l. c.; De Ver. l. c.*
[3] *De Ver. l. c.*
[4] Ad tertium dicendum quod *justificatio* potest sumi dupliciter. Vel secundum quod respondet ad *justificari;* et sic dicit motum ad justitiam praedictam. Vel secundum quod sumitur ad *justificatum esse;* et sic est effectus formalis justitiae praedictae, quia ea aliquid formaliter justificatum
est, sicut albedine albatum.
Sicut autem ab essentia animae potentiae fluunt, ita rectitudo potentiarum a gratia, quae est essentiae perfectio. Et inter ipsas voluntas quae alias
movet eis rectitudinem quodammodo largitur. Et ideo praedictae justitiae cau-

This latter feature of the doctrine of original justice is perfectly clear. Just as original sin is first of all in the essence of the soul [5], so also was original justice. Since it was a gift of nature, it was in the essence of the soul first, then in the will [6].

Consisting in the order or disorder of all the powers of the soul, both original justice and original sin may be called habits: not habits which incline a potency to its operation, but rather the dispositions of a nature composed of many elements, according to which it is well-disposed or ill-disposed to something. Such dispositions are called habits especially when they become almost nature, as in the case of sickness and health. Thus original sin is an inordinate disposition resulting from the destruction of that harmony in which original justice consisted. It is a sickness, a *languor naturae* [7]. Original justice, on the contrary, was the perfect health, the harmony of a nature whose parts were in perfect order [8].

Since it held all the parts of the soul in perfect order, original justice is compared to a bond [9] or a rein [10].

Finally, as we have seen in several texts, the state of rectitude, of perfect order in original justice, is frequently described as the integrity of nature [11].

---

sa prima est gratia, et consequenter caritas, quae voluntatem ad finem perficit, a quo est rectitudo praedicta.

Et propter hoc ipsa justificatio et peccatorum remissio est effectus justitiae generalis sicut causae formalis proximae; sed caritatis et gratiae sicut causarum causae proximae ...

Et quia a proximis causis vel terminis aliquid denominari debet, ideo praedictus motus vel terminatio motus magis denominatur a justitia quam a caritate vel gratia (*In IV Sent.* d. 17, q. 1, a. 1, sol. 1 ad 3).

Ad secundum dicendum, quod iustificatio non dicitur a iustitia legali, quae est omnis virtus; sed a iustitia quae dicit generalem rectitudinem in anima, a qua potius quam a gratia iustificatio denominatur; quia huic iustitiae directe et immediate omne peccatum opponitur, cum omnes potentias animae attingat; gratia vero est in essentia animae (*De Ver.* q. 28, a. 1 ad 2).

[5] *De Malo,* q. 4, a. 4 resp.; *S.T.* I-II, q. 83, a. 2 resp.
[6] *De Malo,* q. 4, a. 4 ad 1; *S.T.* I-II, q. 83, a. 2 ad 2.
[7] *S.T.* I-II, q. 82, a. 1 resp.
[8] *Ibid. l. c.* et a. 2 ad 2.
[9] Cf. *In II Sent.* d. 30, q. 1, a. 3 sol.; *S.T.* I-II, q. 82, a. 4 ad 1.
[10] *De Malo* q. 4, a. 2 ad 4.
[11] *In II Sent.* d. 21, q. 2, a. 2 ad 5; *S.T.* I, q. 94, a. 2 resp.; *Comp. Theol.* c. 192.

CONCLUSION OF PART ONE

From the study of the formulae with which St. Thomas has described original justice we have seen that frequently he uses the term original justice to designate only a part of the perfect order which reigned in human nature in the state of innocence. Usually this limited sense of original justice includes only the two lower subjections: of body to soul, and of the lower powers of the soul to reason. In the hierarchy of the three subjections, the first, that of reason to God, is the cause of the other two. The cause of this first subjection is grace, and there is no other indication of what constituted it. When original justice is clearly distinguished from grace, in *De Malo,* question five, article one, it includes only the two lower subjections, the gifts which remedy the defects of man's lower nature.

Sharply contrasted with this limited sense of original justice is its restricted use to signifiy only the rectitude of the will, in the texts on the formal and material elements of original sin. Though there is one early text in which St. Thomas applies the formal-material terminology to original justice, in general he uses it only in explaining the essence of original sin, and he identifies the formal element of the sin with the privation of original justice, which was in the will. Not only the lack of adequate foundation in the text of St. Thomas, but also the strict limitations of this notion of the rectitude of the will as formal in original justice, make it dangerous to assert simply that the rectitude of the will was the formal cause of original justice. In so far as the will exerts a positive influence, its causality is limited to the subjection of the powers moved by the will: it cannot be extended to explain immortality and freedom from suffering in the body, except in

CONCLUSION OF PART ONE

a very special sense. Moreover, it does not afford a strict formal causality: the will is formal as *moving,* as an efficient cause in human acts, directing them to the last end.

In his treatment of the obscure question of the causes of immortality St. Thomas explains that privilege almost exclusively in terms of the formal causality of the soul, which by a special grace had the power of informing matter more completely and giving it an existence proportioned to the unfailing existence of the soul. There are clear indications that this power was an effect of grace. The emphasis on formal causality, notwithstanding one obscure text on efficient causality, points to the necessity of looking beyond the causal influence of the will to find an adequate theory of the causes of original justice.

St. Thomas attempts to determine the perfection of intellect in the state of innocence in accordance with the needs of that state. Adam had a perfect natural knowledge of God by a type of quasi-angelic contemplation, and a knowledge by faith received through interior illumination. As teacher of his descendants he had a perfect habitual knowledge of all that it is possible for the human intellect to know naturally. Others would have had perfect prudence from the beginning, and would have acquired perfect natural knowledge of other things only gradually. In the state of innocence there was no deception, error, or false opinion.

With regard to the perfection of the will, in St. Thomas' definitive position it is necessary to hold that man was created in grace, since grace is required as the supernatural cause of the rectitude of original justice. Original justice had its root in the supernatural subjection of the reason to God, which is caused by *gratia gratum faciens.* Original justice includes grace. Since the subjection of the human mind to God cannot be firm without grace, original justice is impossible without grace.

Another line of reasoning establishes the necessity of grace in the state of innocence from man's supernatural end. As far as the essential need of grace is concerned, man needed grace as much before as after sin. This need, relative to a super-

natural end, is common to angel and man, to integral and corrupt nature. The other help given to subject the body and
the lower powers of the soul was a disposition for grace in the
state of innocence.

A number of special questions on the need of grace and
the limits of the power of pure nature present some difficulties
because of the apparent contradiction of acts performed without grace, yet only in a state of integral nature which depends
necessarily on grace. The apparent contradiction disappears
when we realize that these acts are proportioned to human nature, and are not caused *per se* by grace. They would be possible naturally in any state in which human nature could be
found uncorrupted by sin. Historically this condition was
verified only in the state of innocence. This solution explains
all difficulties except that of the complete avoidance of venial
sin without grace in the state of integral nature: it seems that
this must always depend necessarily on a supernatural subjection of the lower powers of the soul. Especially fruitful
for our study of the causes of original justice is the discussion
of the natural love of God above all things. The impossibility
of this act without grace in the state of corrupt nature reveals
one of the wounds left in nature by original sin: man's will
now seeks its own individual good above all, and needs the
healing power of grace to be directed again to God as its last
end. Moreover, the discussion of the natural rectitude of the
will and the love of God possible in integral nature without
grace brings out clearly the limits of this perfection, and the
impossibility of finding in it the cause of the whole rectitude
of original justice. Since it is an act proceeding merely from
nature and potency, not from a virtue, this love of God lacks
the promptness, delight, and constancy required for that firm,
continual clinging to God which has been indicated as the principal element of original justice and the cause of the lower
subjections. Moreover, since it is merely a natural act, it cannot be the cause of the other elements of original justice: the
supernatural subjection of the lower powers.

In the state of innocence Adam had sanctifying grace and
all the infused virtues and gifts, for all the virtues were re-

quired for the rectitude of original justice. He had all virtues *in habitu,* and in act he had all except those which involve an imperfection inconsistent with his state of perfection. In general, these gifts were more abundant than they are in the present state. Though Adam's children would not have had all knowledge at birth, they would have had all virtues, since these are required for the perfect union with God demanded by the state of innocence.

Original justice is called justice metaphorically: it involves right order not between individuals, but among the various part of a man. Being a gift of nature, it was first in the essence of the soul, then in the potencies. It was not an operative habit, but it can be called a habit in the sense of a disposition of a nature composed of many elements, according to which it is well-disposed or ill-disposed to something. Thus it is the health of a nature whose parts are in perfect order.

In this preliminary survey of St. Thomas' teaching on original justice our concern has been to follow the essential lines of his treatment, proceeding without special attention to the controversy on the relation of grace to original justice. Yet from time to time we have had occasion to note on the one hand the emphasis given to the role of grace and the virtues in original justice, and on the other hand a number of apparent weaknesses in the theory of the adequate distinction. Thus the text analysis made thus far has established a number of positions which we shall consolidate later. In the following part of our study we shall attempt to determine precisely what is the role of grace and the infused virtues in the constitution of original justice. First of all we must turn to an important issue in the controversy: the distinction between grace and original justice demanded by the distinction between *donum naturae* ande *donum personale.*

PART TWO

GRACE AND ORIGINAL JUSTICE

CHAPTER ONE

DONUM NATURAE AND DONUM PERSONALE

A. SIGNIFICANCE OF THE QUESTION.

One might be tempted to follow the indications given in the preceding survey of St. Thomas' teaching on original justice, and to say simply that since original justice included grace, and since grace clearly was the cause of the subjection of the reason to God and subsequently of the other subjections, clearly grace is an essential part of original justice, and is in fact its formal cause. The matter is not so easy to settle. In fact, in a sense we have not completed our survey of the teaching on original justice, for we have not considered St. Thomas' description of that justice as a gift to nature, and the distinction between such a gift to the nature and a purely personal gift. We must turn now to give full attention to this distinction and to its bearing on the whole question of the relation of grace to original justice. It has an extremely important bearing, since the distinction of *donum naturae* and *donum personale* is perhaps the chief argument advanced to demonstrate the adequate distinction of sanctifying grace and original justice.

Certainly among the modern proponents of the adequate distinction, principally Martin, Bittremieux, and Kors, this argument is fundamental. In the article which began the modern controversy over St. Thomas' teaching on grace and original justice [1] Martin based his thesis largely on the distinction made in the *Contra Gentiles* between a personal good

---

[1] RAYMOND M. MARTIN, O. P., « La doctrina sobre el pecado original en la *Summa contra Gentiles* », *La Ciencia Tomista* 10 (1914-1915) 389-400.

(grace and the right order of the parts of the soul) and a good belonging to the common nature[2].

The importance of the distinction between *donum naturae* and *donum personale* is even greater in Canon Bittremieux's interpretation of St. Thomas. For him this doctrine is the basic, universal teaching which must regulate our exegesis of particular texts in St. Thomas. Early in his study he invokes three rules for discovering the true thought of St. Thomas, calling especially for a sane interpretation of particular texts in the light of principles clearly stated elsewhere[3]. Repeatedly in the course of his article the interpretation of texts to support the adequate distinction between sanctifying grace and original justice is determined according to the « constantly repeated » doctrine that grace is an individual, personal gift[4].

Kors, writing after the controversy had been started, attempts to establish more firmly the person-nature distinction, devoting a special chapter to his interpretation of St. Thomas' teaching on nature and grace[5] as a prerequisite to the proper understanding of the definitive doctrine on original justice. Because original justice pertained properly to human nature and only through it to the person, it was a disposition, or at most an entitative habit, not an operative habit; the act and consequently the habit which is its effect are perfections of the individual[6]. Since grace, a purely personal gift, cannot be part of original justice, a gift to nature, grace cannot be an intrinsic cause of original justice. It is this doctrine on *donum naturae,* then, which prompts Kors to make his challenging assertion that grace is the efficient cause of the rectitude of nature, but in no way the formal cause[7].

---

[2] *C. G.* IV, c. 52.

[3] J. BITTREMIEUX, « La Distinction entre la justice originelle et la grâce sanctifiante d'après saint Thomas d'Aquin », *Revue Thomiste* 26 (1921) 123-124.

[4] Thus, for example, he neutralizes *In II Sent.* d. 20, q. 2, a. 3, which could be used to show that grace can be a gift to the nature (p. 122, note 2); cf. his interpretation of *S.T.* I, q. 95, a. 1 and q. 100, a. 1 ad 2 (pp. 131-135).

[5] J. B. KORS, O. P., *La Justice primitive et le péché originel d'après s. Thomas (Bibliothèque Thomiste* II) Le Saulchoir, Kain, 1922, pp. 114-127.

[6] *Op. cit.* p. 87.

[7] « ... La justice originelle n'est autre chose que la rectitude de la na-

Certainly the theory of *donum naturae* and *peccatum naturae* is fundamental in St. Thomas' theology of original justice and original sin. If the distinction between sanctifying grace as a purely personal gift and original justice as a gift to the nature is essential to that theory, and if like the theory itself this distinction is basic and constantly repeated, then surely we must recognize Bittremieux's right to appeal to it as a principle which must regulate our interpretation of isolated texts. Any attempt to determine the role of sanctifying grace in original justice must, then, include a clarification of this controverted issue. First of all, let us examine the texts of St. Thomas to determine exactly the scope and the significance of the distinction between grace as a personal gift and original justice as a gift to the nature.

B. THREE EARLY TEXTS: VARIETY IN TERMINOLOGY

The first text to be considered here is St. Thomas' first effort to answer the question whether children in the state of innocence would have been born in grace. Setting down the principle that the likeness in generation is confined to those things which pertain to the species, not those characteristics which are proper to the individual, St. Thomas examines the relation of grace to the human species in the state of innocence. It was possible for the first man to have two kinds of justice, original and gratuitous. Original justice consisted in the right relation of body to soul, of the lower powers to the higher, and of the higher to God. This justice by God's grace kept human nature in order from the beginning. Gratuitous justice is the principle of meritorious acts, and concerning it there are two opinions. Some say that the first man was created with only his natural gifts, not with those which are gratuitous. According to this it seems that it was necessary to prepare for such a justice by personal acts; hence according to this opinion

ture dont la grâce est bien la cause effective, mais, en aucune manière, la cause formelle ...» (p. 136). Cf. also p. 139.

grace was a personal property in the soul, and accordingly it could in no way be passed on except in aptitude. Others, however, say that man was created in grace, and according to this it seems that the gift of gratuitous justice was given to human nature itself; consequently in the communication of the nature there would have been simultaneously an infusion of grace [8].

This text has been made to bear much more than its just burden. It is one of the two texts cited by Kors to prove that grace is distinct from original justice. He says that it is obvious that St. Thomas expressly distinguishes original justice from gratuitous justice or sanctifying grace [9]. Bittremieux tries to forestall any use of the second opinion on gratuitous justice as a gift to the nature by saying that here St. Thomas seems to note the thesis later held by Soto, identifying sanctifying grace and original justice, and adds that this is not the opinion of the holy Doctor, who considers grace as a personal gift [10] — which is precisely what we are trying to determine.

Obviously we cannot seek in this early text from the *Sentences* a certain proof of St. Thomas' position: he has not yet chosen between the alternatives — or at least he has not yet chosen to let us know his preference. He simply presents two possibilities. This much, however, we may note. First, the distinction between original justice and gratuitous justice as two distinct and separable justices is given in terms of the opinion that man was not created in grace. Secondly, only in taking gratuitous justice according to this first opinion are we to regard this justice as a personal property, in no way to be passed on. According to the other opinion, that man was created in grace, grace (the justice which is the principle of meritorious act) would be a gift to human nature itself. In this text, therefore, neither the opposition of original justice and gratuitous justice nor the distinction of personal gift and gift to nature has a fixed value. They are functions of the

---

[8] *In II Sent.* d. 20, q. 2, a. 3 sol.

[9] KORS, *op. cit.* p. 90. Later, p. 93, he cites *De Malo* q. 5, a. 1; for the difficulties of this text see above, Part I, chapter I, pp. 24-27.

[10] BITTREMIEUX, *op. cit.* p. 122, note 2.

theory on creation in grace. The text may be used, therefore, as a proof that grace can be a gift to the nature[11].

Another text farther on in the same book of the commentary on the *Sentences* distinguishes clearly between the gifts (*bona*) which had been given to Adam for his personal acts: grace and the virtues; and those which had been given to the whole nature, such as immortality of the body, the obedience of the lower powers to reason, etc.[12]. Yet the distinction has only a relative value here too: St. Thomas is answering the objections not in terms of the theory of creation in grace, but rather supposing that man was created *in naturalibus integris* and that he received grace by turning to God in the instant of creation[13].

The flexibility and variety in the notions of *gratuitum* and personal gift are indicated in the very next article, in which St. Thomas considers the amount of grace which was had before and after the first sin[14]. He distinguishes two genera of gratuitous gifts: those intended for the perfection of the one to whom they are given, and those which are for the help of others (signs, kinds of tongues, etc.). The first class comprises those gifts by which a man is perfected in *his own operations* (*in actibus propriis*). Strangely enough St. Thomas includes under this heading not only *gratia gratum faciens,* the virtues, and the gifts of knowledge and wisdom, but also freedom from suffering in the body, the perfect obedience of the lower powers to reason, and gifts of this kind.

This brief view of early texts may suggest at least this: here in his earliest work, when St. Thomas has not yet taken

---

[11] Cf. R. GARRIGOU-LAGRANGE, O. P., « Utrum Gratia Sanctificans Fuerit in Adamo Dos Naturae an Donum Personae tantum », *Angelicum* 2 (1925) 137-138.

[12] Ad quintum dicendum, quod actus personales non attingunt naturam, sed personam; et ideo Adam, per poenitentiam quam de peccato egit, potuit recuperare illa bona quae sibi ad actus personales data erant, sicut gratiam et virtutes; non autem illa quae toti naturae collata erant, ut immortalitas corporis et obedientia inferiorum virium ad rationem, et hujusmodi (*In II Sent*. d. 29, q. 1, a. 2 ad 5).

[13] *Ibid*. sol.

[14] *In II Sent*. d. 29, q. 1, a. 3 sol.

a strong personal position, his terminology is fluid, and the
distinctions of original and gratuitous justice, and of a gift to
the nature and a gift to the person for his own acts do not
represent fixed classifications of gifts. Grace can be called a
gift to the whole of human nature if one holds that man was
created in grace. On the other hand, freedom from suffering and the perfect obedience of the lower powers to reason,
can be called personal gifts, given to perfect a man in his own
acts. All of these terms have meanings relative to their context, and by no means are they necessarily mutually exclusive.

C. Original Justice as a Donum Naturae.

The doctrine of original justice as a gift to human nature appears clearly in the Commentary on the *Sentences*.
Original justice was a gift to nature, a gift which was not
given to Adam personally, but in so far as he had such a nature, so that all who would receive the nature from him would
acquire this gift. With the propagation of the flesh, therefore, original justice would have been propagated too [15].

Of greater importance for our study is the text of the
Contra Gentiles which has figured prominently in the controversy :

> ... Since sin is a certain evil of rational nature, and evil
> is the privation of good, it is according to the good which is
> removed that one must judge whether some sin pertains to
> the common nature or to some private person. Actual sins,
> therefore, which are committed commonly by men, take away
> a personal good of the sinner, namely grace and the right
> order of the parts of the soul. Hence they are personal, and
> when one sins it is not imputed to another. But the first sin
> of the first man deprived the sinner not only of a private and
> personal good, namely grace and the right order of the soul,
> but also of a good pertaining to the common nature. For as
> has been said above, human nature was so disposed in its
> creation that the lower powers were perfectly subject to

---

[15] *In II Sent*. d. 30, q. 1, a. 2 sol.; d. 31, q. 1, a. 1 sol.

reason, reason to God, and the body to the soul, with God
supplying by grace that which nature lacked for this.   This
gift, which by some is called original justice, was so given
to the first man that it was to be passed on to his descendants
together with human nature ... [16].

Martin [17] and Bittremieux [18] see in this text a clear distinction between sanctifying grace and original justice.
Garrigou-Lagrange contends, on the other hand, that the text
can be read to mean that grace is not only a personal gift, but
also a gift to the nature, especially in the light of later texts [19].
There is some ambiguity in the text.   First of all, as we noted in the study of the formulae of original justice, the text in
the body of this chapter seems to deal with original justice
only in the restricted sense, including the subjection of the
lower powers to reason and the removal of any bodily impediment [20].   Thus original justice remedied the two defects of
human nature.   Although in the text which we are considering St. Thomas uses the threefold formula of perfect subjection, still he refers to his argument in the earlier text.   It would
seem that the formula can be explained by his citation of earlier theologians, and that original justice as distinguished here
from grace includes only the two lower subjections.   Furthermore his statement at the critical point in this text is somewhat
ambiguous : « ... *Primum autem peccatum primi hominis non
solum peccantem destituit proprio et personali bono, scilicet
gratia et debito ordine animae, sed etiam bono ad naturam com-
munem pertinente* ».   It is possible to understand the second
bono as including grace and the right order of the soul.   In
later texts, without distinguishing between grace and the other
gifts, he uses a formula which describes the whole of original
justice as not only a personal gift, but also a gift to the nature :

---

[16] *C. G.* IV, c. 52 ad 1.
[17] Martin, *op. cit.* pp. 398-399.
[18] Bittremieux, *op. cit.* pp. 126, 128.
[19] Garrigou-Lagrange, *op. cit.* pp. 143-144; he cites *De Malo* q. 4, a. 1;
S.T. I-II, q. 81, a. 2 and q. 85, a. 3.
[20] Cf. above, Part I, chapter one, pp. 18-19.

... Hoc autem donum non fuerat datum primo homini ut
singulari personae tantum, sed ut cuidam principio totius humanae naturae, ut scilicet ab eo per originem derivaretur in
posteros ... [21].

... Fuit autem in principio conditionis humanae quoddam
donum gratuitum primo homini divinitus datum non ratione
personae suae tantum, sed ratione totius naturae humanae ab
eo derivandae, quod donum fuit originalis iustitia ... [22].

... Est autem hic defectus, carentia originalis justitiae,
quae erat primo homini divinitus collata, non solum ut erat
persona quaedam singularis, sed etiam ut erat principium
naturae : ut scilicet eam simul cum natura in posteros tradu-
ceret ... [23].

Apart from the single case of this text in the *Contra Gentiles,* the texts which are devoted to the essential theory of
original justice as a gift to the nature do not distinguish between grace and original justice unless they are speaking of
the grace which was given after the first sin, grace which obviously was given only to individual persons, and not as a gift
to human nature [24]. The essential doctrine on the *donum naturae,* fundamental in the explanation of both original justice
and original sin, is simply this : the supernatural gift of original justice was given to Adam not merely as an individual
person, but as the source of human nature. It was to be passed
on with the nature to all his descendants. Thus original
justice was an accident, a property (*accidens consequens naturam speciei*) of human nature, not caused by the principle
of the nature, but a divinely given gift to the whole nature [25].

---

[21] *De Malo,* q. 4, a. 1 resp.

[22] *Ibid.* q. 4, a. 8 resp.

[23] *In Epist. ad Rom.* c. 5, lect. 3, « Et ideo dicendum est ... » (Vivès
ed., vol. 20, p. 451 b).

[24] Cf. the next section of this chapter.

[25] Respondeo dicendum quod naturaliter homo generat sibi simile secundum speciem. Unde quaecumque accidentia consequuntur naturam speciei,
in his necesse est quod filii parentibus similentur, nisi sit error in operatione
naturae, qui in statu innocentiae non fuisset. In accidentibus autem indivi-
dualibus non est necesse quod filii parentibus similentur. Iustitia autem originalis, in qua primus homo conditus fuit, fuit accidens naturae speciei, non

In this essential doctrine of the *donum naturae* in all the texts after the *Contra Gentiles* there is no indication of a distinction between original justice and the grace which was given *before* the first sin. There is nothing in these texts, therefore, which excludes the possibility that grace too was a gift to the nature in the first state, that it was part of original justice.

D. DISTINCTION BETWEEN ORIGINAL JUSTICE AS A GIFT TO THE NATURE AND GRACE AS A PURELY PERSONAL GIFT.

Certainly there are texts in which grace as a purely personal gift is contrasted with original justice as a gift to the whole human nature. In every case, however, there is question of the grace which was given after the first sin, not grace as it was given in the state of innocence. The texts fall into three classes, dealing with the following cases: (1) the effects of the grace in baptism; (2) the power of the grace given to Adam after his sin, and in particular the effects of his penance;

---

quasi ex principiis speciei causatum, sed sicut quoddam donum divinitus datum toti naturae... (*S.T.* I, q. 100, a. 1 resp.).

Ad primum ergo dicendum quod esse perfectum in scientia fuit individuale accidens primi parentis, inquantum scilicet ipse instituebatur ut pater et instructor totius humani generis. Et ideo quantum ad hoc, non generabat filios similes sibi; sed solum quantum ad accidentia naturalia vel gratuita totius naturae (*S.T.* I, q. 101, a. 1 ad 1).

... Impossibile est quod aliqua peccata proximorum parentum, vel etiam primi parentis praeter primum, per originem traducantur. Cujus ratio est quia homo generat sibi idem in specie, non autem secundum individuum. Et ideo ea quae directe pertinent ad individuum, sicut personales actus et quae ad eos pertinent, non traducuntur a parentibus in filios: non enim grammaticus traducit in filium scientiam grammaticae, quam proprio studio acquisivit. Sed ea quae pertinent ad naturam speciei, traducuntur a parentibus in filios, nisi sit defectus naturae... Et si natura sit fortis, etiam aliqua accidentia individualia propagantur in filios, pertinentia ad dispositionem naturae, sicut velocitas corporis, bonitas ingenii, et alia hujusmodi: nullo autem modo ea quae sunt pure personalia, ut dictum est.

Sicut autem ad personam pertinet aliquid secundum seipsam, et aliquid ex dono gratiae, ita etiam ad naturam potest aliquid pertinere secundum seipsam, scilicet quod causatur ex principiis eius, et aliquid ex dono gratiae. Et hoc modo iustitia originalis, sicut in Primo dictum est, erat quoddam donum gratiae toti humanae naturae divinitus collatum in primo parente... (*S.T.* I-II, q. 81, a. 2 resp.).

(3) the contrast between original sin, which removed a good of nature, and other actual sins, which remove a purely personal good.

It is necessary for all men descended from Adam to be born in original sin because a defective nature is incapable of generating an individual without the defect. Only a perfect restoration of the nature could change this. But human nature in the present state is not restored in what pertains to the nature, though by grace it is restored in what pertains to the person. In the future it will be restored completely in the blessed [26]. Bodily generation terminates *per se* in the nature, since the form is the term of generation, but spiritual generation terminates in the perfection of the person, which is caused by grace [27]. Baptism removes what has carried over to the person from the corruption of the nature. Thus it removes the guilt affecting the person, and the punishment which deprived him of a personal act: the lack of the beatific vision. It does not remove the infection in so far as it affects the nature [28]. The process in original sin was this: first a person infected the nature, then the nature infected the person. Christ has reversed this order, repairing first what pertains to the person. Later He will repair in all at once what pertains to the nature [29].

----

[26] ... Natura vero humana in statu hujus viae non reintegratur quantum ad id quod naturae est, etsi per gratiam reintegratur quantum ad hoc quod ad personam pertinet; sed in futuro perfecte reintegrabitur in beatis ... (*In II Sent.* d. 31, q. 1, a. 2 sol.; cf. d. 32, q. 1, a. 2 sol.).

[27] Ad tertium dicendum, quod generatio spiritualis efficacior est in eo ad quod ordinatur, quam generatio corporalis. Generatio autem corporalis terminatur per se ad naturam, quia forma est terminus generationis; sed generatio spiritualis terminatur ad perfectionem personae, quae est per gratiam; et ideo plus mundat generatio spiritualis personam, quam generatio corporalis inficere possit ... (*In II Sent.* d. 32, q. 1, a. 2 ad 3.). This is one of Bittremieux's texts.

[28] *In IV Sent.* d. 4, q. 2, a. 1 resp. ad q. 3. Cfr. *De Ver.* q. 25, a. 7 ad 5.

[29] Ad tertium dicendum quod, sicut in Secunda Parte dictum est, peccatum originale hoc modo processit quod primo persona infecit naturam, postmodum vero natura infecit personam. Christus vero converso ordine prius reparat id quod personae est, postmodum simul in omnibus reparabit id quod naturae est. Et ideo culpam originalis peccati, et etiam poenam ca-

Though Adam by his sin infected the whole of human nature, he could not repair the whole of human nature by his penance or any other merit.   His penance was the act of an individual person, and its principle was a grace given to that man personally.   The act of an individual is unable to affect the nature of the whole species.   The vitiation of the whole nature by the sin of the first parent followed *per accidens,* in so far as when he had been deprived of the state of innocence, it could not pass on to others through him.   Though by penance he returned to grace, he could not return to that pristine innocence to which God had given the gift of original justice [30].

The contrast between actual sin and original sin frequently serves to bring out the opposition between grace as a personal gift and original justice as a gift to nature.   In the text already cited from the *Contra Gentiles,* as we have seen, St. Thomas distinguishes between actual sin, which takes away a personal good (grace and the right order of the parts of the soul) and the first sin of the first parent, which deprived the sinner not only of his personal good (grace and the right order of the

---

rentiae visionis divinae, quae respiciunt personam, statim per baptismum tollit ab homine. Sed poenalitates praesentis vitae, sicut mors, fames, sitis et alia huiusmodi, respiciunt naturam, ex cuius principiis causantur, prout est destituta originali iustitia. Et ideo isti defectus non tollentur nisi in ultima reparatione naturae per resurrectionem gloriosam (*S.T.* III, q. 69, q. 3 ad 3).

[30] Quamvis autem peccatum primi parentis totam humanam naturam infecerit, non tamen potuit per eius poenitentiam vel quodcumque eius meritum tota natura reparari. Manifestum est enim quod poenitentia Adae, vel quodcumque aliud eius meritum, fuit actus singularis personae, actus autem alicuius individui non potest in totam naturam speciei. Causae enim quae possunt in totam speciem, sunt causae aequivocae, et non univocae. Sol enim est causa generationis in tota specie humana, sed homo est causa generationis huius hominis. Singulare ergo meritum Adae, vel cuiuscumque puri hominis sufficiens esse non poterat ad totam naturam reintegrandam. Quod autem per actum singularem primi hominis tota natura est vitiata, per accidens est consecutum, inquantum eo privato innocentiae statu, per ipsum in alios derivari non potuit. Et quamvis per poenitentiam redierit ad gratiam, non tamen redire potuit ad pristinam innocentiam, cui divinitus praedictum originalis iustitiae donum concessum erat ... (*Comp. Theol.* c. 198, Marietti ed. n. 376). Cf. *De Malo* q. 4, a. 6 ad 19: «...Bonum autem poenitentiae ipsius non est transfusum ad alios, quia eius principium fuit gratia personaliter illi homini data.

soul) but also the good pertaining to the common nature
(original justice, consisting in the threefold subjection)[31]. We
have already noted the obscurity of this text and the controversy
over its interpretation. Later texts, as far as I have been able
to observe, eliminate the confusing distinction within the goods
lost through the first sin, and merely speak of the distinction
between the whole of original justice as a gift to the nature
and the merely personal gift of grace which is lost through
actual sins. The chief text is that of the *De Malo,* in which
St. Thomas is showing why the sins of the nearer ancestors
do not pass on to their descendants. The principle from which
he argues is again that in generation it is the specific nature
and the accidents following upon it which are communicated
to the offspring. Sometimes individual accidents affecting the
body are passed on, but never those which pertain to the intellectual soul only. The first sin of the first parent differs
from all other actual sins in the good which it took away.
Original justice was a gift to the first man not for his own
person only, but for the whole human nature to be derived
from him. For two reasons it would have been passed on to
his descendants : first, because it followed upon human nature
by God's favor, though not by nature's order; secondly, because it extended even to the body, which is passed on by
generation. This gift was taken away by the first sin of the
first parent. Hence reasonably that sin too for the same reasons
descends by generation to his offspring. But the other actual
sins either of the first parent or of others are opposed to a
gift of grace divinely given to someone for his own person
only; moreover, it resides only in the intellectual part and does
not extend to the body to remove its corruptibility. Therefore
neither this grace nor the actual sins of any parents, even of
Adam himself, except his first sin, are passed on by generation
to their descendants[32]. Clearly in this text and in corresponding later texts, the opposition between grace as a purely personal gift and original justice as a gift to the nature always

[31] *C. G.* IV, c. 52.
[32] *De Malo* q. 4, a. 8 resp. Cf. *S.T.* I-II, q. 81, a. 2 resp. (quoted
above in note 25) and *In Epist. ad Rom.* c. 5, lect. 3.

involves the grace given after the first sin. These texts, therefore, in no way support the thesis holding an adequate distinction between original justice and the sanctifying grace which
was given to Adam in the state of innocence.

E. SANCTIFYING GRACE AS A GIFT TO THE NATURE

Our examination of the texts thus far has shown that
there is nothing in St. Thomas' teaching on the *donum naturae*
which excludes the sanctifying grace given to Adam in the state
of innocence. It is time now to consider positive indications
that sanctifying grace can be a *donum naturae,* and that in
fact it was in the first state of nature.

The first text, already familiar, is that in which St. Thomas
gives the two chief opinions on *iustitia gratuita.* For those
who hold that man was created *in naturalibus tantum,* gratuitous justice, which performs meritorious acts, is a purely personal grace, requiring personal acts as a preparation. According
to the opinion that man was created in grace, the gift of
gratuitous justice was given to human nature itself, and it
would have been infused simultaneously with the transmission
of the nature [33].

In connection with the effects of original sin remaining
after baptism, we find another interesting text in the Commentary on the *Sentences.* In the solution St. Thomas has
explained why effects such as concupiscence and mortality remain. Original sin is first of all a sin of nature, and consequently it infects the person in so far as the disposition of

---

[33] *In II Sent.* d. 20, q. 2, a. 3 sol. BITTREMIEUX attempts to eliminate
any serious consideration of this text on the grounds that in it St. Thomas
is noting a position later to be taken by Soto. His reason for refusing
to see here the opinion of St. Thomas is that he believes that for St. Thomas
grace is a purely personal gift. Our study of the texts has already removed
most of the props which seemed to support Bittremieux. As for the opinion
given in this text, it does not represent St. Thomas' mind in this sense:
he has not yet taken a stand on the question of creation in grace. The text
indicates, however, that *if* one holds that man was created in grace, then
grace is to be regarded as a gift to human nature.

nature affects the person. There are, then, two punishments of original sin. One affects the person: the lack of the divine vision, for the vision is an act, and all acts pertain to the person. The other affects the nature, involving the necessity of dying, suffering, the rebellion of the flesh against the spirit, etc. Baptism removes original sin only in so far as it has infected the person, but it does not remove the infection of nature in what pertains to the nature itself. The fifth objection is that since the grace given in baptism decreases the tinder of sin, it could be increased enough to remove the tinder completely. St. Thomas replies that whatever degree of the baptismal grace is infused in baptism, it can never effect the complete removal of the tinder, since that grace is intended only to heal the infection of the person, which proceeds from the infection of the nature. God could, however, infuse another kind of grace by which it would be completely removed, so that thus simultaneously the infection of person and nature would yield to grace[34].

The phrase *alterius generis gratiam* is obscure. One might say that it refers to a completely different grace, and so is irrelevant to our present question. It is possible, however, that St. Thomas means *gratia gratum faciens* not limited to the effects which it now produces in baptism, but with the fulness of effects which it could have, and did have in the state of innocence. Not much can be concluded from this text alone, but we may look to later texts for more light.

In the *De Veritate,* having shown the impossibility of the remission of sins without grace, St. Thomas answers an objection concerning the state of innocence. The objection is that it is possible to have the remission of sins without grace, since it is not necessary that either of these contraries be present. In Adam, according to this opinion, there was a state midway between the state of grace and the state of sin. St. Thomas

---

[34] Ad quintum dicendum, quod quantumcumque de gratia baptismali in baptismo infundatur, nunquam tamen potest hoc efficere ut ex toto tollat fomitem; quia gratia illa non est ordinata nisi ad curandum infectionem personae ex infectione naturae procedentem. Posset tamen Deus alterius generis gratiam infundere, per quam totum tolleretur; ut sic simul et personae et naturae infectio gratiae cederet (*In II Sent.* d. 32, q. 1, a. 2 ad 5).

answers in terms of that opinion not widely held, that for some time Adam had neither grace nor sin. During that time such a neutral condition may have been possible. « But after that time when Adam received grace, or could receive it, in such a way that *it would pass on to all his descendants,* no one is without grace except through actual or original sin » [35]. One may protest that St. Thomas is not solving the objection in terms of his own position. Yet he is proposing something which he regards as possible, and the significant thing is not whether or not he holds that there was a time when Adam had neither grace nor sin. The important thing is that he speaks of Adam's receiving grace in such a way that it was to pass on to all his descendants. He is speaking of *gratia gratum faciens,* and what he says fits perfectly into his doctrine of the *donum naturae.*

It is not surprising, then, to find the same notion further developed and included in his treatise on the state of innocence in the *Summa Theologiae.* Children would have been born in justice, because original justice was an accident of the specific nature, not caused by the principles of the species, but as a divine gift to the whole nature [36]. The second objection is that children would not have been born in justice because this would involve the transmission of grace, the cause of justice. Grace cannot be transmitted, because thus it would be natural. It is infused by God alone. St. Thomas answers:

> Some say that children would not have been born with gratuitous justice, which is the principle of merit, but with original justice. But since the root of original justice, in whose rectitude man was made, consists in the supernatural subjection of the reason to God, which is caused by *gratia gratum faciens,* as has been said above, it is necessary to say that if children would have been born in original justice, they would have been born also with grace; as we said above

---

[35] ... Sed post illud tempus quo Adam gratiam accepit vel accipere potuit, ita quod in omnes eius posteros transiret, nullus caret gratia nisi per culpam actualem vel originalem (*De Ver.* q. 28, a. 2 ad 4).

[36] *S. T.* I, q. 100, a. I resp.

concerning the first man, that he was created with grace. Nor on this account would grace have been natural, since it would not have been transmitted by the power of the seed, but would have been given to man as soon as he had a rational soul. Similarly as soon as the body is disposed, the rational soul is infused by God. It is not, however, from the seed (*traduce*) [37].

Finally, we may cite two texts of the *De Malo*. First, original justice seems to be considered a principle of merit. The text is not perfectly clear. The objection is that original sin cannot be passed on to Adam's descendants because the good which he did, his penance, is not passed on. The principle is that *sicut bonum est diffusivum ita malum est constrictivum*. St. Thomas answers that the principle of sin is from us, but the principle of meritorious good is from God. Hence in Adam there was some good that he could communicate to all, namely original justice, which however he had from God. The evil which he transmitted to others he had from himself. Thus one could say that it is God who passes on the good, but man who passes on evil. The good of his penance, however, was not passed on to others, because its principle was a grace given personally to that man [38]. The sense of the text seems to be that both original justice and the grace by which Adam did penance were principles of merit; hence they depended on God, and it was God who determined that one was to be a merely personal gift, and the other a gift to be passed on to all of Adam's descendants. In calling original justice a principle of merit St. Thomas would seem to be including in it *gratia gratum faciens*.

In the second text the grace by which one arrives at the beatific vision is called a *bonum naturae*. The question is whether the lack of the vision of God is a suitable punishment of original sin. The objection is that original sin should have a milder punishment than venial sin; but venial sin is not punished with the loss of the vision of God. St. Thomas answers

[37] *Ibid.* ad 2.
[38] *De Malo*, q. 4, q. 6 ad 19.

DONUM NATURAE AND DONUM PERSONALE 113

that venial sin in comparison with original sin is in a way greater, in a way smaller. Venial sin in relation to this or that person has more of the nature of sin than has original sin, since venial sin is voluntary with the will of this person, but original sin is not. However original sin is greater in relation to the nature, because it deprives the nature of a greater good than that of which venial sin deprives the person, namely the good of grace. On this account there is due to it the loss of the divine vision, because one does not arrive at the divine vision except through grace, which venial sin does not exclude [39]. Certainly he is speaking of *gratia gratum faciens,* for it is grace which is the means of arriving at the divine vision. This grace is a *bonum naturae,* as opposed to a good of the person.

Briefly, then, we may summarize the indications that for St. Thomas grace can be a gift to nature, and in fact was a gift to nature in the state of innocence. (1) According to the opinion holding that man was created in grace, the gift of gratuitous justice was given to human nature itself, and it would have been infused simultaneously with the transmission of the nature. (2) Though the grace of baptism removes the infection of original sin in so far as it affects the person, leaving those defects which belong to the nature itself, God could infuse another kind of grace which would remove simultaneously the infection of person and nature. (3) When Adam received grace, he received it in such a way that it would pass on to all his descendants. (4) It is necessary to say that if Adam's children would have been born in original justice, they would have been born also with grace. Grace would not have been natural on this account, for it would not have been transmitted by the power of the seed, but would have been given to man as soon as he had a rational soul, just as the soul is infused by God as soon as the body is disposed. (5) Though the text is not perfectly clear, St. Thomas seems to say that original justice was a principle of meritorious good: necessarily, then, it included *gratia gratum faciens.* (6) The grace by which one

[39] *De Malo* q. 5, a. 1 ad 9.

8 — W. A. VAN ROO, S. I. - *Grace and original justice.*

arrives at the beatific vision is called a good of the nature, in a text which contrasts the personal good lost through venial sin and the good of the nature lost through original sin.

In this series of texts I have included only those which directly bear on the *donum naturae*. One might add the other texts which implicitly indicate that grace is a gift to nature by saying that grace is included in original justice. We shall have occasion to deal with those texts later in connection with the role of sanctifying grace in original justice.

What, then, are the conclusions which we may draw from the examination of the texts on original justice as a *donum naturae*? First, in the essential theory of original justice as a *donum naturae,* apart from one doubtful text in the *Contra Gentiles,* the distinction between grace as a purely personal gift and original justice as a gift to the nature does not appear. The essentials of the theory are these : the supernatural gift of original justice was given to Adam not merely as an individual person, but as the source of human nature; it was to be passed on to all his descendants as an accident (property) of human nature, not caused by the principles of the nature, but a divinely given gift to the whole nature. Secondly, with the sole exception of the same controverted text of the *Contra Gentiles,* the distinction between sanctifying grace as a purely personal gift and original justice as a gift to the whole nature always deals with the grace given after the first sin, never with sanctifying grace as given in the state of innocence. All such texts, concerning the effects of baptismal grace, the efficacy of Adam's penance, and the contrast between actual personal sins and the sin of the nature, are irrelevant when there is question precisely of the grace given to Adam in the state of innocence. Thirdly, not only is there no textual basis for denying that sanctifying grace can be a gift to the whole nature, but also there are several positive indications that it can be and that in fact it was a *donum naturae* in the state of innocence.

F. Examination of the Arguments of Martin, Bittremieux, and Kors

Against the background of this study of the texts of St. Thomas let us examine the arguments advanced to prove the adequate distinction between sanctifying grace as a purely personal gift and original justice as a gift to the whole nature.

A great weakness in Martin's position is that he limits his discussion to the single text in the *Contra Gentiles*. Notwithstanding his claim that this text represents the definitive teaching of St. Thomas on original sin and original justice, the text does not suffice by itself to give a full, clear statement of the doctrine. I have already pointed out the obscurity of the text, and the fact that if it means what Martin says it means, it is unique among the texts on the *donum naturae*. Moreover, the very scope of this chapter in the *Contra Gentiles* suggests some of its limitations: St. Thomas is trying to show the harmony of reason and faith, as Martin observes [40], and in the body of the article he uses arguments from divine providence and the dignity of the soul to show that probably God would remedy the weakness of nature. The formula describing original justice here seems to consider it in the limited sense, including only the two lower subjections [41]. There is no indication of what constituted the subjection of the reason to God, which is mentioned only in the answer to the first objection, where St. Thomas cites the threefold formula of earlier theologians. Perhaps because he has confined his treatment to a text in which the argument from reason and harmony with nature is so prominent, Martin has seized upon the naturalness of original justice as its chief characteristic, and *donum naturae* to him seems to mean first of all a gift *in linea naturae*. I believe that he has exaggerated this aspect of St. Thomas' treatment of original justice. It is true that in a sense original justice is natural, as corresponding to the dignity of

[40] Martin, *op. cit.* p. 393.
[41] Cf. the exegesis of *C. G.* IV, c. 52 given above in Part I, Chapter One, pp. 18-19.

the soul. St. Thomas, however, never says, as does Martin, that the gift was entirely *in linea naturae*. In St. Thomas' description of the *donum naturae* the essential thing is not that it is entirely within the order of nature, but rather that it is a gift given to the whole nature, a gift which may be in part strictly supernatural. He simply speaks of it as a supernatural gift, a gift of grace.

Bittremieux's article is more formidable. His texts, however, do not bear scrutiny. To prove the adequate distinction between sanctifying grace as a personal gift and original justice as a gift to nature he cites four texts, all of which deal with the grace given after the first sin [42]. Two of these texts also speak of original justice as a gift to Adam not only as an individual person but also as the principle of human nature to be derived from him [43], and thus they fall into the first class of texts considered in the preceding section of this chapter, dealing with the essential doctrine of the *donum naturae,* but not distinguishing between grace and original justice in the state of innocence. His texts, therefore, are irrelevant: in so far as they prove a distinction between grace and original justice, they treat the grace given after the first sin. Bittremieux himself admits that « some » of the texts bear on the grace given after the first sin, but even in these texts, he says, « ... the thought of St. Thomas is surely that sanctifying grace necessarily, of its nature, is a gift given to the person » [44]. Why say « even in these texts », when as a matter of fact his distinction is found *only* in these texts, and without anything to show that sanctifying grace of its nature necessarily is only a personal gift? Bittremieux then offers two more confirmatory texts: one is our familiar chapter of the *Contra Gentiles*; the other

---

[42] BITTREMIEUX, *op. cit.* p. 126: his texts are in *In II Sent.* d. 32, q. 1, a. 2 ad 3; *De Malo* q. 4, a. 6 ad 19 and a. 8 resp.; *In Epist. ad Rom.* c. 5, lect. 3. I have discussed these texts in the preceding section of this chapter.
[43] *De Malo* q. 4, a. 8 resp.; *In Epist. ad Rom.* c. 5, lect. 3.
[44] *Op. cit.* p. 128.

is a text in the *Summa Theologiae* where St. Thomas enumerates three kinds of goods of nature without mentioning
grace[45]. Enough has been said about the first text. Concerning
the other, Bittremieux is taking for granted, of course, that
in mentioning original justice, St. Thomas is not including
sanctifying grace — in spite of the clear statements that original
justice does include it. Moreover, an argument from silence
should be based on more than a momentary silence : a man
cannot say everything at once. We have already heard St.
Thomas say that grace is a *bonum naturae*[46].

In answer to an objection on the basis of St. Thomas'
statement that children in the state of innocence would have
been born with grace[47], Bittremieux says that they would have
received grace as a personal gift, not a gift to the nature, and
he takes this occasion to develope an elaborate argument from
the fact that St. Thomas denies that grace is transmitted, but
affirms this of original justice. St. Thomas says that grace
would have been *infused* into the soul, but that original justice
would have been propagated, communicated, derived, transmitted together with the nature. Thus Bittremieux lists the
terms used : *transfundi, traduci, derivari, propagari, transire ad
posteros.* Grace, on the other hand, is a purely personal gift,
an accidental property of the soul alone, which could not be
transmitted by way of origin[48]. One can refute this argument
by turning it upon its author : if one would hold with Bittremieux that sanctifying grace was the efficient cause of original
justice[49], the problem of transmitting original justice without

---

[45] Respondeo dicendum quod bonum naturae humanae potest tripliciter
dici. Primo, ipsa principia naturae, ex quibus natura constituitur, et proprietates ex his causatae, sicut potentiae animae et alia huiusmodi. Secundo,
quia homo a natura habet inclinationem ad virtutem, ut supra habitum est,
ipsa inclinatio ad virtutem est quoddam bonum naturae. Tertio modo potest
dici bonum naturae donum originalis iustitiae, quod fuit in primo homine
collatum toti humanae naturae... (*S.T.* I-II, q. 85, a. 1 resp.).

[46] *De Malo* q. 5 a. 1 ad 9. Cf. the preceding section of this chapter,
p. 147 and note 39.

[47] *S.T.* I, q. 100, a. 1 resp. et ad 2.

[48] *Op. cit.,* pp. 129-130.

[49] *Op. cit.,* p. 139.

transmitting grace would be equally embarrassing [50]. Actually
Bittremieux's argument has not much force. The very same
difference in terminology occurs in the question of the transmission of human nature itself. Human nature is propagated,
transmitted, etc. None of these terms, however, can be used
of the human soul. Shall we say, then, that the soul does not
pertain to human nature, that it is purely personal, in no sense
a part of the nature? If Bittremieux had found twice as many
terms and ten times as many texts to prove the adequate distinction between sanctifying grace and original justice on the
basis of this difference in terminology, his argument would be
equally ineffective. The difficulties and the solutions of the
problems of the transmission of original justice and that of
human nature itself are analogous. Human nature can be said
to be transmitted, though its principal part is not transmitted,
but infused when the matter is disposed. Original justice, a
gift of grace not confined to the rational soul alone but extend-
ing in its effects to the whole nature, even to the body, can be
said like the nature itself to be transmitted, though its principal part, sanctifying grace, be infused only at the instant when
the soul itself is infused. As for the questions concerning disposition and kinds of causality, we must reserve their discussion for the later chapters of this study.

What, then, is to be said of Bittremieux's position? There
are not merely isolated weaknesses in his arguments. Rather
there is question of the whole textual foundation for his thesis
of the adequate distinction between sanctifying grace and original justice as proved from the doctrine of the *donum naturae*.
He has appealed constantly to this doctrine as fundamental
in St. Thomas, and in the question of the role of sanctifying
grace in original justice he has insisted on interpreting texts
always to agree with what he has termed St. Thomas' « constant teaching » that sanctifying grace is a purely personal gift.
This so-called constant teaching of St. Thomas is non-existent,

---

[50] Cf. the refutations made by G. HUARTE, S. J., « De Distinctione
inter justitiam Originalem et Gratiam Sanctificantem », *Gregorianum* 5 (1924)
195: and JOHANN STUFLER, S. J., in his review of Kors' book in *Zeitschrift
für katholische Theologie* 47 (1923) 80.

and Bittremieux is utterly without sound textual support for
his principal thesis.

Kors does not offer direct textual proof in his use of the
donum naturae theory to prove the adequate distinction between sanctifying grace and original justice. He is concerned
rather with a general interpretation of St. Thomas' theories
of nature, person, and grace. Original justice pertains properly to human nature, and through it to the person. That is
why it is a disposition, or at most an entitative habit, not an
act or operative habit. An act and the habit which is its effect
are perfections of the individual [51]. We may note that what
Kors says of habit is true only of acquired habits. He is thinking of the habit not so much as a principle of operation, but
as the effect of personal acts.

Kors gives three arguments to prove that grace is essentially a personal gift and so is distinct from original justice,
a gift to the nature [52]. The first argument is based on the

---

[51] KORS, *op. cit.* p. 87. For his statement on act and habit Kors has
partial support in the text which he cites: « Actus autem omnis personae
est, quia actus individuorum sunt, ut dicit Philosophus » (*In II Sent.* d. 32,
q. 1, a. 2 sol.).

[52] Actually he has two overlapping series of arguments. First, in a
special chapter on nature and grace in St. Thomas, he tries to prove that
grace is a purely personal gift. There are three arguments: (1) the position
of the treatises on grace and on original justice in the *Summa Theologiae;*
(2) grace as a participation in the divine life and cause of our adoptive
sonship; (3) grace as a principle of the personal acts by which we may
attain our supernatural end (pp. 124-126). Then in his treatment of St. Thomas' definitive doctrine on original justice, he gives three proofs to show
that grace is distinct from original justice: (A) a negative argument:
St. Thomas never affirms their identity; (B) grace is a personal gift, and
original justice is a gift to the nature; (C) grace is supernatural, infinitely
exceeding the dignity of the soul, whereas original justice was given because
of the dignity of the soul and perfected it only in its own order (pp. 134-135).
These last two positive arguments are based on the first series of three,
which I am examining in the text. As for the negative argument, it is
wide of the mark. Kors, like Bittremieux before him (*op. cit.,* p. 134) is
principally concerned with refuting Soto's opinion identifying sanctifying
grace and original justice, and like Bittremieux too (*op. cit.,* p. 122, note
and 141-142) is intent upon establishing the other extreme: the complete
distinction of the two. As a matter of fact, perhaps most of the modern
disciples of St. Thomas do not hold that the two were identical, but that
grace was part of original justice. St. Thomas says that original justice
included grace, and the position which can be demonstrated against Kors

location of the treatise on grace in the *Summa Theologiae*.
Grace is treated in the Second Part of the *Summa,* among the
causes of human acts.   It is considered, therefore, in its relation to the human act [53].   From this essential relation of
grace to operation it follows that grace properly concerns the
person, to whom the actions pertain [54].   St. Thomas gives his
exposition of original justice apart from the treatise on original sin.   Original justice is treated in the First Part of the
Summa, among the works of God, manifesting His goodness.
As man proceeded from the hand of God, he shared in that
goodness, for « God made man right ».   This is the principle
on which St. Thomas establishes his whole doctrine of original justice, and it is the reason why he separates this doctrine
from the treatise on original sin.   Original justice is the work
of God and the effect of His infinite goodness; original sin is
the work of man.   Thus the doctrine on original sin must take
its place in the Second Part of the *Summa,* where St. Thomas
considers the relations of man to God and treats human acts,
that is to say virtues and sins.   The place given to the two
treatises in the systematic arrangement of the *Summa* is noteworthy, Kors says, for it sheds light on the general conception
of the nature of both original sin and original justice [55].

The second argument is drawn from the nature of grace.
It is a participation in the divine nature, making us adoptive
sons of God.   Clearly, therefore, grace is personal, since
adoption does not pertain to the nature, but to the person.   It is
a personal property : one does not adopt a nature, but only an
individual [56].

The third argument is drawn from the purpose for which
grace is given to us : to direct us to our supernatural end.   But
the end of man consists in the beatific vision, in the possession

---

is that grace is distinct from original justice as a part from the whole,
the distinction which is now commonly called a real, inadequate distinction.

53 *Op. cit.* p. 124.
54 *Ibid.* p. 125.
55 *Ibid.* pp. 128-129.
56 *Ibid.* pp. 125-126.

of God by the act of our intellect. The end, therefore, is essentially personal. We must merit it by our own acts. That
is why the grace given in view of this end must itself be a
personal gift. Through it man attains God personally [57].

What is to be said of these arguments to prove that grace
is an essentially personal gift, and that consequently it is opposed to original justice, which is a gift to the nature? The
principle which underlies his first argument is this: the human
act and whatever pertains to it, as its principle or as its effect,
are proper to the person. The principle is good; it holds
strictly for human acts, according to the axiom *actus sunt sup-
positorum,* or *actus individuorum sunt* [58]. Moreover, one can
draw a number of reasonable conclusions from this principle.
Thus one may say that original justice and original sin pertain first to the essence of the soul, then to the potencies; for
they are the gift and the sin of the nature, whereas the potencies *seem* to pertain rather to the person, since they are the
principles of personal acts. Consequently the potencies are the
proper subjects of actual sins, which are personal sins [59].
Again, a grace given only to one person to enable him to attain the beatific vision can be called a personal grace: it is given
to him personally, and it is given as a principle of his personal
meritorious acts. Certainly acts belong to the person: they
are performed only by human nature as it is concreted in this
or that individual; they are attributable only to the person who
acts; they affect the nature only as it is found in this person.
And one can say that what is a more proximate principle of
operation in a sense seems to pertain rather to the person than

[57] *Ibid.* p. 126; cf. p. 134.
[58] Kors cites *In II Sent.,* d. 32, q. 1, a. 2 sol., where St. Thomas
applies the Aristotelian principle: « ... actus autem omnis personae est, quia
actus individuorum sunt, ut dicit Philosophus ».
[59] Ad secundum dicendum quod etiam originalis iustitia pertinebat primordialiter ad essentiam animae: erat enim donum divinitus datum humanae
naturae, quam *per prius* respicit essentia animae quam potentiae. Potentiae
enim *magis videntur* pertinere ad personam, inquantum sunt principia personalium actuum. Unde sunt propria subiecta peccatorum actualium, quae
sunt peccata personalia (*S.T.* I-II, q. 83, a. 2 ad 2).

to the nature⁶⁰. But these are rather persuasive arguments
than strict demonstrations. When St. Thomas sets about demonstrating that original sin is first of all in the essence of the
soul, his reason is that it is the essence of the soul which is
reached first by the movement of generation causing the sin⁶¹.
On the other hand, actual sins are in the potencies which are
their principles, because the sins introduce a disorder directly
in the potency⁶². With regard to St. Thomas' use of the
nature-person distinction in these matters, then, it is undeniable
that he cautiously extends to the potencies a principle which
holds strictly for acts.

There is no such caution or care for reasonable limits in
Kors' interpretation. He goes all the way: whatever is a principle or an effect of human acts is essentially a personal gift
and does not pertain to the nature. Thus he explains why
original justice is a disposition or an entitative habit, not an
operative habit; thus he excludes grace and all virtues. Carried to its logical consequences, his principle would involve
many absurdities. Not only the virtues, but also the potencies must be assigned to the person as opposed to the nature,
since they are meaningless except in so far as they are principles of operation. And best of all, the nature must be said
to pertain to the person, not to the nature, because it too is
unintelligible except in relation to the operations by which and
in which it attains its end. The dynamic character of every
nature, of every form, is essential to the philosophy and theology of St. Thomas. Every form, every nature has a twofold
act: it is a principle of being and of operation; and the inclination to operation is inseparable from the nature. Kors' interpretation simply does not fit. One cannot set up a radical
opposition between *bonum naturae* and *donum naturae* on the
one hand and all principles of human acts on the other. When

---

⁶⁰ St. Thomas is careful to say « Potentiae enim *magis videntur* pertinere ad personam, *inquantum* sunt principia personalium actuum » (*loc. cit.*),
just as he says that original sin as a sin of the nature is *first* in the
essence of the soul, though it is also in the will and other potencies (*Ibid.*
a. 2, a. 3).
⁶¹ *Ibid.* a. 2 resp.
⁶² *Ibid.* q. 74, a. 1 resp.

St. Thomas enumerates as *bona naturae* the principles constituting the nature: the properties caused by them, such as the
potencies of the soul; the inclination to virtue; and the gift of
original justice, how is it possible to oppose these to principles
of human acts? Within the gift of original justice itself, what
does the rectitude of the will mean, if it does not refer to the
will's habitual right inclination to seek God in its operations?
And the will is the cause of the rectitude of the lower powers
only in so far as *in act, in operation,* it moves them to the last
end. Human nature and all of the properties which follow
upon it are *bona naturae*: common to the whole nature, to be
found in every individual of that nature. But in this or that
person, all of these natural endowments are the principles of
his personal acts, and as they are concreted in this individual
they are personal endowments [63]. In the present state of mankind, grace is a personal gift in two senses: first, it elevates
the person to a share in the divine life and makes him capable

---

[63] Compare the very interesting text *In II Sent.* d. 32, q. 1, a. 3 sol.,
in which the nature-person distinction as involved in perfections of person
and of nature, and infection of the person and of the nature, do not involve essentially different perfections and infections, but rather a twofold
consideration of nature: Respondeo dicendum, quod cum corruptio fomitis
sit per se infectio humanae naturae, oportet idem esse judicium de intensione ejus et de intensione humanae naturae. Natura autem ipsa potest considerari dupliciter: vel quantum ad rationem speciei, et sic aequaliter in
omnibus invenitur; vel inquantum redundat perfectio naturae in perfectionem
individui per modum quo ex principiis speciei sequuntur operationem individuorum, et secundum hoc unus homo alio est potentior in explendis ope-
rationibus speciem consequentibus; unus enim alio promptior est ad intel-
ligendum vel ad ratiocinandum, et sic de aliis. Similiter est etiam de corruptione fomitis: quia si consideretur secundum quod per se naturam respicit, sic proculdubio aequaliter in omnibus invenitur, et haec est absoluta
consideratio ejus. Quod enim subtrahatur rectitudo illa quae omnes vires
animae in unum continebat, hoc omnibus aequaliter convenit: quia privatio,
quantum in se est, non suscipit magis et minus. Sed si consideretur secundum hoc quod infectio originalis redundat in infectionem personae, inquantum
potentiae sua rectitudine carentes in turpes operationes inclinant; sic in
uno est major corruptio fomitis quam in alio, scilicet inquantum vel per
naturalem complexionem, vel per consuetudinem, concupiscibilis vel irascibilis in uno est efficacior et ferventior ad suum actum quam in alio: et per
hunc etiam modum fomes dicitur post baptismum diminui, inquantum gratia
retardat impetum concupiscibilis et irascibilis, in contrarios actus inclinans.

of personal meritorious acts; secondly, it is given to the person
in such a way that it is not to be passed on by generation.
There is nothing to prevent God's having determined that
grace be a *bonum naturae,* a gift to the whole nature, an *accidens gratuitum totius naturae,* part of the gift of original
justice. As such it was to be received by all who would receive
human nature by descent from Adam. In every person it
would be the principle of his personal meritorious acts, just as
all the other goods of the nature are principles of his personal
acts.

Thus Kors' argument from the structure of the *Summa
Theologiae,* based on the principle that grace must be a purely
personal gift because it is a principle of human acts, is not
sound. Moreover, one may note that even his distinction between the treatises on original justice and grace breaks down.
In the First Part of the *Summa,* where St. Thomas treats original justice, he includes grace and all the virtues as necessary
for that rectitude. For the explanation of how the virtues
were necessary for the rectitude of original justice, he refers
to his treatise on the virtues in the Second Part. [64]. The line
of division between the First and Second Parts of the *Summa*
is not an uncrossable frontier for St. Thomas. Grace and the
virtues pertain to the treatise on original justice. They cannot be fully developed here: St. Thomas cannot do everything
at once, nor can he give two full treatises on grace and the
virtues.

The second argument, from adoptive sonship as an effect
of grace, certainly proves that grace is a personal gift. It does
not, however, exclude the possibility that grace be also, under certain conditions, a gift to the nature. The argument is
akin to the argument from grace as a principle of human acts:
Kors would exclude from the notion of a good of the nature
anything which is the principle of a personal good. Basically
these arguments involve a distortion of the notion of *bonum
naturae* or *donum naturae.* Though grace be a principle of
personal acts and of an adoptive sonship proper to the person,

---

[64] Cf. *S. T.* I, q. 95, a. 3 resp.

it can be a gift to the whole human nature if its effects can extend beyond the soul to the body, and especially if God gives it with the intention that it be passed on with the nature (that is: infused simultaneously with the soul). Only this second condition seems to be essential to St. Thomas' notion of a gift to the nature. Certainly the argument proposed by Kors does not seem to have occurred as a difficulty to prevent St. Thomas' calling grace a *bonum naturae* [65].

The third argument, that grace must be a purely personal gift because it is the principle of the personal acts by which we merit the beatific vision, rests in part on the first argument, excluding from the *donum naturae* any principle of human acts. In part, like the argument from adoptive sonship and participation in the divine nature, it follows from an exaggeration of the *naturalness* of original justice, by which it would be opposed to the supernatural. The advocates of the adequate distinction between grace and original justice generally interpret the *donum naturae* as being entirely within the order of nature, *in linea naturae*. They base their contention on the texts in which St. Thomas says that the subjection of the lower powers to reason, and of the body to the soul, was somehow natural as befitting the dignity of the rational soul. However they go considerably beyond St. Thomas, who speaks of the perfect subjection as a supernatural gift, beyond the powers of nature. Moreover they seem to disregard the beginning of their favorite text, the response in *De Malo,* question five, article one, in which St. Thomas, speaking as a theologian who is giving more than probable arguments from the reasonableness of original justice, describes the real dignity and the pre-eminence of the rational creature as consisting in its capacity for the supreme good to be attained through the vision and

---

[65] *De Malo* q. 5, a. 1 ad 9; cf. the discussion of the text above, pp. 112-113.

With regard to adoptive sonship we may note St. Thomas' solution of the difficulty concerning Christ, who had grace but was not an adopted son. Grace pertains to the nature, whereas sonship refers to the person (*In III Sent.* d. 13, q. 1, a. 1 ad 1; *De Ver.* q. 29, a. 1 ad 1). Though the solution is not relevant to our present argument, the use of the nature-person distinction in these texts is interesting.

enjoyment of God. It is in relation to this supernatural end that he shows the need of both sanctifying grace and original justice (taken in the restricted sense as including only the two lower subjections). No one will deny that the two lower subjections are somehow in the order of nature, and that if original justice be taken in the restricted sense as including only these it is certainly distinct from sanctifying grace. But, as we have seen, original justice fully understood includes the higher subjection of reason to God, and according to the obvious meaning of the text of St. Thomas it includes sanctifying grace. There is no longer any justification for the refusal to take the obvious meaning of the many texts which we have already seen.

Correctly understood, the theory of the *donum naturae* does not rule out the possibility of including grace as a part of original justice. The arguments of Martin, Bittremieux, and Kors do not rest on a solid textual foundation, and the authors do not succeed in their attempt to prove that the complete distinction between sanctifying grace and original justice is the teaching of St. Thomas. Thus, I believe, the rule which has determined the exegesis of many texts in their interpretation seems quite unreasonable. We may turn now to the text of St. Thomas to determine positively what was the role of grace and the virtues in original justice.

CHAPTER TWO

THE ROLE OF SANCTIFYING GRACE AND
THE INFUSED VIRTUES IN ORIGINAL JUSTICE

In the first part of this study of St. Thomas' theology of original justice we made a preliminary survey of the principal features of his teaching concerning the perfection of the first state of man. Grace and virtues were an important part of that perfection. To this point in our inquiry, however, we have not determined exactly the relation of grace and the virtues to original justice itself. Because of the controversy over the relation of grace to original justice it has been necessary to allow for the possibility that they were completely distinct. We must turn now to consider that relationship, to determine as fully and exactly as possible St. Thomas' conception of the nature of original justice. Was it a rectitude which was constituted principally by *gratia gratum faciens* and the infused virtues, a justice which, apart from certain special effects of grace in that state, was essentially similar to the justice which is received by grace in the present state of human nature? Or was it a unique rectitude, natural rather than supernatural, not constituted by grace and the virtues (and according to Kors in no sense including virtues)?

In examining the texts we shall consider first the comparison between original justice and the justice which is received through baptism. Then, at greater length, we shall endeavor to find in St. Thomas' description of original justice what he conceived to be the role of grace and the virtues.

A. A Comparison of Original Justice and Gratuitous Justice

In any effort to determine the relation of gratuitous justice to original justice in the theology of St. Thomas, one should recognize that the very terminology which is used in proposing the question is somewhat prejudicial. The distinction between the two justices comes from the doctrine of those who held that the first man was not created in grace. Use of the two terms, and the discussion of the relation between the two justices, then, would tend to involve presumptions in favor of the complete distinction of the two. It seems, however, that from the outset St. Thomas would wish to indicate that the distinction between the two justices will depend on one's theory on creation in grace. If one holds that the first man was created in grace, then grace was a gift to human nature itself [1], and the complete distinction between original justice and gratuitous justice vanishes: in part, the two justices coincide. What, then, is the relation between the two justices in the teaching of St. Thomas, and in particular, how do they compare with regard to the role of grace and the infused virtues? I shall propose three groups of texts, concerned with the following themes: (1) direct comparison of the two justices; (2) the comparison involved in texts on original sin and the effects of baptism; (3) the analogy with the justice of Christ and the Blessed Virgin Mary.

1. *Direct Comparison of the Two Justices*

The first text is from the Commentary on the *Sentences*, in the discussion of whether or not the punishment due to original sin should remain after baptism. In the solution St. Thomas has shown that baptism removes the infection of original sin only in so far as it affects the person, not in so far as it affects the nature itself. Consequently the punishment

---

[1] *In II Sent.* d. 20, q. 2, a. 3 sol.

due to the person, the lack of the beatific vision, is taken away; but there remain the punishments due to the sin as it affects the nature. The objection is that since gratuitous justice is more powerful than original justice, the punishment of original sin should not remain after baptism; for while original justice was in the soul, there was no rebellion of the flesh nor corruption nor possibility of suffering. St. Thomas answers:

> In every effect which pertains essentially to justice (*quod per se justitiae est*) gratuitous justice is more powerful than original justice. The exclusion of such penalties, however, is not the effect of justice in so far as it is justice: but it was the effect of original justice by reason of a certain accident added to it: that is to say, in so far as it was continuous and unbroken in human nature. For it was fitting that as the soul through justice was directed to God without interruption, so also the body should obey the soul completely and without interruption. Consequently it is not necessary that that effect belong to gratuitous justice, since there has been an interruption of the right order of human nature with respect to God [2].

The text is interesting because it suggests that original justice and gratuitous justice are similar in what is essential to justice. It is not perfectly clear, however, because it does not state what it is that is essential to justice, and because in the comparison of the two, they are not said to be alike in essentials: gratuitous justice is said to be more powerful. It would be possible, then, to say that the text does not prove that sanctifying grace was part of original justice, and to explain that gratuitous justice is more powerful because it elevates man to the supernatural life, whereas original justice was merely a perfect harmony among the parts of human nature which did not surpass the order of created nature. I think it is more reasonable, however, to regard the text as an indication that justice in both cases is a supernatural justice constituted essentially by sanctifying grace and the virtues.

---

[2] *In II Sent.* d. 32, q. 1, a. 2 ad 2.

Taking this interpretation, that there is an essential similarity between the two, we can explain from the immediate context in what sense gratuitous justice is more powerful: whereas the first justice had been given to man with a nature unspoiled by sin, did not involve a cleansing from sin, and was opposed only to original sin; the second justice (there is question of the justice given in baptism) cleanses not only of original sin but also of actual sin. Even this, however, can be drawn only indirectly from the answer to the third objection[3], and the text remains obscure. Nor does the answer to the last objection dispel the clouds: it is the text in which we have already seen St. Thomas explain that baptismal grace, no matter how abundantly given, could never remove completely the tinder of sin, since it is not intended for that, but that God could infuse another kind of grace by which it would be completely removed[4]. From the evidence of this text and context alone, then, one could say no more than that it is probable that St. Thomas regards original justice as essentially similar to gratuitous justice.

Another probable argument for the essential similarity of the two justices can be found in the *De Veritate*. In the question concerning the justification of the sinner, St. Thomas is inquiring whether this justification is the remission of sins. If justification be regarded as the movement (*motus*) terminating in justice, there is one and the same movement by which sin is removed and justice is introduced: justification differs only in concept, then, from the remission of sins. If justification be regarded as a change (*mutatio*) the generation of

---

[3] Ad tertium dicendum, quod generatio spiritualis efficacior est in eo ad quod ordinatur, quam generatio corporalis. Generatio autem corporalis terminatur per se ad naturam, quia forma est terminus generationis; sed generatio spiritualis terminatur ad perfectionem personae, quae est per gratiam; et ideo plus mundat generatio spiritualis personam, quam generatio corporalis inficere possit. Generatio enim corporalis non potest inficere personam nisi infectione originalis; sed generatio spiritualis purgat personam a culpa originali et actuali ... (*Ibid.* ad 3).

[4] ... Posset tamen Deus alterius generis gratiam infundere, per quam totum tolleretur; ut sic simul et personae et naturae infectio gratiae cederet (*Ibid.* ad 5).

justice is different from the destruction of sin: the two are not identical except in that they occur together. Whichever way justification be understood, it must be taken in reference to that justice which is opposed to any sin: not the cardinal virtue of justice, therefore, nor legal justice, but the justice which Aristotle called metaphorical. This justice signifies a certain fitting state in which a man is well disposed toward God, his neighbor, and himself; so that his lower powers are subject to his higher. This justice is opposed to all sin, since any sin destroys something of that order [5]. The justice in question, then, is clearly that of which *gratia gratum faciens* is the formal cause. The comparison with Adam's justice occurs in connection with the twelfth objection. Since Christ and the first man in the state of innocence — if he had grace — were justified without the remission of sin, justification is not the remission of sins. St. Thomas answers that justification as such is the conferring of justice. In so far as it is the justification of a sinner, it involves the remission of sins. In this sense it did not apply to Christ, nor to man in the state of innocence [6].

From this text too one can draw no more than a probable argument for the essential similarity of original justice and gratuitous justice. Certainly it indicates that Adam had a supernatural justice like ours. It does not exclude the possibility that this justice which he had through grace was distinct from an original justice which was merely in the order of nature.

The last and clearest text, in the *Summa Theologiae,* is much stronger. In the whole text there is question of supernatural justification: St. Thomas is considering the effects of grace [7]. Adam's justification differs from the justification of

---

[5] *De Ver.* q. 28, a. 1 resp. Cf. the parallel treatment of this justice in *In IV Sent.* d. 17, q. 1, a. 1 qc. 1. where this justice is called *general* because it includes all the virtues.

[6] Ad duodecimum dicendum, quod ad iustificationem, in quantum huiusmodi, pertinet iustitiae collatio; sed in quantum est impii iustificatio, sic ad eam pertinet peccatorum remissio; et hoc modo Christo non competit, nec etiam homini in statu innocentiae (*Ibid.* ad 12).

[7] *S.T.* I-II, q. 113, « De Effectibus Gratiae, et primo, de Iustificatione Impii ».

the sinner only in that it was *per modum simplicis generationis,* since there was no sin to be remitted. The loophole left in the other text for a distinction between Adam's gratuitous justice and his original justice is closed in this text, for St. Thomas speaks explicitly of Adam's reception of original justice[8]. This text, therefore, gives a much stronger proof of the essential similarity of original and gratuitous justice: original justice is a justice constituted principally by grace and the virtues; it is not, therefore, to be distinguished completely from grace.

2. *Original Sin and the Effects of Baptism*

There is an implicit but very clear comparison between original justice and the justice received in baptism, a comparison involved in the texts on original sin and the effects of baptism. As we have seen in the study of the *formalis-materialis* terminology as it is applied to original sin, the formal element of original sin is opposed to original justice, understood in the restricted sense of the rectitude of the will (or the higher part of the soul)[9]. In the texts on the remission of original sin through baptism we find the counterpart: by baptism the formal element of original sin is destroyed, and the justice

---

[8] Respondeo dicendum quod iustificatio passive accepta importat motum ad iustitiam; sicut et calefactio motum ad calorem. Cum autem iustitia de sui ratione importet quandam rectitudinem ordinis, dupliciter accipi potest. Uno modo, secundum quod importat ordinem rectum in ipso actu hominis ...

Alio modo dicitur iustitia prout importat rectitudinem quandam ordinis in ipsa interiori dispositione hominis: prout scilicet supremum hominis subditur Deo, et inferiores vires animae subduntur supremae, scilicet rationi. Et hanc etiam dispositionem vocat Philosophus, in V Ethic., iustitiam metaphorice dictam. Haec autem iustitia in homine potest fieri dupliciter. Uno quidem modo, per modum simplicis generationis, quae est ex privatione ad formam. Et hoc modo iustificatio posset competere etiam ei qui non esset in peccato, dum huiusmodi iustitiam a Deo acciperet: *sicut Adam dicitur accepisse originalem iustitiam.*

Alio modo potest fieri huiusmodi iustitia in homine secundum rationem motus qui est de contrario in contrarium. Et secundum hoc, iustificatio importat transmutationem quandam de statu iniustitiae ad statum iustitiae praedictae. Et hoc modo loquimur hic de iustificatione impii ... (*S.T.* I-II, q. 113, a. 1 resp.).

[9] Cf. Part I, chapter two.

which is received is identified with original justice in so far as it concerned the higher part of the soul.

We have noted that though the *formalis-materialis* terminology is applied to original justice directly only in one text, it occurs commonly in the analysis of original sin. In the definition of original sin as *concupiscentia cum carentia originalis iustitiae* [10], concupiscence or the disorder of the lower powers is material, and the lack of original justice is formal. Sometimes, when comparing the powers of the soul, this formal element is indicated simply as the disorder of the will: for the will has a primacy, since it moves all the other powers subject to it. Yet this is a limited consideration of original sin as it affects the powers of the soul. In a wider sense, the formal element of original sin is the lack of right order in the higher part of the soul [11]. In all these texts on the formal element in original sin, the discussion is limited to the powers or parts of the soul. But prior even to the disorder of the will is that of the essence of the soul. St. Thomas teaches constantly that original sin is first in the essence of the soul [12]. The disorder of the essence of the soul is the opposite of order caused by grace [13]. Though in actual sin the privation of grace

---

[10] *De Malo,* q. 4, a. 2 resp.

[11] Sic ergo in peccato primi parentis fuit aliquid formale, scilicet aversio ab incommutabili bono, et aliquid materiale, scilicet conversio ad bonum commutabile. Ex hoc autem quod aversus fuit ab incommutabili bono, donum originalis iustitiae amisit; ex hoc vero quod conversus est inordinate ad commutabile bonum, inferiores vires quae erigi debebant ad rationem, depressae sunt ad inferiora. Sic ergo in his quae ex eius stirpe oriuntur, et superior pars animae caret debito ordine ad Deum, qui erat per originalem iustitiam, et inferiores vires non subduntur rationi, sed ad inferiora convertuntur secundum proprium impetum: et ipsum etiam corpus in corruptionem tendit secundum inclinationem contrariorum ex quibus componitur. (*Ibid.*).

[12] *In II Sent.* d. 31, q. 2, a. 1 sol.; *De Ver.* q. 27, a. 6, ad 2; *De Malo,* q. 4, a. 4 resp.; *S.T.* I-II, q. 83, a. 2 resp.

[13] Ad secundum dicendum, quod culpa actualis non potest esse nisi in potentia, quae sit principium actus. Culpa autem originalis est in anima secundum suam essentiam, per quam coniungitur ut forma carni, ex qua infectio originalis in anima contrahitur. Et quamvis ab anima nihil essentialium auferatur, impeditur tamen ordo ipsius essentiae animae per modum

is not of the essence of the fault, but rather is its effect and punishment [14], the case is different in original sin: here the disorder of the nature, caused by the withdrawal of original justice, is of the essence of original sin [15]. The formal element of original sin, therefore, is the lack of original justice, the lack of that order which was in the essence of the soul and in the will. Implicitly in these texts original justice is restricted to the order of the highest part of the soul.

Keeping in mind this opposition between original justice and the formal element of original sin, let us examine the texts in which St. Thomas discusses the removal of the sin through baptism. In a text which we have seen in the question of the *donum naturae,* St. Thomas explains why original sin must be passed on by all descendants of Adam. Human nature in the present state is not restored in what pertains to the nature, though by grace it is restored in what pertains to the person [16]. Again, discussing the removal of original sin by baptism, he repeats the same teaching and then gives an interesting answer to an objection. The difficulty is that a privation is not removed unless the opposite possession is restored. Original justice, of which original sin is the privation, is not restored by baptism, since the right order of the lower powers to reason does not remain. Therefore original sin is not removed by baptism. St. Thomas answers that in original jus-

---

cuiusdam elongationis, sicut contrariae dispositiones elongant potentiam materiae ab actu formae. (*De Ver.* q. 27, a. 6 ad 2).

[14] *De Malo* q. 2, a. 2 ad 9.

[15] Ad decimum dicendum, quod concupiscentia secundum quod est aliquid originalis peccati, non nominat necessitatem consentiendi motibus concupiscentiae inordinatis, sed nominat necessitatem sentiendi, quae quidem manet post baptismum; sed non manet cum carentia originalis iustitiae, ex qua est reatus poenae. Et ideo dicitur, quod manet actu, et transit reatu. Nec tamen oportet quod necessitas sentiendi concupiscentiae motus, non habet rationem originalis peccati, propter hoc quod sentire huiusmodi motus non habet rationem peccati actualis propter carentiam gratiae: quia peccatum actuale in actu consistit, est enim actus inordinatus. Et ideo defectus qui constituit actuale peccatum, est ipsa inordinatio actus, non autem carentia gratiae, quae est defectus in subiecto peccati. Sed peccatum originale est peccatum naturae; et ideo inordinatio naturae per subtractionem originalis iustitiae facit rationem originalis peccati (*De Malo* q. 4, a. 2 ad 10).

[16] *In II Sent.* d. 31, q. 1, a. 2 sol.

tice there was something quasi formal, the rectitude of the will; and in this original justice was opposed to the deformity of sin. There was also something quasi material, the right order impressed upon the lower powers; in this it was opposed to concupiscence and the tinder of sin. Although *original justice* is not restored in its material element, *it is restored in what concerns the rectitude of the will,* the privation of which constituted the sin. Therefore the sin is removed in baptism, but the other punishment remains [17]. The text is important for the implicit comparison between original justice and the justice conferred by baptism. The rectitude of will caused by baptism, a rectitude constituted by grace and charity especially, is a restoration of part of original justice.

In the capital text of the *De Malo* on the nature of original sin, after defining original sin as *concupiscentia cum carentia originalis iustitiae,* St. Thomas defends the definition against an objection that concupiscence cannot in any way be original sin. Concupiscence in so far as it is part of original sin does not mean the necessity of consenting to the movements of concupiscence, but rather the necessity of feeling them. This remains after baptism, but *it does not remain with the lack of original justice,* which makes one liable to punishment. Accordingly it is said to remain, though the guilt passes away [18].

In the same article he answers substantially the same objection which was considered in the Commentary on the *Sentences*: original justice is not restored by baptism because the lower powers still resist reason; if therefore original sin were the lack of original justice, it would follow that it would not be remitted by baptism, which is heretical. The answer is that

---

[17] Ad primum ergo dicendum, quod in originali justitia erat aliquid quasi formale, scilicet ipsa rectitudo voluntatis, et secundum hoc sibi opponitur culpae deformitas. Erat in ea etiam aliquid quasi materiale, scilicet ordo rectitudinis impressus in inferioribus viribus; et quantum ad hoc opponitur sibi concupiscentia et fomes. Quamvis ergo non restituatur originalis justitia quantum ad id quod materiale in ipsa erat, restituitur tamen quantum ad rectitudinem voluntatis, ex cujus privatione ratio culpae inerat: et propter hoc id quod culpae est tollitur per baptismum, sed aliud poenale remanet (*Ibid.* d. 32, q. 1, a. 1 ad 1).

[18] *De Malo* q. 4, a. 2 ad 10 (text quoted above in note 15).

original justice is restored in baptism, in what concerns the
union of the higher part of the soul with God (the privation
of this union was the cause of guilt) but not in what concerns
the subjection of the lower powers to reason. This defect
is the cause of concupiscence, which remains after baptism [19].

There is a third text farther on in the same question of
the *De Malo*. Original sin is opposed to original justice, by
which the higher part of the soul was united with God, commanded the lower powers, and could preserve the body from
corruption. By baptism, then, original sin is removed in so
far as grace is given, by which the higher part of the soul is
united with God. But the soul is not given the power by which
it could preserve the body from corruption or by which the
higher part of the soul could keep the lower powers from all
rebellion. Hence there remain after baptism both the necessity
of dying and concupiscence, which is material in original sin.
Thus, in what concerns the higher part of the soul the baptized
shares in the newness of Christ; but in what concerns the lower
powers of the soul and also the body there remains still the
oldness which comes from Adam [20].

These three texts of the *De Malo* certainly imply a partial
identity of original justice and the justice received in baptism.
Though concupiscence remains after baptism, it does not remain with the lack of original justice: part of original justice
is restored in baptism, in so far as grace is given to restore the
union of the higher part of the soul with God. The same
implication is contained, though less clearly, in a similar text
of the *Summa Theologiae*: the guilt of original sin is removed

---

[19] Ad secundum dicendum, quod iustitia originalis restituitur in baptismo quantum ad hoc quod superior pars animae coniungitur Deo, per
cuius privationem inerat reatus culpae, sed non quantum ad hoc quod rationi
subiiciantur inferiores vires; ex huiusmodi enim defectu est concupiscentia
quae manet post baptismum (*Ibid.,* ad 2 in contr., third series of objections,
23 in the Marietti edition).
[20] *Ibid.* q. 4, a. 6 ad 4. Note that in this text St. Thomas does not
apply the definition of original sin as *concupiscentia cum carentia originalis
iustitiae.* Instead he simply opposes original justice and original sin.

by baptism in so far as the soul *recovers* grace in what concerns the mind [21].

What, then, is the evidence of these texts on original sin and the effects of baptism? Though they offer only an implicit comparison of original justice and the justice of the baptized, I believe that they give a clear indication, if not an adequate proof, that St. Thomas regards the chief element of original justice, the rectitude of the higher part of the soul, as a justice which is constituted by sanctifying grace and charity uniting the soul with God.

3. *Analogy with the Justice of Christ and of the Blessed Virgin Mary*

The problem in the theology of original justice is to give as far as possible a reasonable explanation of the revealed data concerning the first state of man, to explain the nature and the intrinsic principles of the perfect rectitude of original justice. Thus in the question of immortality we have seen how St. Thomas endeavors to explain the created causes of this privilege [22]. Just as in that question we can profit by the study of his treatment of the analogous prerogatives of the glorified body, so in the attempt to determine St. Thomas' explanation of the complete subjection of the lower powers to reason we can learn something from his explanation of the same phenomenon in Christ and the Blessed Virgin Mary. In both of these cases St. Thomas himself makes the comparison with original justice.

In his discussion of the defects of soul which Christ as-

---

[21] Ad secundum dicendum quod peccatum originale per baptismum aufertur reatu, inquantum anima recuperat gratiam quantum ad mentem. Remanet tamen peccatum originale actu quantum ad fomitem, qui est inordinatio inferiorum partium animae et ipsius corporis, secundum quod homo generat, et non secundum mentem. Et ideo baptizati traducunt peccatum originale: non enim generant inquantum sunt renovati per baptismum, sed inquantum retinent adhuc aliquid de vetustate primi peccati (*S.T.* I-II, q. 81, a. 3 ad 2).

[22] Part I, chapter three.

sumed in human nature St. Thomas replies as follows to the
question whether Christ had the *fomes peccati*:

> As has been said above, Christ had grace and all the
> virtues most perfectly. Now a moral virtue which is in the
> irrational part of the soul makes it subject to reason, and
> so much the more as the virtue is more perfect: as temper-
> ance (subjects) the concupiscible, and fortitude and meek-
> ness the irascible, as has been said in the Second Part. But
> the inclination of the sense appetite to that which is against
> reason is of the essence of the tinder. Thus therefore it is
> evident that the more perfect one's virtue is, the more the
> power of the tinder is weakened in him. Since, then, in
> Christ there was virtue in the most perfect degree, it follows
> that in Him there was no tinder of sin: since that defect too
> is not capable of being directed to satisfaction, but rather
> inclines to the opposite of satisfaction [23].

Obviously there is question of the same phenomenon which
is to be explained in original justice [24]. The complete freedom

------

[23] *S.T.* III, q. 15, a. 2 resp.

[24] Cf. *Comp. Theol.* c. 224: «... Sed beata Virgo Maria tanta abundantia gratiae sanctificata fuit, ut deinceps ab omni peccato conservetur im-
munis non solum mortali sed etiam veniali. § Et quia veniale peccatum
interdum ex surreptione contingit, ex hoc scilicet quod aliquis inordinatus
concupiscentiae motus insurgit, aut alterius passionis, praeveniens rationem,
ratione cuius primi motus dicuntur esse peccata, consequens est quod beata
Virgo Maria numquam peccavit venialiter, eo quod inordinatos passionum
motus non sensit. Contingunt autem huiusmodi motus inordinati ex hoc
quod appetitus sensitivus, qui est harum passionum subiectum, non sic su-
biicitur rationi quin interdum ad aliquid praeter ordinationem rationis moveatur, et quandoque contra rationem, in quo consistit motus peccati. Sic
igitur fuit in beata Virgine appetitus sensitivus rationi subiectus per virtutem gratiae ipsum sanctificantis, quod nunquam contra rationem movebatur,
sed secundum ordinem rationis; poterat tamen habere aliquos motus subitos
non ordinatos ratione. § In domino autem Iesu Christo aliquid amplius fuit.
Sic enim inferior appetitus in eo rationi subiiciebatur ut ad nihil moveretur,
nisi secundum ordinem rationis, secundum scilicet quod ratio ordinabat, vel
permittebat appetitum inferiorem moveri proprio motu. *Hoc autem videtur
ad integritatem primi status pertinuisse,* ut inferiores vires totaliter rationi
subderentur: quae quidem subiectio per peccatum primi parentis est sublata
non solum in ipso, sed etiam in aliis qui ab eo contrahunt peccatum originale,
in quibus etiam postquam a peccato mundantur per gratiae sacramentum,
remanet rebellio vel inobedientia inferiorum virium ad rationem, quae dicitur fomes peccati, quae in Christo nullatenus fuit secundum praedicta. § Sed

from the *fomes peccati,* the perfect subjection of the lower powers to reason, is caused by the perfect grace and virtues in the soul of Christ.

In the Blessed Virgin Mary the ligation of the *fomes* was the effect of the grace of sanctification which she received. The matter is obscured by St. Thomas' difficulty concerning the Immaculate Conception [25]. Of the two explanations from which he finally makes his choice, one held that the *fomes* was completely removed by the first grace of sanctification, so that in this respect it had the power of original justice. St. Thomas rejects this as detracting somewhat from the dignity of Christ: it was not fitting that anyone should have this privilege before Christ himself had it. Consequently he explains that before the Incarnation Mary had the *fomes,* but it was bound by the abundant grace of sanctification and especially through Divine Providence. Later, in the very conception of Christ, she shared in His complete freedom from the tinder of sin [26]. Despite the

---

quia in beata Virgine Maria non erant inferiores vires totaliter rationi subiectae, ut scilicet nullum motum haberent a ratione non praeordinatum, et tamen sic cohibebantur per virtutem gratiae, ut nullo modo contra rationem moverentur, propter hoc solet dici, quod in beata Virgine post sanctificationem remansit quidem fomes peccati secundum substantiam, sed ligatus. (Marietti ed. nn. 461-464).

[25] *Ibid.* c. 224, nn. 457-461.

[26] Restat igitur ut dicamus quod vel totaliter fomes fuerit ab ea sublatus per primam sanctificationem: vel quod fuerit ligatus. Posset tamen intelligi quod totaliter fuit sublatus fomes hoc modo, quod praestitum fuerit Beatae Virgini, ex abundantia gratiae descendentis in ipsam, ut talis esset dispositio virium animae in ipsa quod inferiores vires nunquam moverentur sine arbitrio rationis: sicut dictum est fuisse in Christo, quem constat peccati fomitem non habuisse: et *sicut fuit in Adam ante peccatum per originalem iustitiam; ita quod, quantum ad hoc, gratia sanctificationis in Virgine habuit vim originalis iustitiae.* Et quamvis haec positio ad dignitatem Virginis Matris pertinere videatur, derogat tamen in aliquo dignitati Christi... Et ideo melius videtur dicendum quod per sanctificationem in utero non fuit sublatus Virgini fomes secundum essentiam, sed remansit ligatus: non quidem per actum rationis suae, sicut in viris sanctis, quia non statim habuit usum liberi arbitrii adhuc in ventre matris existens, hoc enim speciale privilegium Christi fuit; sed per gratiam abundantem quam in sanctificationem recepit; et etiam perfectius per divinam providentiam sensualitatem eius ab omni inordinato motu prohibentem. Postmodum vero, in ipsa conceptione carnis Christi, in qua primo debuit refulgere peccati immunitas, credendum est quod ex prole redundaverit in matrem totaliter a fomite subtractio... (*S.T.* III, q. 27, a. 2 resp.).

difficulties of the text, it is clear that the intrinsic principle of Mary's freedom from concupiscence was the abundant grace conferred on her.

St. Thomas' treatment of the complete subjection of the lower powers to reason in Christ and in the Blessed Virgin is another indication that we may expect him to explain that element of original justice as the effect of the abundance of sanctifying grace and the infused virtues. We may observe once again the difference between this subjection of the lower powers commanded by the will and that other perfect subjection of body to soul which resulted in immortality and the freedom from suffering. The first subjection can be explained in terms of virtues subjecting the irrational powers to reason. The second cannot be caused by the virtues, for it concerns forces which are not subject to the will. Thus St. Thomas explains that the perfection of virtue which freed Christ from concupiscence did not free Him from suffering [27].

B. Subjection of the Lower Powers to Reason

Having considered the comparisons of original justice and gratuitous justice and the analogy with the justice of Christ and the Blessed Virgin Mary, let us turn now to examine directly St. Thomas' teaching on the role of grace and the virtues in original justice. First, what are the intrinsic principles of man's freedom from concupiscence in the state of innocence : what caused the complete subjection of the lower powers to reason?

---

[27] Ad primum ergo dicendum quod inferiores vires pertinentes ad sensibilem appetitum, naturaliter sunt obedibiles rationi : non autem vires corporales, vel humorum corporalium, vel etiam ipsius animae vegetabilis, ut patet in I *Ethic.* Et ideo perfectio virtutis, quae est secundum rationem rectam, non excludit passibilitatem corporis : excludit autem fomitem peccati, cuius ratio consistit in resistentia sensibilis appetitus ad rationem (*S. T.* III, q. 15, a. 2 ad 1).

For the differences in the causality involved in the two subjections, see Part I, chapters two and three.

The answer is given in a single text in which St. Thomas considers whether Adam had all the virtues:

> Man in the state of innocence somehow had all the virtues: this can be clear from what has been said: ... the rectitude of the first man was such that reason was subject to God, and the lower powers to reason. But the virtues are nothing else than certain perfections by which reason is directed to God, and the lower powers are disposed according to the rule of reason, as will be more evident when we treat the virtues ... [28].

For St. Thomas the problem is quite simple: the perfect rectitude of reason and of the lower powers subject to reason was the effect of grace [29] and the virtues. And if any commentary be needed on this text, St. Thomas himself indicates where it is to be found: in his theory of the virtues. It is not necessary here to go into a thorough exposition of that theory, and it is beyond the reasonable limits of this study to do so. Suffice it to recall a few details of his treatment of the virtues which are especially pertinent to the question of the subjection of the lower powers.

With regard to the general teaching on *habitus,* though there is a distinction between operative habits and what may be called entitative habits (directly intended to perfect the nature), still all habits are somehow directed to operation, since the nature itself is directed to operation or to the product of an operation as to its end [30]. Entitative habits, therefore, are

---

[28] *S.T.* I, q. 95, a. 3 resp.

[29] *S.T.* I, q. 95, a. 1 resp.

[30] Respondeo dicendum quod habere ordinem ad actum potest competere habitui et secundum rationem habitus; et secundum rationem subiecti in quo est habitus. Secundum quidem rationem habitus, convenit omni habitui aliquo modo habere ordinem ad actum. Est enim de ratione habitus ut importet habitudinem quandam in ordine ad naturam rei, secundum quod convenit vel non convenit. Sed natura rei, quae est finis generationis, ulterius etiam ordinatur ad alium finem, qui vel est operatio, vel aliquod operatum, ad quod quis pervenit per operationem. Unde habitus non solum importat ordinem ad ipsam naturam rei, sed etiam consequenter ad operationem, inquantum est finis naturae, vel perducens ad finem. Unde et in V *Metaphys.* dicitur in definitione

not without their relation to operation. On the other hand, though the human virtues are operative habits [31], yet they are a certain well-ordered disposition in the soul itself, for this right disposition in the agent is prerequisite to perfect operation. Thus a virtue is a proper disposition of the soul, in so far as the potencies of the soul are somehow in order with respect to each other and to that which is outside. As a suitable disposition of the soul the virtue is compared with health and beauty, which are the right dispositions of the body. Still it is also a principle of operation [32].

In the question of the perfect subjection of the lower powers to reason, we are concerned with the virtues as they affect the concupiscible and the irascible powers. In so far as these powers participate reason, since they are intended to obey reason, they can be the subject of human virtues. The virtue which is in the irascible and concupiscible part is nothing else than a certain habitual conformity of those powers to reason [33].

---

habitus, quod est dispositio secundum quam bene vel male disponitur dispositum aut secundum se, idest secundum suam naturam, aut ad aliud, idest in ordine ad finem... (*S. T.* I-II, q. 449, a. 3 resp.).

[31] *Ibid.* q. 55, a. 2 resp.

[32] Ad primum ergo dicendum quod modus actionis sequitur dispositionem agentis: unumquodque enim quale est talia operatur. Et ideo, cum virtus sit principium aliqualis operationis, oportet quod in operante praeexistat secundum virtutem aliqua conformis dispositio. Facit autem virtus operationem ordinatam. Et ideo ipsa virtus est quaedam dispositio ordinata in anima: secundum scilicet quod potentiae animae ordinantur aliqualiter ad invicem, et ad id quod est extra. Et ideo virtus, inquantum est conveniens dispositio animae, assimilatur sanitati et pulchritudini, quae sunt debitae dispositiones corporis. Sed per hoc non excluditur quin virtus etiam sit operationis principium (*Ibid.* ad 1).

[33] Respondeo dicendum quod irascibilis et concupiscibilis dupliciter considerari possunt. Uno modo secundum se, inquantum sunt partes appetitus sensitivi. Et hoc modo, non competit eis quod sint subiectum virtutis. Alio modo possunt considerari inquantum participant rationem, per hoc quod natae sunt rationi obedire. Et sic irascibilis vel concupiscibilis potest esse subiectum virtutis humanae: sic enim est principium humani actus, inquantum participat rationem. Et in his potentiis necesse est ponere virtutes.

Quod enim in irascibili et concupiscibili sint aliquae virtutes, patet. Actus enim qui progreditur ab una potentia secundum quod est ab alia mota, non potest esse perfectus, nisi utraque potentia, sit bene disposita ad actum: sicut actus artificis non potest esse congruus, nisi et artifex sit bene dispositus ad agendum, et etiam ipsum instrumentum. In his igitur circa quae

I believe that it is sufficiently clear that according to St. Thomas the perfect subjection of the lower powers to reason is to be explained in terms of the perfection of the virtues. This is the clear indication, and the only indication, which he has given of an intrinsic principle (as contrasted, for example, with Divine Providence as the extrinsic principle). It is the explanation in the analogous case of Christ's perfection. Given the Thomist theory of the necessity and the function of the virtues, it seems impossible to conceive of any other explanation which would fit the theology of St. Thomas [34].

In St. Thomas' theology of original justice, then, properly speaking there is no so-called preternatural gift of integrity distinct from the virtues. The sole intrinsic principles of the perfect subjection of the lower powers to reason are the perfect infused virtues. Thus we may understand better why St. Thomas simply speaks of this subjection as not natural, requiring as its cause the supernatural gift of grace [35].

C. SUBJECTION OF REASON TO GOD

In the earlier stages of this investigation we have often had occasion to observe details of St. Thomas' teaching concerning the subjection of the higher part of the soul to God. Before attempting to complete our study of this most im-

---

operatur irascibilis et concupiscibilis secundum quod sunt a ratione motae, necesse est ut aliquis habitus perficiens ad bene agendum sit non solum in ratione, sed etiam in irascibili et concupiscibili. Et quia bona dispositio potentiae moventis motae attenditur secundum conformitatem ad potentiam moventem; ideo virtus quae est in irascibili et concupiscibili nihil aliud est quam quaedam habitualis conformitas istarum potentiarum ad rationem (*Ibid.* q. 56, a. 4 resp.). Cf. q. 59, a. 4 resp.

[34] In fact, no real alternative has been suggested in the controversy over St. Thomas' doctrine on original justice. The proponents of the adequate distinction between grace and original justice speak vaguely of a force or power given to the soul, but they make no effort to explain precisely what those words stand for. They make no reference to the role of the virtues in the state of innocence, and one is left to suppose that the rectitude of original justice was completely mysterious and unique.

[35] *S.T.* I, q. 95, a. 1 resp.

portant element of original justice, let us recall the conclusions already reached :

(1) When the cause of the subjection of reason to God is indicated, it is *gratia gratum faciens* [36].

(2) Where original justice is clearly distinguished from sanctifying grace, it includes only the two lower subjections, only the gifts which remedy the defects of man's lower nature. There is no indication that original justice so distinguished from grace includes a « preternatural » rectitude of the will [37].

(3) In the texts in which original justice is opposed to the formal element of original sin, the justice is understood in the restricted sense of the rectitude of the will, or of the higher part of the soul [38]. That this rectitude was the supernatural rectitude of grace and the virtues is indicated in the texts on the effects of baptism : by baptism original justice is restored in what concerns the higher part of the soul [39].

(4) The argument which St. Thomas uses to prove that the first man was created in grace indicates that for St. Thomas the rectitude of grace and charity is the only possible supernatural rectitude of the will, the only possible cause of the lower subjections [40].

(5) *Gratia gratum faciens* was necessary in the state of innocence not merely as the cause of the supernatural rectitude of the lower powers and of the complete subjection of the body, but also because man was destined to a supernatural end. Original justice (in the restricted sense of the two lower subjections) was given to dispose man properly for this grace [41].

(6) The natural rectitude of the will in a human nature unspoiled by sin does not suffice to constitute the principal element of original justice and the cause of the lower subjections. First, since the love of God of which it is capable is a natural act, proceeding from the faculty alone, not perfected by a vir-

---

[36] Part I, chapter one, concluding summary, p. 30.
[37] *Ibid. loc. cit.*
[38] Part I, chapter two, p. 43.
[39] Part II, chapter two, pp. 132-137.
[40] Part I, chapter five, pp. 57-59.
[41] *Ibid.* pp. 63-64.

tue, it lacks the qualities which a virtue would contribute: promptness, constancy, and delight.   It cannot explain the firm, continual union with God which is required for the rectitude of original justice.   Secondly, since original justice was given in view of a supernatural end, and involved not only charity and other infused virtues, but also a supernatural subjection of the body and the lower powers of the soul, it could not be caused by a purely natural rectitude of the will [42].

(7) Original justice was first of all in the essence of the soul, then in the will.   It was the perfect health or harmony of a nature whose parts were in perfect order [43].

(8) The theory of the *donum naturae* in no way excluded the possibility that sanctifying grace was part of original justice: on the contrary St. Thomas indicates that in the state of innocence grace was a *donum naturae* [44].

(8) From the explicit and implicit comparisons to be found in various questions treated by St. Thomas it seems clear that original justice and the justice received in baptism are essentially similar.   Though there are differences in perfection and in certain of their effects, grace and the virtues are the principles of both justices [45].

All of the evidence leads to one conclusion: the rectitude of the higher part of the soul, the principal element of original justice, was a rectitude constituted by grace and the infused virtues, especially charity.

In the earlier texts St. Thomas holds that the whole order of original justice depended on the order of the highest part of man, which clings to the end [46].   The end to which man is directed is beyond the power of created nature, a beatitude consisting in the vision of God.   It is only with his highest part that man could cling by love to his last end and arrive at its possession.   To enable that part to tend to God freely and without impediment, the lower powers were made subject

---

[42] *Ibid.* pp. 75-76.
[43] *Ibid.* p. 89.
[44] Part II, chapter one.
[45] Part II, chapter two.
[46] *In II Sent.* d. 21, q. 2, a. 3 ad 6.

to it, and the body was freed from suffering [47]. The rectitude of original justice involved a continual clinging to God [48], a perfect union with God which required all the virtues [49].

In the definitive doctrine of the *Summa Theologiae* and the *De Malo,* notwithstanding the objections and the alternative exegesis which have been proposed, grace and charity are intrinsic principles of the rectitude of original justice.

The subjection of man's reason to God in original justice was not merely natural, but was caused by the supernatural gift of grace, since this subjection was the cause of the subjection of the lower powers and of the body, which was not natural [50]. As we have seen, the subjection of the lower powers to reason was caused by the perfect infused virtues in the irascible and concupiscible powers. Consequently the need of grace and charity as principles of the higher subjection is evident not only from the axiom cited by St. Thomas, « *non enim potest esse quod effectus sit potior quam causa* », but also more particularly from his theory of the connection of the infused virtues among themselves and with grace. As for immortality and the freedom from suffering, they were due to the special information by the soul perfected by grace [51].

Again in the question concerning Adam's virtues, it is evident that the rectitude of reason is to be explained by infused virtues :

> The rectitude of the first man was such that reason was subject to God, and the lower powers to reason. But the virtues are nothing else than certain perfections by which *reason is directed to God,* and the lower powers are disposed according to the rule of reason, as will be more evident when we treat the virtues ... [52].

Among the virtues which he mentions explicitly are charity, faith, and hope.

---

[47] *Ibid.* d. 30, q. 1, a. 1 sol; cf. above, p. 62; *De Ver.* q. 14, a. 10 ad 2.
[48] *In II Sent.* d. 33, q. 1, a. 1 sol.
[49] *De Ver.* q. 18, a. 7 ad 2.
[50] *S.T.* I, q. 95, a. 1 resp.
[51] Cf. above, Part I, chapter three.
[52] *S.T.* I, q. 95, a. 3 resp.

The root of original justice, in whose rectitude man was made, consists in the supernatural subjection of the reason to God, which is caused by *gratia gratum faciens*. Therefore it is necessary to say that if children would have born in original justice, they would have been born with grace, as the first man was created with grace [53]. Original justice includes *gratia gratum faciens* [54] Original justice is restored in baptism in so far as the higher part of the soul is joined to God [55]. *Gratia gratum faciens* is included in the concept of original justice [56].

I believe that the obvious meaning of these texts, in harmony with all other evidences of St. Thomas' teaching, is that grace is part of original justice, or rather that the rectitude of the highest part of the soul was a supernatural rectitude constituted by grace and the infused virtues.

Against this interpretation of the texts we have the objections principally of Bittremieux and Kors. Thus the former holds that children in the state of innocence would have received grace as a personal gift, not as a gift to the nature [57]. Again, the subjection of reason to God was formally a perfection of nature, *in linea naturae,* but it was caused by the supernatural gift of grace. This interpretation is necessary

---

[53] *Ibid.* q. 100, a. 1 ad 2.

[54] *De Malo* q. 4, a. 2 ad 1 in contr. (third series of objections).

[55] *Ibid.* ad 2 in contr.

[56] Ad decimum dicendum, quod ratio illa procedit secundum opinionem ponentium quod gratia gratum faciens non includatur in ratione originalis iustitiae; quod tamen credo esse falsum, quia cum originalis iustitia primordialiter consistat in subiectione humanae mentis ad Deum, quae firma esse non potest nisi per gratiam, iustitia originalis sine gratia esse non potuit ... (*Ibid.* q. 5, a. 1 ad 13).

Dom O. Lottin, O. S. B., « Le Péché originel chez Albert le Grand, Bonaventure et Thomas d'Aquin », *Recherches de Théologie Ancienne et Médiévale* 12 (1940) 305, especially note 72, holding the text to the meaning required by the immediate context, says that it means only that grace is the condition *sine qua non* of original justice, or at most its efficient cause, but not the formal cause. Granting that one cannot say immediately how much is meant by *in ratione originalis iustitiae* from the immediate context, certainly the whole pattern of the texts which we have seen gives us reason for holding that grace is more than a condition *sine qua non*. Cf. *Psychologie et Morale,* IV, I, 256-257.

[57] Bittremieux, *op. cit.* p. 129.

to harmonize with St. Thomas' teaching that original justice was a perfection of the nature, to be transmitted by generation, whereas sanctifying grace was a gift to the person, incapable of transmission by heredity [58]. Again, though the root of original justice was the supernatural subjection of the reason to God, we must not say that this is the first element of original justice (since grace and the formal effects of grace are purely personal gifts) : rather, this supernatural subjection, the formal effect of grace, is the cause of the whole of original justice, and therefore of another subjection of the will *in linea naturae* [59].

The constant motive in these objections and the constant rule of exegesis is the Bittremieux-Kors interpretation of St. Thomas' teaching on the *donum naturae* : all must be made to harmonize with this « constantly repeated » teaching. As we have seen, that interpretation is illusory, completely lacking in solid textual foundation, and actually inconsistent with the theology of St. Thomas.

Moreover, there is no trace in St. Thomas of the special rectitude of the will « in linea naturae », postulated by these authors as the principal element of original justice. Nor does it seem possible to find any place for such a rectitude. In what would it consist? For Kors at least, it could not be a virtue, since every virtue is an operative habit, a principle of operation, and therefore, according to him, a purely personal gift. What kind of perfection could be added to the will which would not be a habit, a virtue? Apart from this particular difficulty arising from Kors' interpretation, how could one explain such a perfection consistently with St. Thomas' theory of the will and his theory of habit and virtue? A rectitude *in linea naturae* would be a rectitude of the will with respect to an ultimate end proportioned to its nature. With respect to such a good, however, the will needs no added perfection. What the virtues add to other potencies the will has by its

---

[58] *Ibid.* pp. 132-133.
[59] *Ibid.* pp. 133-135. KORS, too, holds that grace was the root of original justice, but not part of it (*op. cit.* pp. 138-139).

very nature as a potency: its object is the good, and its natural inclination, unerring and necessary, tends to the good, to the final end of beatitude proportioned to its nature [60]. As we have seen, a will uncorrupted by sin is capable of a natural love of God above all things [61]. Such a will has no need of a remedy for the weakness of human nature, such as the weakness of the lower powers and of the body, which were reme-

---

[60] Respondeo. Dicendum, quod per habitum virtutis potentia quae ei subicitur, respectu sui actus complementum acquirit. Unde ad id ad quod potentia aliqua se extendit ex ipsa ratione potentiae, non est necessarius habitus virtutis. Virtus autem ordinat potentias ad bonum; ipsa enim est quae bonum facit habentem, et opus eius bonum reddit.

Voluntas autem hoc quod virtus facit circa alias potentias, habet ex ipsa ratione suae potentiae: nam eius obiectum est bonum. Unde tendere in bonum hoc modo se habet ad voluntatem sicut tendere in delectabile ad concupiscibilem, et sicut ordinari ad sonum se habet ad auditum. Unde voluntas non indiget aliquo habitu virtutis inclinante ipsam ad bonum quod est sibi proportionatum, quia in hoc ex ipsa ratione potentiae tendit; sed ad bonum quod transcendit proportionem potentiae, indiget habitu virtutis.

Cum autem uniuscuiusque appetitus tendat in proprium bonum appetentis; dupliciter aliquod bonum potest excedere voluntatis proportionem. Uno modo ratione speciei; alio modo ratione individui.

Ratione quidem speciei, ut voluntas elevetur ad aliquod bonum quod excedit limites humani boni: et dico humanum id quod ex viribus naturae homo potest. Sed supra humanum bonum est bonum divinum, in quod voluntatem hominis caritas elevet, et similiter spes.

Ratione autem individui, hoc modo quod aliquis quaerat id quod est alterius bonum, licet voluntas extra limites boni humani non feratur; et sic voluntatem perficit iustitia, et omnes virtutes in aliud tendentes, ut liberalitas, et alia huiusmodi. Nam iustitia est alterius bonum, ut Philosophus dicit in V *Ethic.* (*De Virt.* a. 5 resp.). Cf. *S.T.* I, q. 60, a. 1 resp. et ad 3.

I quote most of this text because I do not wish to seem to dodge one possible explanation which can be offered. It seems that there could be a natural virtue of love to perfect the will in the natural love of God above all things. It would afford the promptness, constancy, and delight which were lacking to the act of the natural love of God proceeding merely from the potency. Furthermore, it seems that such a natural virtue could have been infused, since St. Thomas holds that Adam had infused natural science.

So much for the possibility of such a recondite solution. There is no evidence in the expositions of Kors or Bittremieux that they had threaded their way to such an explanation (for Kors, of course, such a virtue is also ruled out). But above all, we are concerned with what St. Thomas actually taught about the rectitude of the will, and there is not a shred of evidence that this was his explanation. Only the unfounded premises of the Bittremieux-Kors theory would force us to turn from the obvious meaning of texts.

[61] Cf. *supra,* pp. 66-76.

died by the two lower subjections in original justice. The
natural rectitude of the will was not a special gift of grace.
Nor, as we have seen, could it suffice to explain the perfect
subjection of the will to God which was the cause of the other
rectitudes in original justice [62]. It is in relation to a good
which transcends the proportion of the potency that the will
needs to be perfected, that is: needs virtues [63].

Thus, in the state of innocence, man was directed to the
supernatural end of a beatitude consisting in the vision of God.
By grace and charity he received a new inclination to an end
completely transcending created nature. In the state of grace
he was intimately united to God by grace and charity, and the
perfect subjection of his reason to God was a supernatural
subjection, the formal effect of grace and charity, directing
all of his actions to a supernatural end. This is the rectitude
which was the cause of the rectitude of the lower powers and
of the perfect subjection of the body. There is no trace of a
second, « preternatural » rectitude of the will [64].

Finally, the theory of Bittremieux and Kors seems to end
in unintelligibility in what concerns the essence of the soul.
They hold, of course, that according to St. Thomas original
justice was first of all in the essence of the soul. Moreover
Kors says that it was an entitative habit, *in linea naturae*. Again
there seems to be nothing to correspond to this in the theology
of St. Thomas. As far as the perfection of human nature is
concerned, the soul is not the subject of a habit perfecting the
nature directly, since the soul itself is the form which completes
human nature. There could be a habit or disposition perfecting
the body in relation to the soul, but not the reverse. If, however, we speak of a higher nature, which man can participate,

---

[62] Cf. *supra*, pp. 75-76.

[63] *De Virt.*. a. 5 resp.; for text see note 60 above.

[64] Thus one is inclined to agree with MICHEL: « Je ne comprends donc
pas que l'on puisse concevoir en Adam une rectitude de la raison et de la vo-
lonté, composée pour ainsi dire de deux rectitudes subordonnées: 'sujétion
naturelle', 'rectitude surnaturelle'. Au fond, sous ces formules, n'y aurait-il
simplement que des mots? » (« La Grâce sanctifiante et la justice originelle »,
Revue Thomiste 26 (1921) 426).

THE ROLE OF SANCTIFYING GRACE AND THE INFUSED VIRTUES

there is nothing to prevent there being some habit in the essence of the soul, namely *grace* [65].

In conclusion, then, I believe that we may say with certainty that grace and the infused virtues are part of original justice in the theology of St. Thomas. There is an essential similarity between original justice and gratuitous justice. Though grace and the virtues were more perfect generally in the state of innocence, and though they had more far-reaching effects than they have in the present order, their role in original justice was essentially the same as in the justice of the baptized. The rectitude of the highest part of the soul was constituted by grace and the infused virtues in the intellect and will. The perfect subjection of the lower powers to reason was caused immediately by the perfect infused virtues in the irascible and concupiscible powers. Freedom from suffering and death, as far as it is explained by intrinsic principles, was caused by the special information of the body by a soul which was perfected by an abundant grace.

To this point, then, we have determined the role of grace and the virtues in original justice, without attempting to clarify the question of the kind of causality which they exercised. Having established the essential similarity of the two justices, however, we are at least in a position to approach the problem of causality with some hope of finding adequate textual basis for a solution. On the basis of only the scattered texts on original justice it would be impossible to answer the question. If original justice were utterly unique, and if grace and the virtues were completely distinct from original justice, there would be no way of controlling such statements as have been

---

[65] Respondeo dicendum quod, sicut supra dictum est, habitus importat dispositionem quandam in ordine ad naturam, vel ad operationem. Si ergo accipiatur habitus secundum quod habet ordinem ad naturam, sic non potest esse in anima, si tamen de natura humana loquamur: quia ipsa anima est forma completiva humanae naturae: unde secundum hoc, magis potest esse aliquis habitus vel dispositio in corpore per ordinem ad animam, quam in anima per ordinem ad corpus. Sed si loquamur de aliqua superiori natura, cuius homo potest esse particeps, secundum illud II Petr. 1, *ut simus consortes naturae divinae*: sic nihil prohibet in anima secundum suam essentiam esse aliquem habitum, scilicet gratiam, ut infra dicetur (*S.T.* I-II, q. 50, a. 2 resp.).

made concerning the exclusively efficient causality of grace.
As it is, however, we may use the full riches of St. Thomas'
teaching on the causality involved in grace and the virtues.
In the remaining part of this study we shall attempt to clarify
somewhat this very difficult and obscure question.

PART THREE

FORMAL AND EFFICIENT CAUSALITY
IN ORIGINAL JUSTICE

CHAPTER ONE

OBSERVATIONS ON FORMAL AND EFFICIENT CAUSALITY

A. The Problem

In the controversy over St. Thomas' theology of original justice the question of the kind of causality exercised by grace has been a simple corollary of the positions taken on the questions which we have already considered. Thus the advocates of the complete distinction between sanctifying grace and original justice have held that grace cannot be the formal cause, since it is not part of the justice: therefore it is the efficient cause. Those who hold that grace was part of original justice maintain that it was the formal cause. If the matter could be settled so simply, we could say now without further inquiry that the second position is more in accord with St. Thomas' teaching. One cannot, however, move so quickly to this final resolution of the problem without some misgivings.

Since original justice is essentially similar to gratuitous justice, and the role of grace and the virtues in both is essentially the same, the question of the kind of causality exercised by grace can be answered only in the light of St. Thomas' general teaching on grace and the virtues. There are many indications that this matter of causality is very complicated, that the structure of causal relationship is extremely varied and delicate. The relation of grace to the virtues is analogous to that of the essence to its properties, the soul to its faculties, charity to all other virtues, and prudence to the moral virtues. With regard to the soul, there are texts which indicate a coincidence of two or three types of causality: the soul is the

final, material, and somehow efficient cause of its potencies [1];
it is the formal, efficient, and final cause of the body [2]. Not
only are there many kinds of causality involved, but the terminology varies considerably, especially in the case of *forma*
and *formalis*. Thus, when charity is said to be the form of
the virtues, *form* and *formal* clearly mean *movens*, with over-
tones of final, formal, and exemplary causality in many of the
earlier texts [3].

Much of what has been written concerning the causality
of grace in original justice has been dialectical rather than
historical. Without inquiry into the exact meaning of the terms
involved in St. Thomas' treatment of grace and the virtues,
this question has been settled on the basis of the general notions
of the genera of cause.

Holding the complete distinction between grace and original justice because of his interpretation of the theory of the
donum naturae, Bittremieux simply takes for granted that when
grace is called the cause of original justice, it is the efficient
cause[4]. Kors, too, regarding the complete distinction as a certainty, simply states that grace was the efficient cause of the
rectitude of nature, and in no way the formal cause [5]. He
explains that grace was needed as the supernatural cause of
the natural rectitude of the will, to give a continual confirmation of the will in its natural love of God. There is no
apparent concern for how this fits St. Thomas' theory of the
will and the virtues, nor any reason given for calling the causality efficient — the reason is simply that on Kors' premises one
cannot call it formal: it cannot be part of original justice.

On the other side, the proponents of formal causality have
in general a solid position, for as we have seen, it is certain
that they are right in maintaining that sanctifying grace was
an intrinsic principle of original justice. Yet at times their
case is weakened by recourse to arguments of a purely dialectical

---

[1] *S.T.* I, q. 77, a. 6 resp. et ad 1, 2, 3.
[2] *De Anima* a. 8, 9.
[3] Cf. below, chapter two.
[4] BITTREMIEUX, *op. cit.* pp. 131-135; 139.
[5] KORS, *op. cit.* pp. 136, 139.

nature. They have seized upon texts which speak of grace as
the *root* of original justice, or as being included in the *ratio*
of original justice, and they have argued from these general
notions. Especially in the case of the expression « *in ratione
originalis iustitiae* » one may be too prone to say that it means
clearly that grace is in the very definition of original justice,
and therefore is its intrinsic, formal cause. It is interesting
to watch these words *radix* and *ratio* in the texts. To give
only some examples of their many uses, cupidity [6], pride [7], and
the will itself [8] are the root of all sin. The soul is the root of
its potencies [9]. Charity is the root of the virtues [10], reason the
root of man's good [11], the Divine Goodness the root of all
created good [12], and God the root of beatitude [13]. How is it
possible to say simply that *radix* necessarily means something
intrinsic — or extrinsic? Nor does the simple occurrence of
the word *ratio*, even where it means definition, assure one that
there is question of an intrinsic principle, part of the essence.
In the definition of every accident one places its proper subject.
Moreover, in a perfect definition of anything one gives all its
causes, not merely its intrinsic principles [14].

We know that grace was part of original justice. But of
what kind of whole was it a part? What was the nature and
unity of original justice, and what were its causes? In a matter
as complicated as the principles of human operation, where one
is dealing constantly with analogy and with a chameleonic terminology, where *formalis* does not necessarily mean formal as
opposed to efficient or moving, there is no safe method but
that of painstaking text-analysis, with constant attention to
the evolution in St. Thomas' thought. This is the work which

[6] *S.T.* I-II, q. 84, a. 1 resp.
[7] *De Malo* q. 8, a. 2 resp.
[8] *Ibid.* q. 2, a. 2 ad 2.
[9] *De Spir. Creat.* a. 4 ad 3; *Comp. Theol.* c. 89.
[10] *De Car.* a. 3 resp.
[11] *S. T.* I-II, q. 24, a. 3 resp.
[12] *Comp. Theol.* c. 102.
[13] *De Car.* a. 7 resp.
[14] *S.T.* I-II, q. 55, a. 4 resp.

remains to be done before we can say — and know what we mean — that grace was the formal cause or efficient cause (or both) of original justice.

B. The Two Effects of Every Form

One constantly-recurring principle in our texts is this: grace and charity, like all other forms, have two effects. In *actu primo* they are principles of being, perfecting the essence of the soul and the will in supernatural being: this is strictly formal causality. In *actu secundo* they are principles of operation: thus they exercise efficient causality.

The principle is clear even in the earliest texts, where St. Thomas, before considering whether charity and grace are distinct, is concerned with showing that charity must be a created habit in the soul, distinct from the Holy Spirit. All being must be from some inherent form: hence the need of grace and charity perfecting the soul in its gratuitous being. Since an act cannot be perfect unless it proceeds from a potency perfected by a habit, charity must be a created habit in the soul [15]. Thus there is a twofold operation of the Holy Spirit in making the soul pleasing to God. One terminates in *esse*, in the first act, which is to be pleasing by having the habit of charity. The second causes the second act, the operation moving the will to the work of love. With regard to the first act, which is *esse gratiae*, charity is a *formal cause*; with regard to the second act it is an *efficient cause*, since the virtue which is a principle of operation is reduced to an agent cause [16].

In the being both of nature and of grace, the form which is the principle of being is at once the terminus of the action of the agent which caused the being, and the principle of the operations which God performs in the creature [17].

Though the use of the terms *gratia operans* and *gratia*

[15] *In I Sent.* d. 17, q. 1, a. 1 sol.
[16] *Ibid.* ad 1.
[17] *Ibid.* a. 3.

cooperans varies, in so far as grace is a principle of being in the soul, making a man pleasing to God, it is a formal cause; in so far as it causes a meritorious action it is an efficient cause [18]. When grace is considered as an habitual gift, it has two effects, as does any other form: the first is *esse,* the second is operation [19].

The same principle is involved in the many texts which are concerned with the soul as form and moving cause: it is the principle of being and of operation [20]. Again, in the general theory of habit and virtue, the habit is a *forma quiescens* remaining in the subject, by which one can act when he wishes [21]. The habit is an efficient cause of the act [22].

Just as two effects are attributed to every form, one due to formal causality and the other to efficient causality, so there is a twofold use of the words *agere* and *facere,* one properly referring to efficient causality, the other by extension referring to formal causality. Thus in justification God acts as the efficient cause, charity and grace act as formal causes [23]. To avoid misunderstanding, St. Thomas indicates how these terms are to be understood. *Agere* is said properly only of the agent which produces the act; improperly it is said of that by which the agent acts [24]. Non-subsistent forms, called beings in so far as by them something is, do not have their own operation, but are said to act in so far as through them the subjects act [25].

C. The Meanings of *Forma* and *Formalis*

It is essential in our present problem to understand what St. Thomas means by the terms *forma, formalis, informa-*

---

[18] *In II Sent.* d. 26, q. 1, a. 5 sol. et ad 1, 2, 3, 4. Cf. *De Ver.* q. 27, a. 5 ad 1, 2, 17, 18.

[19] *S.T.* I-II, q. 111, a. 2 resp. et ad 4.

[20] Cf. *De Anima* a. 8 resp.; a. 9 resp.

[21] *De Virt.* a. 1 resp.

[22] *Ibid.* a. 12 ad 5.

[23] *In I Sent.* d. 17, q. 1, a. 1 ad 5; a. 2 ad 4; *In II Sent.* d. 26, q. 1, a. 1 ad 4.

[24] *De Malo* q. 2, a. 11 resp.

[25] *De Anima* a. 19 resp.

tio, etc.   Without attempting a complete study of the meanings
of these terms, we may review the principal uses in the texts
which are relevant to our question.   Clarification of this terminology will help to understand how charity and grace are
said to be the form of the virtues, and to determine the kinds
of causality involved.

1. *Strict Formal Causality*

Obviously in many of the texts which concern us there
is question of a strict formal causality attributed to an inherent
form which is the intrinsic principle of being, substantial or
accidental, natural or supernatural.   Thus charity and grace
are forms [26], and every virtue has its own form, according to
the potency which it perfects and to its own proper object [27].
The human soul is both form of the body and mover, principle
of being and of operation [28].   As form it is united immediately
with the body in all its parts, though as mover it moves
mediately through its potencies and the parts of the body [29].
Since matter and form are intrinsic principles constituting a
thing, it is impossible for anything to receive its *esse* and its
species from something separate as from its formal cause [30].

2. *Principium Formale*

Since the form is a principle of both being and operation,
the term *principium formale* may designate formal or efficient
cause, depending on the context.   Thus charity, besides being
a form perfecting the will in supernatural being, is called the
principium formale of the act of love [31].   As such it is an
efficient cause, since all operative habits are efficient causes

---

[26] *S.T.* I-II, q. 111, a. 1 ad 1, *et passim.*
[27] *In III Sent.* d. 27, q. 2, a. 4, sol. 3 ad 5.
[28] *S.T.* I, q. 76, aa. 1, 4, 6, 7; *De Anima* a. 8.
[29] *S. T.* I, q. 76, aa. 1, 6, 7, 8; *De Anima* a. 9 resp. et ad 1, 2, 5, 14.
[30] *De Anima* a. 10 resp.
[31] *De Car.* a. 1 resp.

of their acts [32]. In a variation of the formula it is called a *principium activum formale* [33].

3. *The Object as Formal*

There is a twofold diversity in powers or habits: from their objects and from the different manner in which they act. The diversity according to objects is essential; the other is the difference between the complete and the incomplete [34]. Since a potency as such is ordered to act, the nature of a potency can be understood from the act to which it is ordered. Consequently potencies are distinguished according to the distinction of their acts. The nature of an act, however, is distinguished according to the difference in the nature of the object. Every action pertains to an active potency or to a passive potency. The object is compared to the act of a passive potency as its principle and moving cause. To the act of an active potency the object is compared as terminus and end. From these two an action receives its species: from its principle or from its end or terminus. Necessarily, then, potencies are diversified according to acts and objects [35].

The object moves by determining the act in the manner of a formal principle, from which action is specified in things of nature. Thus the intellect moves the will as that which presents its object [36]. Just as the first goodness of a natural thing is considered from its form, so the first goodness of a moral act is considered from its suitable object [37].

Since a difference taken from a more particular form is more specific, and a more universal agent gives a more universal form, and a more remote end corresponds to a more universal agent, it follows that the specific difference which is from the end is more general, and the difference which is from an object essentially ordered to such an end is specific with

---

[32] *De Virt.* a. 12 ad 5; cf. *In I Sent.* d. 17, q. 1, a. 1 ad 1.
[33] *De Car.* a. 1 ad 13.
[34] *De Ver.* q. 14, a. 7 resp.; cf. *In III Sent.* d. 27, q. 2, a. 4 sol. 3 ad 5.
[35] *S.T.* I, q. 77, a. 3 resp.
[36] *S.T.* I-II, q. 9, a. 1 resp.
[37] *Ibid.* q. 18, a. 2 resp.

respect to it.   For the will, whose proper object is the end, is
the universal mover with respect to all the potencies of the
soul, whose proper objects are the objects of particular acts [38].

4. *The End as Formal in Human Acts*

In all voluntary acts that which concerns the end is formal.
The reason is that every act receives its form and species according to the form of the agent.   The form of the will is its
object, which is the good and the end [39].   Thus the end in
what pertains to operation is like the principle in the speculative
intellect [40].

5. *The* Movens *as Formal*

Closely related to the role of the end as being somehow
formal is the function of the cause which moves to the end.
Where there are two or more powers one moving the other,
the first mover, the highest power, that which tends to the
highest end, is formal with respect to the lower powers [41].
Lower powers do not have the perfection of virtue except
through participation from higher powers.   Since the higher
are formal with respect to the lower, as being more perfect,
that which is participated from the higher is formal in the
lower. Hence for the perfection of virtue in a potency as many
forms are required as there are higher principles with respect
to that potency [42].   Thus the will is formal with respect to all

---

[38] *Ibid.* a. 7 resp.; cf. q. 19, a. 2 ad 1.

[39] *De Car.* a. 3 resp.; cf. *S.T.* II-II, q. 23, a. 8.

[40] Cf. *S.T.* I, q. 60, a. 2 resp.; q. 82, a. 1 resp.   Though the end is said
to be formal, the comparison with the principle in the speculative intellect
suggests a causality which is rather efficient than formal, since the principle
is related to its conclusion in a demonstration as efficient cause to effect (Cf.
In Post. Anal. I, lect. 3, number 1 in the Leonine edition).

[41] *In II Sent.* d. 26, q. 1, a. 4 ad 5; *In III Sent.* d. 23, q. 3, a. 1, sol. 1;
d. 27, q. 2, a. 4, sol. 3 ad 2; *De Malo* q. 2, a. 11; *De Car.* a. 3 resp.

[42] Ad secundum dicendum quod inferiores vires non perficiuntur perfec-
tione virtutis, nisi per participationem perfectionis a superioribus. Cum autem
superiora sint formalia respectu inferiorum, quasi perfectiora, quod partici-
patur a superioribus in inferioribus formale est. Unde ad perfectionem virtutis in aliqua potentia tot formae exiguntur quot superiora sunt respectu illius
potentiae. Sicut ratio superior est quam concupiscibilis quasi ordinans ipsam.
Et ideo *prudentia* quae est perfectio rationis, est *forma temperantiae* quae
est virtus concupiscibilis. Similiter voluntas est superior ratione, secundum

the other powers, since it moves all [43].   Charity is formal with respect to the other virtues, since it commands and moves all to the last end [44].   The interior act of the will is formal with respect to the external act, of which the will is the efficient cause [45].   Since the will, moving all the other powers, is formal with respect to them, the disorder in the will is formal in original sin, as we have seen, and the rectitude of the will may be called formal in original justice.

6. *Forma Exemplaris*

Since prudence, charity, and grace are somehow formal with respect to the virtues and yet are not forms which are intrinsic, pertaining to the essence of the virtues, St. Thomas attempts frequently in the earlier texts to explain their causality as that of an exemplar whose perfection is shared by the lower powers.   There is more than a mere likeness involved: the lower powers somehow participate in the being of the higher, though they need not be of the same species as the exemplar, which has the perfection essentially, not merely by participation [46].   Though the habit of charity is not intrinsic to faith, it can be called the exemplary form, and there is some effect of charity which is intrinsic to faith [47].   What faith receives from charity is accidental according to its natural genus, but essential according to its moral genus [48].   Though the exemplary

---

quod actus rationis consideratur ut voluntarius et meritorius. Et ideo *caritas est forma prudentiae et temperantiae*. Similiter essentia animae est superior voluntate, inquantum ab essentia et voluntas et omnes aliae vires animae fluunt. Et ideo *gratia* quae est perfectio essentiae animae, constituens ipsam in esse spirituali, est *forma et caritatis et prudentiae et temperantiae*. Nec caritas esset virtus si esset sine gratia, sicut nec prudentia si est [sic] sine caritate, loquendo de virtutibus infusis ordinatis ad merendum, neque temperantia sine caritate et prudentia (*In III Sent.* d. 27, q. 2, a. 4 sol. 3 ad 2).

[43] *In III Sent.* d. 23, q. 3, a. 1 sol. 1; *De Car.* a. 3 ad 12.
[44] *In II Sent.* d. 26, q. 1, a. 4 ad 5; *De Malo* q. 8, a. 2 resp.; *De Car.* a. 3 resp.
[45] *S.T. I-II,* q. 18, a. 6; q. 20, a. 1 ad 3.
[46] *In III Sent.* d. 27, q. 2, a. 4 sol. 3 ad 1; *De Ver.* q. 14, a. 5 ad 1, 3.
[47] *De Ver.* q. 14, a. 5 ad 4.
[48] *Ibid.* q. 14, a. 6 ad 1.

causality remains in the explanation given in the *De Caritate,* the emphasis is shifting to efficient causality: the virtues are not generated in the likeness of charity, but somehow they operate in its likeness [49]. Charity is an *exemplar effectivum* [50].

7. *Other Uses of* Forma *and* Formalis.

Finally we may note a few other variations in the terminology. An act proceeding from a virtue is informed by the virtue [51], perfected in the manner of action [52] by a *forma superinducta* [53] which comes from the habit eliciting the act. Reason is formal with respect to the will in the act of election, which is substantially an act of the will, receiving from reason its order with respect to the end. St. Thomas invokes the general principle: « *Quandocumque autem duo concurrunt ad aliquid unum constituendum, unum eorum est ut formale respectu alterius* » [54]. Likewise reason is the commanding and moving principle from which the appetitive part receives its form, participating reason [55]. That which is the *ratio* of another thing is related to it as formal to material. Thus light is related to color; the end to that which is ordered to the end; principle to conclusion; act of the will to the exterior act. Since the two are related as form and matter, they form one: from color and light there is one visible object; the act of the will and the external act are one sin [56].

---

[49] *De Car.* a. 3 ad 6
[50] *Ibid.* ad 8.
[51] *In II Sent.* d. 24, q. 1, a. 4 ad 4; d. 28, q. 1, a. 1 ad 5.
[52] *De Ver.* q. 14, a. 7 resp.
[53] *Ibid.* q. 23, a. 7 resp.
[54] *S.T.* I-II, q. 13, a. 1 resp.
[55] *Ibid.* q. 60, a. 1 resp.; q. 61, a. 1 ad 1; q. 66, a. 2 resp.
[56] *De Malo* q. 2, a. 2 ad 5, 11.

CHAPTER TWO

CHARITY AS THE FORM OF THE VIRTUES

St. Thomas' explanation of how charity is the form of the virtues underwent a considerable development, and recent studies have set forth clearly the stages in the evolution of his teaching [1]. The causality of charity, which is described in the earlier works as efficient, final, formal, and somehow exemplary, is reduced in the *Summa Theologiae* to efficient causality principally, with some mention of finality. Moreover, there is a tendency in the texts to concentrate on the influence of charity on the acts of the other virtues, disregarding the thesis of the earlier texts that charity was the form somehow perfecting not only the acts, but also the virtues themselves [2]. There is no further need of studying these texts to settle any serious controversy in the matter, but the very substance of the texts is relevant to our study, and it seems necessary to present here the chief lines of development.

In the Commentary on the *Sentences* St. Thomas begins

---

[1] Dom ODON LOTTIN, O. S. B., *Principes de Morale* (2 vols., Louvain, 1947) esp. vol. 2, pp. 204-211. GEORGE P. KLUBERTANZ, S. J., « The Unity of Human Activity », *The Modern Schoolman* 27 (1950) 76-85.

For other studies of charity as the form of the virtues, see the works of Gilleman, Carpentier, Chenu, Deman, Falanga, Lottin, Lumbreras, Parente, Van Roey, Schultes, Simonin, and Urmanowicz listed in the bibliography.

[2] Dom LOTTIN in his solution of the controversy between those who held an intrinsic modification of the virtues themselves (CAJETAN, SALMANTICENSES, URMANOWICZ) and those who rejected this in favor of a purely extrinsic, moral influence (RIPALDA, VAN ROEY) speaks only in terms of the acts (*op. cit.*, pp. 210-211). Father KLUBERTANZ takes the dictum *caritas est forma virtutum* to mean « Charity is the form of the acts of the virtues » (*op. cit.*, pp. 77, 85), regards this as St. Thomas' consistent point of view, and in his discussion of the texts says nothing more of the statements to the effect that the virtues themselves are perfected by charity.

by pointing out a contrast between charity and grace as the form of the virtues. Whereas grace informs the virtues as that from which they have their origin, charity is the form of the virtues in what regards their acts, in so far as it gathers all the acts of the virtues to its own end, since its object is the last end. Thus in all potencies and acts which are ordered, that which regards the higher end gives a form to the art which is beneath it, whose act is directed to its end. Hence charity informs the virtues as one virtue informing another [3]. Certainly here the information pertains not only to the act, but also to the virtue. When it is said that charity is the form *ex parte actus* this qualification is opposed to *per modum originis*: charity is not a principle of the very *esse* of the virtues, as is the case with grace. It perfects them in relation to their operation, and the words *potencies, art,* and *virtues* indicate that he is speaking of a perfection of the virtues themselves.

Both faith and charity direct to the ultimate end exceeding the power of nature: faith by pointing it out, charity by giving an inclination to the end, as a natural form inclines to its end [4].

Charity is the *motor, finis,* and *forma* of the virtues. It is the *mover,* because the good which is its object is the end of the virtues, and it commands the acts of the lower powers and habits. It is likewise called the *mother* of the virtues, because it produces their acts from the conception of the end, which is like a seed. It is the end of the virtues, since the ends of the lower powers or habits are directed to the end of the higher. It is the *form* perfecting every virtue in the nature of virtue (*in ratione virtutis*) [5]. Lower powers are not perfected with the perfection of virtue except through participation of the perfection of the higher powers. Since the higher are formal with respect to the lower, as being more perfect, what is participated from the higher powers is formal in the lower. Hence for the perfection of virtue in a potency,

---

[3] *In II Sent.* d. 26, q. 1, a. 4 ad 5.
[4] *Ibid.* d. 41, q. 1, a.1 sol.
[5] *In III Sent.* d. 27, q. 2, a. 4 sol. 3.

as many forms are required as there are higher principles
with respect to that potency. Thus, since reason is higher than
the concupiscible power, prudence is the form of temperance.
Since the will is higher than reason considered as voluntary
and meritorious, charity is the form of prudence and temperance. Since the essence of the soul is higher than the will,
because the will and all other powers flow from the essence
of the soul, hence grace, which is the perfection of the essence
of the soul, constituting it in spiritual being, is the form of
charity and prudence and temperance[6]. This is one way in
which charity is the form of the virtues, but there are two
others, for both the mover and the end are somehow formal
in so far as the mover puts its mode in the instrument, and
those things which are relative to an end are directed according to the nature of the end (*ex ratione finis*)[7].

Charity is the *exemplary form* of the virtues : not merely
one which is represented by something, as a thing is the exemplar of its picture; but rather an exemplary form in whose
likeness something is made and whose being it participates.
Thus the Divine Goodness is the exemplary form of all goodness, and the Divine Wisdom of all wisdom. Such an exemplary form need not be of the same species as the things caused
by it, since participants do not always participate according
to the manner of that which is participated[8]. An exemplary
form can be numerically one with the agent and the end, though
an intrinsic form cannot[9].

Substantially the same doctrine is found in the *De Veritate*,
somewhat more fully developed. St. Thomas rejects as impossible the view that grace is the form of faith, and not charity, except in so far as it is essentially identical with grace.
Grace pertains to the essence of the soul, and virtue to a potency. Though the essence is the root of all the potencies,
yet they do not all flow equally from the essence : some are
prior and move others. It is necessary, therefore, that habits

---

[6] *Ibid.* ad 2.
[7] *Ibid.* sol. 3.
[8] *Ibid.* ad 1.
[9] *Ibid.* ad 4.

in the inferior powers be formed by habits in the superior.
Thus the formation of the lower virtues must be from some
higher virtue, not immediately from grace. Charity, then, as
the chief of the virtues, is commonly called the form of the
virtues. The explanation of the manner in which it is the
form is again that of two moving principles or agents which
are ordered to each other: that which is in the effect from
the higher agent is as it were formal; that which is from the
lower agent is as it were material. Since reason commands
the lower powers, the concupiscible and the irascible, in the
habit of the concupiscible that which is from the concupiscible,
namely a certain proneness to use somehow the objects of
desire, is quasi material in temperance; but the order and rectitude which come from reason are its quasi form. Since
faith is in the intellect according as it is moved and commanded
by the will, the element of knowledge is quasi material in it:
but its formation must be had from the side of the will. Accordingly, since charity is the perfection of the will, faith is
informed by charity. So it is with all other virtues as they
are considered by the theologian, as principles of a meritorious
act [10].

Charity is not an intrinsic form, not part of the essence
of faith, but is like an exemplary form whose perfection is
participated by the other virtues: what charity has essentially
faith and the other virtues have by participation. Though the
habit of charity is not intrinsic to faith, neither its substantial
nor accidental form, yet something of charity is intrinsic in
faith. The form which faith receives from charity is accidental according to the natural genus (*genus naturae*) but essential according to its moral genus (*genus moris*) [11].

What has been clear from the manner in which he has
spoken in these texts, St. Thomas states explicitly: there is
question of the information of the virtue, not merely of the
act. When a superior power is perfect, something of its perfection is left in the lower power. Thus, since charity is in

<hr>

[10] *De Ver.* q. 14, a. 5 resp.
[11] *Ibid.* ad 1, 3, 4; a. 6 ad 1.

the will, its perfection somehow flows into the intellect. Thus charity informs not only the act of the faith, but faith itself [12]. Formed and unformed faith are not two different habits, but they differ in their manner of acting, as perfect and imperfect habits [13]. Though two accidents do not form one, yet one accident can be perfected by another. Thus faith is perfected by charity [14].

In a single text of the *De Malo* charity is called the form and mother of all the virtues because it commands all. Thus, though it is a special virtue, if its proper object is considered, still according to a certain *diffusion of its command* it is common to all the virtues [15]. A text from the *De Virtutibus* on the analogous case of prudence reduces its influence to a kind of efficient causality. The right reason of prudence is not placed in the definition of a moral virtue as something of its essence, but as the cause which somehow produces it, or its cause through participation, for a moral virtue is nothing else than a certain participation of right reason in the appetitive part [16].

All of the elements of the earlier explanations remain in the *De Caritate,* but there is a noticeable trend to efficient causality. We must judge habits according to their acts. Hence, when that which pertains to one habit is formal in the act of another habit, necessarily one habit is as form of the other. In all voluntary acts that which pertains to the end is formal, since every act receives its form and species according to the form of the agent. But the form of the will is its object, which is the good and the end. Consequently, that which pertains to the end is formal in the act of the will. The acts of all other virtues are directed to the proper end of charity, which is its object, namely the highest good. Hence clearly in all the acts of all the virtues that which pertains to charity is the form. It is called *the form of all virtues in so far as*

---

[12] *Ibid.* a. 5 ad 9.
[13] *Ibid.* a. 7 resp.
[14] *Ibid.* a. 7 ad 5.
[15] *De Malo* q. 8, a. 2 resp.
[16] *De Virt. in Comm.* a. 12 ad 16.

all the acts of all the virtues are directed to the highest good
which is loved [17].

Charity is not an intrinsic form, not part of the essence
of the virtues, but an « informing form » which does not give
the virtue its proper species, but gives it the common species of
virtue, in so far as we speak of virtue as a principle of merit [18].

Charity is the exemplary form of the virtues, not because
they are produced in its likeness, but because they somehow
operate in its likeness [19].   It has not only the character of exemplar with regard to an act, but also an efficient and motive
power (*virtutem motivam et effectivam*).   An efficient exemplar (*effectivum*) is not without its copy, since it produces it
(*producit illud in esse*): thus charity is not without the other
virtues [20].   This text is somewhat ambiguous: in so far as it
refers to charity as producing the acts of the virtues, it agrees
with what has been said consistently; seemingly, however, St.
Thomas extends the notion to include the production of the
virtues, and his meaning is not clear.

The grace of God is called the form of the virtues in
so far as it gives spiritual being to the soul, so that it be capable
of receiving the virtues.   Charity is the form of the virtues
in so far as it forms their operations [21].

Finally in the *Summa Theologiae* we can observe the result of the two tendencies already noted: (1) charity is the
form of the virtues in so far as it forms their acts [22]; (2) its

---

[17] *De Caritate* a. 3 resp.   In the same text he repeats that charity is
the *mover* of all the virtues since it commands the acts of all; and the *mother*,
because from the conception of its end are producted the acts of all the
virtues.   For the same reason it is called the *root* of the virtues.

[18] *Ibid.* ad 18, 16, 3.

[19] *Ibid.* ad 6.

[20] *Ibid.* ad 8.

[21] *Ibid.* ad 19.

[22] ... Et ideo caritas dicitur forma fidei, *inquantum per caritatem actus
fidei perficitur et formatur* (*S.T.* II-II, q. 4, a. 3 resp.) ... Caritas dicitur
esse forma fidei *inquantum informat actum ipsius*. Nihil autem prohibet unum
actum a diversis habitibus informari, et secundum hoc ad diversas species
reduci ordine quodam ... (*Ibid.* ad 1).   Respondeo dicendum quod in moralibus
forma actus attenditur principaliter ex parte finis: cuius ratio est quia principium moralium actuum est voluntas, cuius obiectum et quasi forma est finis.
Semper autem forma actus consequitur formam agentis.   Unde oportet quod

influence on the virtues is reduced to efficient causality: the form of the act follows the form of the agent; charity is an efficient form, in so far as it imposes a form on all the virtues [23]. Though it is still called the end of the virtues, it is not properly their end: rather it directs all other virtues to its own end [24].

With regard to the development of St. Thomas' thought as it is revealed in this series of texts, we may make two observations. The first is that the reduction of the influence of charity on the virtues to efficient or moving causality in no way rejects the teaching that charity does cause an intrinsic modification of the act which it moves to its end. It was the realization that charity somehow perfected the acts of the other virtues which seems to have inspired the early efforts to explain how charity was somehow an exemplary form whose perfection was participated by its copy. Gradually it became clear that the causality must be explained as simply efficient; that like any other efficient cause which itself is extrinsic to the effect it produces, charity does produce a perfection intrinsic to the act which it moves to its end. Both Lottin and Klubertanz have contributed to the understanding of how the causality is to be explained, and of the nature of the effect which is intrinsic to the act moved by charity. Dom Lottin has applied the teaching on *intentio,* an act of the will directing other acts to the end, impregnating them with its own dynamism,

---

in moralibus id quod dat actui ordinem ad finem, det ei et formam. Manifestum est autem secundum praedicta quod per caritatem ordinantur actus omnium aliarum virtutum ad ultimum finem. Et secundum hoc *ipsa dat formam actibus omnium aliarum virtutum. Et pro tanto dicitur esse forma virtutum*: nam et ipsae virtutes dicuntur in ordine ad actus formatos (*Ibid.* q. 23, a. 8 resp.).

[23] ... Caritas dicitur esse forma fidei inquantum informat actum ipsius ... Semper autem forma actus consequitur formam agentis ... (*Ibid.*). Ad primum ergo dicendum quod caritas dicitur esse forma aliarum virtutum *non quidem exemplariter aut essentialiter, sed magis effective*: inquantum scilicet omnibus formam imponit secundum modum praedictum (*Ibid.* ad 1).

[24] Ad tertium dicendum quod caritas dicitur finis aliarum virtutum quia omnes alias virtutes ordinat ad finem suum. Et quia mater est quae in se concipit ex alio, ex hac ratione dicitur mater aliarum virtutum, quia ex appetitu finis ultimi concipit actus aliarum virtutum, imperando ipsos (*Ibid.* ad 3).

causing 'n them an intrinsic intentional mode of being, an accidental modification which ceases when the influence of the intention ceases [25].   Father Klubertanz, studying the unity of human action, has considered the case of charity and the virtues in the light of the teaching on *imperium* and the commanded act, *imperium* and *consilium,* and the act of choice.   These are only some of the examples of human activity in which there is an act proceeding from two or more powers and virtues, receiving the influence of all, having a unity of composition in which the effect of the higher principle is related to that of the lower as form to matter [26].

Secondly, it seems that one must say that according to St. Thomas charity informs not only the acts of the other virtues, but the virtues themselves.   We have already noted that this is true in the earlier texts [27].   Even in the *Summa Theologiae,* though the discussion is concerned explicitly with the formation of the acts, the formation of the virtues is implicit.   Thus, though we do find in the *Summa Theologiae* a corrective with regard to the kind of causality involved, limiting it to efficient causality and rejecting the earlier exemplary causality, there is no similar rejection of the earlier explicit teaching that the virtues themselves are informed by charity. Attention is directed to the acts because we are to judge the virtues according to their acts : they are called *virtues* (in the full theological sense) with respect to acts which are formed [28]. Unformed faith is not a virtue because it lacks the perfection due on the part of the will [29].   Formed faith receives an orientation to the good as it is the object of the will [30].   Formed and unformed faith differ as the perfect and the imperfect in

---

[25] LOTTIN, *Principes de Morale,* vol. 2, pp. 210-211.

[26] KLUBERTANZ, « The Unity of Human Activity », *The Modern Schoolman* 27 (1950) 75-103.

[27] *In II Sent.* d. 26, q. 1, a. 4 ad 5; *In III Sent.* d. 23, q. 3, a. 1 sol. 1; d. 27, q. 2, a. 4 sol. 3 et ad 2; *De Ver.* q. 14, a. 5 resp. et ad 9; a. 7 resp.; *De Car.* a. 3 resp.

[28] *S.T.* II-II, q. 23, a. 8 resp.

[29] *Ibid.* q. 4, a. 5 resp.

[30] *Ibid.* ad 1.

the same species [31].   Absolutely speaking, a true virtue directs
to the principal good of man.   A virtue is imperfect unless it
is referred to the final and perfect good [32].

We can hardly say, then, that St. Thomas meant in the
later texts to confine the formation by charity to the acts of
the other virtues.   The analogy constantly employed is that
of ordered movers.   It would not suffice to explain how in
the act we find the effects of two or more movers, as if the
moving principles converged upon the act, or exercised a parallel causality.   Rather, the lower virtue is impregnated with
the force of the higher : the first and principal mover has its
proper effect on the act *through* the subordinated movers which
are its instruments.   In the very operation, then, the lower
habit as well as the act receives the influence and the formation
of the higher virtues.   Moreover it seems necessary to say that
even as habits, and not merely in their acts, the virtues are
perfected by charity, participating its order with respect to the
final and perfect good.   In their very being they are in a more
perfect state, participating the order and perfection of a will
informed by charity.   It is not that charity informs the virtues as an accident, but that the perfection brought to the soul
by charity changes the proportion of act to potency involved
between the powers and their virtues.   By charity faith itself
— as faith — is not changed : but the subject of faith, the
soul, is changed, and the virtue of faith in such a soul participates the new perfection.   The nature of this intrinsic modification of the virtue is no more difficult to explain than that
of the act.   It is a modification of the moral genus of the virtue, in no sense affecting its *genus naturae*.   The virtue is a
perfect virtue because existing in the soul perfected by grace
and charity it participates the soul's orientation to its last end [33].

What, then, it to be said of the causality of charity in
both original and gratuitous justice?   First, there is a strict

---

[31] *Ibid.* ad 3.

[32] *Ibid.* q. 23, a. 7 resp.

[33] For a study of charity as form not only of the acts of the virtues,
but also of the virtues themselves, see P. LUMBRERAS, O. P., « Notes on the
Connection of the Virtues », *The Thomist* 11 (1948) 234-240.

formal causality which we have not considered, since we have
examined only the texts bearing on the special question of
charity as the form of the virtues.   As a habit perfecting the
will to render it capable of an act of love completely exceeding
the power of nature, inclining it to the act of charity, and making its act prompt and delightful, charity is a form, and its
causality is purely formal [34].   Secondly, charity exercises a twofold efficient causality.   It elicits its own acts of love, of which
it is the formal active principle [35], as any habit is said to be
an efficient cause of its act.   Moreover it moves all the acts
of all the other virtues to its own end, as we have seen, im-
posing upon them its own order.

The role of charity in justice, therefore, is twofold.   It
constitutes formally the rectitude of the will, the principal element of justice in so far as it concerns the powers of the soul.
It commands and moves all the other virtues to the end, to
God as the source of supernatural beatitude; and thus it maintains the order of all the lower powers subject to the will.
In original justice charity was perfect, and, as we have seen,
through the other virtues the lower powers were kept in complete subjection to reason and thus participated the perfect order of the highest part of the soul.

---

[34] *S.T.* II-II, q. 23, a. 2 resp. et ad 2; *De Car.* a. 1 resp. et ad 1, 10, 13, 17.
[35] *De Car.* a. 1 resp. et ad 13.

CHAPTER THREE

GRACE AS THE FORM OF THE VIRTUES.
THE CAUSALITY OF GRACE IN JUSTICE.

Grace, like charity, is called the form of the virtues, and to a certain extent its causality in justice is indicated by this formula. As we shall see, however, the notion of *forma virtutum* plays a less prominent role in the texts on the causality of grace than it did in those on charity. Let us examine the texts in order of time, gathering what we can first from the direct teaching on grace, and then considering what further light can be cast on our subject from the study of the analogies which St. Thomas suggests.

A. TEXTS ON THE CAUSALITY OF GRACE.

1. *The Commentary on the* Sentences.

The texts of the Commentary on the *Sentences* are concerned largely with two aspects of the causality of grace: as a form perfecting the essence of the soul, and as the form of the virtues.

Grace is an accident formally uniting the soul to its last end [1], cleansing it and making it pleasing [2], elevating the essence of the soul to a certain divine being, so that it may be fit for divine operations [3]. Though it belongs to the first species of quality, yet it is not properly a habit, since it is not

---

[1] *In II Sent.* d. 26, q. 1, a. 2 sol.
[2] *Ibid.* ad 4.
[3] *Ibid.* a. 3 sol.; a. 5 sol.

immediately ordered to act; but it is like a disposition (*habitudo*), as health is with regard to the body.   Accordingly Chrysostom says that grace is the health of the mind [4].

As a potency is the principle of a given operation only as it flows from the principles of a given essence, so also the perfection of the potency is able to inform an act in virtue of the grace perfecting the essence itself. Accordingly grace is said not only to make the essence of the soul pleasing, but to render its act pleasing, not as the proximate *informing* principle, but as the first, which elevates the nature to a higher being [5].

Grace differs essentially from the virtues. It is necessary that perfections be proportioned to the things perfected. Hence, as from the essence of the soul there flow potencies essentially different from it, as accident from its subject, and yet all are united in the essence of the soul as in a root; so also grace is the perfection of the essence, and from it flow the virtues which are the perfections of the potencies, essentially different from grace itself. In grace, however, they are united as in their origin, as different rays proceed from the same luminous body [6].

Charity is called the form of the virtues in a different way than grace. Charity is the form of the virtues in what regards their acts, in so far as it gathers all the acts of the virtues to its own end, since its object is the last end. But grace informs the virtues as that from which they have their origin, that is: because from grace itself somehow formally arise the habits of the virtues, diffused through the different potencies. That which has its origin from another draws its form and species from it, and remains in its vigor as long as it is connected with its origin. Therefore it is not necessary that grace be the same as charity, though charity can never exist without grace [7].

Many potencies flow from one essence, but the essence remains one. All are alike in what pertains to them in so far

[4] *Ibid.* a. 4 ad 1.
[5] *Ibid.* a. 3 ad 2.
[6] *Ibid.* a. 4 sol.
[7] *Ibid.* a. 4 ad 5.

as they are in such a nature, but they are distinguished according to the different natures of the potencies. So also many virtues flow from one grace. They are alike in being meritorious, which pertains to them as they arise from grace. They differ according to their proper natures in so far as they are virtues [8]. Grace is not the intrinsic form, constituting the virtues, but is as the principle from which the virtues originate formally (*a quo virtutes formaliter oriuntur*) [9]. Thus faith is formed by grace by means of charity [10], and grace is the form successively of charity, prudence, and temperance [11]. Charity is the form of the virtues, with which all the virtues are infused simultaneously. Grace is as a potential whole with respect to the virtues: from it somehow the virtues flow, as the potencies flow from the essence of the soul [12].

Justification in the sense of *iustificatum esse* is the formal effect of metaphorical justice, the rectitude which includes all the virtues, not as a whole which is universal, but as an integral whole. As the potencies flow from the essence of the soul, so the rectitude of the potencies flows from grace, which is the perfection of the essence. And among the potencies the will which moves the others, somehow gives them a rectitude. Accordingly, the first cause of the aforesaid justice is grace, and then charity, which perfects the will with respect to the end, from which rectitude is had. On this account, the justification itself and the remission of sins is the effect of general justice as of the proximate formal cause, but of charity and grace as of the causes of the proximate cause [13].

---

[8] *Ibid.* a. 6 sol.
[9] *Ibid.* a. 6 ad 3.
[10] *In III Sent.* d. 23, q. 3, a. 1, sol. 1 ad 3.
[11] *Ibid.* d. 27, q. 2, a. 4, sol. 3 ad 3.
[12] *Ibid.* d. 36, a. 2 resp.
[13] *In IV Sent.* d. 17, q. 1, a. 1 sol. 1 et ad 3. As I have noted above, pp. 87-88, this text is a somewhat strained effort to explain why justification has its name from *iustitia*, rather than from *caritas* or *gratia*. Hence justification is confined to the potencies, and grace is not its formal cause (as in later texts) but rather the cause of its proximate cause.

2. *The* De Veritate.

Substantially the same doctrine is found in the *De Veritate*. Grace is the formal cause of our gratuitous spiritual being [14], uniting the rational mind immediately with the ultimate end [15]. Through grace God inhabits the minds, and the mind clings to God himself through the love of charity [16]. By grace the soul shares in the Divine nature by a certain assimilation [17]. In the remission and expulsion of sin grace acts as a formal cause, not an efficient cause [18].

Grace is as the first perfection of the virtues; charity, the proximate perfection [19]. Grace is the form of the virtues, not as an essential part, but in so far as it formally completes the act of virtue. There is a threefold information of the act of virtue: by prudence, charity, and grace. Grace gives efficacy in meriting. Thus grace is said to be the form of charity and of the other virtues [20].

Along with this twofold function of grace as form perfecting the essence of the soul and as form of the virtues we find in the *De Veritate* a development of one of the distinctions of *gratia operans* and *cooperans* given in the Commentary on the *Sentences* [21]. Grace is *operans* in so far as it *informs* the soul; *cooperans* in so far as it *inclines* to the interior and ex-

---

[14] *De Ver.* q. 27, a. 1 ad 3; a. 5 ad 17.
[15] *Ibid.* a. 3 resp.; q. 28, a. 2 resp.
[16] *Ibid.* q. 28, a. 2 resp.
[17] *Ibid.* q. 27, a. 6 resp.
[18] *Ibid.* q. 28, a. 2 ad 8, 9.
[19] *Ibid.* q. 14, a. 5 ad 6.
[20] *Ibid.* q. 27, a. 5 ad 5; cf. a. 1 ad 7; a. 2 ad 6; a. 5 ad 9; a. 6 ad 7.
[21] ... Sed distinctio gratiae operantis et cooperantis proprie accipitur tantum prout pertinet ad statum vitae praesentis: unde dupliciter distingui potest. Uno modo ut per gratiam operantem significetur ipsa gratia, prout esse divinum in anima operatur, secundum quod gratum facit habentem; et per gratiam cooperantem significetur ipsa gratia secundum quod opus meritorium causat, prout opus hominis gratum reddit. Alio modo secundum quod gratia operans dicitur, prout causat voluntatis actum; et cooperans secundum quod causat exteriorem actum in quo voluntas completur, vel perseverantiam in illo. Et utroque modo cooperans et operans dicitur idem quod praeveniens et subsequens (*In II Sent.* d. 26, q. 1, a. 5 sol.).

terior act, and gives facility in persevering to the end [22]. Thus there are various effects of grace: it informs the soul, elicits the interior and exterior act, and somehow causes perseverance. There are ordered effects of one grace [23].

Finally, we may note some interesting and rather difficult texts of the *De Veritate* concerning the relation of the infusion of grace to the remission of sin and to the acts of free will involved in justification. The question whether the remission of sins precedes the infusion of grace is settled in terms of the kinds of causality involved. When one thing precedes and follows another according to different genera of cause, that is said to be prior absolutely which is prior according to a genus of cause which has priority in causality. The first cause is the end. Since the remission of sin, like the expulsion of the preceding form, is a disposition for the new form and therefore is reduced to material causality, the remission of sin is prior according to this genus of cause. The infusion of grace is prior in the order of formal causality, and since the form is numerically one with the end and specifically one with the efficient cause, this priority is absolute in the order of nature [24]. This much is clear. There is some obscurity, however, in St. Thomas' discussion of the relation of grace to the acts of free will.

There are three opinions as to whether the acts of free will precede the infusion of grace. According to the first opinion, the acts of free will naturally precede the infusion of grace. The acts involved are attrition and unformed faith, not contrition and formed faith. St. Thomas rejects the position as irrelevant; we are inquiring about the acts which are simultaneous with the infusion of grace, without which there can be no justification in adults. The second opinion holds that the acts are meritorious, informed by grace, and consequently following grace. However, they are naturally prior to the remission of sin, since grace effects (*operatur*) the re-

---

[22] *De Ver.* q. 27, a. 5 ad 1.
[23] *Ibid.* ad 2; cf. ad 17, 18.
[24] *Ibid.* q. 28, a. 7 resp.

mission of sin through these acts.   This, St. Thomas says, is
impossible.   That which causes through its operation causes
as an efficient cause.   That is impossible in this case, for an
efficient cause destroying something is in existence before that
which it destroys cases to exist.   It is impossible for grace to
be in the soul before sin has been remitted.   Therefore grace
does not cause the remission of sin by some operation, but by
information of the subject, which is caused by the infusion
of grace and the remission of sin.   Accordingly there is nothing
intermediate between the infusion of grace and the remission
of sin.   One must say, then, according to another opinion, that
there is a mutual priority.   With regard to the material cause
the acts of free will precede the infusion of grace naturally, as
the disposition of matter precedes the form.   With regard to
the formal cause, the opposite is true.   Similarly in natural
things the disposition of matter, which pertains to matter, is
prior to the substantial form from the point of view of the
material cause; but considering the formal cause, the substantial form is prior, in so far as it perfects both the matter and
the material accidents [25].

The difficulty in this text lies in St. Thomas' reason for
rejecting the second opinion: his argument seems to involve
a difficulty in his own position.   He holds that grace cannot
remit sin through its operation, since existence is prior to
operation.   One must suppose, then, prior to operation, the
coexistence of grace and sin in the soul, which is impossible.
But one may say similarly that acts which are dispositions
involve an operation which presupposes existence.   Grace must
be regarded, then, as existing prior to performing the acts which
are necessary dispositions for its existence.   We shall have
another occasion to note this difficulty when we consider the
texts on form and disposition.

---

[25] *De Ver.* q. 28, a. 8 resp.

3. *Other Texts Prior to the* Prima-Secundae.

The *Contra Gentiles* describes a twofold function of grace: it is a supernatural form and perfection added to man to give him a continual orientation to his end [26]; and it is the cause of love, faith, and hope [27]. There is no indication of the kind of causality involved [28]. Among the other scattered texts we may single out a reply to an objection in the *De Caritate*. As far as I have been able to observe, it is the only text after the *De Veritate* in which grace is called the form of the virtues: the grace of God is said to be the form of the virtues, in so far as it gives spiritual being to the soul, so that it may be able to receive the virtues; charity is the form of the virtues in so far as it forms their operations [29].

4. *The* Summa Theologiae.

Grace is a form, a supernatural quality perfecting the essence of the soul as a formal cause [30]; by it the Holy Trinity dwells in the soul [31], which participates in the Divine nature [32], is made pleasing to God [33] and united with Him [34].

By grace a man is the adopted son of God, worthy of eternal life [35]. Grace is a habit perfecting the essence of the soul in relation to a higher nature which man can participate [36],

---

[26] *C.G.* III, c. 150.

[27] *Ibid.* cc. 151, 152, 153.

[28] Nor does SYLVESTER OF FERRARA succeed notably in clarifying the matter. According to him, the causality is neither formal nor properly efficient. It may be called a kind of improper efficient causality or instrumentality. In the final analysis it is simply this: according to the order of Divine Providence, charity follows upon grace by a natural and necessary concomitance (In *C.G.* III, c. 151, Leonine edition vol. 14, p. 446).

[29] *De Car.* a. 3 ad 19.

[30] *S.T.* I-II, q. 110, a. 2 resp.; a. 4 resp.

[31] *S.T.* I, q. 43, a. 4 ad 2; a. 5 resp.

[32] *S. T.* I-II, q. 110, a. 3 resp.; a. 4 resp.

[33] *Ibid.* q. 111, a. 1 ad 1.

[34] *Ibid.* resp.

[35] *Ibid.* a. 114, a. 3 resp.; I, q. 24, a. 3 resp.

[36] *S.T.* I-II, q. 50, a. 2 resp.

a habit comparable with health, strength, and beauty in the
body [37].

Grace is presupposed to the infused virtues as their principle and root [38]. As from the essence of the soul flow its
potencies, which are the principles of operations, so from grace
itself flow the virtues to the potencies of the soul, by which
the potencies are moved to their acts. According to this, grace
is compared to the will as mover to moved, which is the comparison of rider to horse: not as accident to subject [39]. Grace
is the cause of faith (from the comparisons it would seem to
be somehow an efficient cause) [40] and in general the virtues and
gifts are effects of grace [41].

Like any other form, grace as an habitual gift has two
effects: the first is *esse,* the second is operation. Thus, in so
far as it heals or justifies, it is called *gratia operans*; in so far
as it is the principle of meritorious works, which also proceed
from the free will, it is called *cooperans* [42]. *Gratia operans*
and *gratia cooperans* are the same grace [43], distinguished by different effects. Five successive effects of grace are these: that
the soul be healed, that it will the good, efficaciously perform
the good which it wills, persevere in the good, and attain glory.
As causing the first is it prevenient with respect to the second;
as causing the second it is subsequent to the first. As one
effect is posterior to one and prior to another, grace may be
called prevenient and subsequent with regard to the same effect

---

[37] *Ibid.* q. 50, a. 1 resp.; q. 54, a. 1 resp.
[38] *Ibid.* q. 110, a. 3 ad 3.
[39] *Ibid.* q. 110, a. 4 ad 1.
[40] Ad tertium dicendum quod gratia facit fidem non solum quando fides
de novo incipit esse in homine, sed etiam quandiu fides durat: dictum est
enim supra quod Deus semper operatur iustificationem hominis, sicut sol
semper operatur illuminationem aeris. Unde gratia non minus facit adveniens fideli quam adveniens infideli: quia in utroque operatur fidem, in uno
quidem confirmando eam et perficiendo, in alio de novo creando.
Vel potest dici quod hoc est per accidens, scilicet propter dispositionem
subiecti, quod gratia non causat fidem in eo qui habet. Sicut e contrario secundum peccatum mortale non tollit gratiam ab eo qui eam amisit per peccatum mortale praecedens (*S.T.* II-II, q. 4, a. 4 ad 3).
[41] *S.T.* III, q. 7, a. 9 resp.
[42] *S.T.* I-II, q. 111, a. 2 resp.
[43] *Ibid.* ad 4.

as referred to different effects [44]. Grace suffices for man in all
things by which he is directed to beatitude. Some of these it
accomplishes itself, immediately, such as to make pleasing to
God; some it accomplishes by means of the virtues, which flow
from grace [45].

Finally, we may note some details of the teaching on justification. Some preparation is required for habitual grace as
a disposition for the form [46], a disposition caused by God himself [47]. In the instant of justification the disposition for grace
consists in a single movement of free will moved by God, an
act by which simultaneously a man turns to God and detests
his sin, a single act proceeding from many virtues: faith,
charity, filial fear, humility, according as one commands and
another is commanded [48].

We may reduce the teaching on the causality of grace to
a threefold function: information of the soul, emanation of the
virtues, and meritorious operation through the virtues. The
first is clearly formal causality, and although the enumeration
of the formal effects varies somewhat through the series of
texts, the doctrine is constant. The third function is clearly
efficient causality. It does not appear clearly in the text of the
Commentary on the *Sentences,* where the emphasis is rather
on grace as the form of the virtues. Beginning in the *De Veritate* this aspect is evident. In so far as it is *cooperans,* grace
inclines to the interior and exterior acts, and is said to elicit
these acts. In the discussion of justification, the operation of
grace through the virtues is reduced to efficient causality and
opposed to its information of the soul. In the *Summa Theologiae* there is a clear distinction between two effects of grace,
as of any form: *esse* and operation. With regard to the first
and third functions of grace, then, there is no problem: the

---

[44] *Ibid.* a. 3 resp.
[45] *S.T.* III, q. 7, a. 2 ad 1.
[46] *S.T.* I-II, q. 112, a. 2 resp.
[47] *Ibid.* ad 3.
[48] *Ibid.* q. 113, a. 3 resp.; a. 4 resp. et ad 1; a. 5 resp.; a. 6 resp. et ad 3;
a. 7 resp. et ad 1, 2, 4; a. 8 resp. et ad 1, 2.
For a full study of the question, see MAURIZIO FLICK, S. J., *L'attimo
della giustificazione secondo S. Tommaso* (*Analecta Gregoriana*) Romae, 1947.

former is clearly formal causality, the latter clearly efficient. As to the second function, the role of grace in the origin or emanation of the virtues, the doctrine is obscure.

The one constant element in the texts is this : the virtues flow from grace as potencies flow from the essence of the soul. In the earlier texts grace is called the form of the virtues : not their proximate informing principle, but the first principle, elevating the nature to a higher being; giving them their form and species as *meritorious* virtues; it is not an intrinsic form constituting the virtues, but a potential whole, the principle from which they originate formally. In the *Contra Gentiles* grace is simply described as the cause of love, faith, and hope. In the *Summa Theologiae* it is called the principle and root of the infused virtues, and examples given to illustrate suggest efficient causality, without affording any solid basis for a conclusion concerning grace itself. One further hint is given in the texts on justification, in which the act of free will in the instant of justification is as the ultimate disposition to grace.

Beyond this, as far as I can discover, there is no evidence of what kind of causality is involved in the emanation of the virtues from grace. We may turn now to consider the analogies suggested by St. Thomas : first, the emanation of the potencies from the essence of the soul; secondly, the relationship of form and disposition.

B. PRINCIPAL ANALOGIES

1 .*The Soul and its Potencies*

Though there are many texts in which St. Thomas mentions that the potencies flow from the essence of the soul, only three articles are devoted directly to the question of the origin of the potencies. The first, in the Commentary on the *Sentences,* deals with the origin of the potencies from the essence of the soul, and the order in which one potency proceeds from another, but there is no indication of the kind of causality

involved [49].   In the *Summa Theologiae* we have a much more
thorough study, in which St. Thomas discusses separately the
questions of the order of the potencies, their procession from
the essence of the soul, and the origin of one potency from
another [50].   In the article dealing with the latter two questions
we have his only treatment of the problem of causality.

The question of the origin of the potencies from the essence of the soul is reduced to the general question of the
origin of proper accidents from their subjects [51].   The solution
is found in the difference between substantial and accidental
forms.   In the first place, the substantial form causes to be
simply, and its subject is being in potency only.   On the
contrary, the accidental form does not cause to be simply, but
to be such, or so great, or somehow disposed; and its subject
is being in act.   Hence, whereas the substantial form has a
priority of act over its subject and causes its subject to be in
act, the subject has a priority of act over the accidental form
and causes it to be in act.   Thus, in so far as it is in potency,
the subject is susceptible of the accidental form; in so far as
it is in act, the subject is productive of it.   This is true only
of the proper and essential (*per se*) accident, for with respect
to an extraneous accident the subject is merely susceptible : the
productive principle of such an accident is an extrinsic agent.
Secondly, whereas matter is ordered to the substantial form,
the accidental form is ordered to the completion of the subject.

Since the subject of the potencies is either the soul or the
composite, which is in act because of the soul, all the potencies
flow from the essence of the soul as from their principle, for
an accident is caused by the subject in so far as the latter is
in act, and is received by the subject in so far as it is in
potency [52].

The subject is the final, somehow active, and material cause
of its proper accidents.   Thus, therefore, the soul is the end and

---

[49] *In II Sent.* d. 24, q. 1, a. 2 sol.
[50] *S.T.* I, q. 77, aa. 4, 6, 7.
[51] *Ibid.* a. 5.
[52] *Ibid.* a. 6 resp.

the active principle of all its potencies and is the subject of
some of them [53]. The emanation of the proper accidents is not
effected by a change (*transmutatio*) but by a natural consequence, as one thing naturally results from another, as color
from light [54]. Since this is the manner in which the potencies
flow from the soul, they are created simultaneously with it [55].

Two aspects of this teaching in the *Summa Theologiae*
are clear : first, the relation of soul to potency is a particular
case of the relation of subject to proper accident; secondly,
the soul is somehow the efficient cause of its potencies. Both
points are confirmed in other texts. Several texts describe the
potencies as the properties or proper accidents of the soul [56].
The efficient causality of the essence of the soul with respect
to its rational potencies is indicated somewhat obscurely in a
text of the *De Malo* [57], but there is a strong confirmation of the
thesis on efficient causality in the discussion of the larger
question of subject and proper accident, especially in the commentary on the *Posterior Analytics* [58]. Here, in the treatment
of the various modes of predication *per se,* it is shown that
when *per* signifies a causal relationship, the causality may be
formal, or material, or efficient. The example of the last is
that of subject and proper accidents.

The clearest texts, therefore, indicate that the emanation
of the potencies from the essence of the soul is a particular

---

[53] Ad secundum dicendum quod subiectum est causa proprii accidentis et
finalis, et *quodammodo activa*; et etiam ut materialis, inquantum est susceptivum accidentis. Et ex hoc potest accipi quod essentia animae est causa
omnium potentiarum sicut finis et sicut principium activum; quarundam
autem sicut susceptivum (*Ibid.* ad 2).

[54] Ad tertium dicendum quod emanatio propriorum accidentium a subiecto non est per aliquam transmutationem; sed per aliquam naturalem resultationem, sicut ex uno naturaliter aliud resultat, ut ex luce color (*Ibid.* ad 3).
Cf. a. 7 ad 1.

[55] *Ibid.* a. 7 ad 1.

[56] *De Spir. Creat.* a. 11 resp.; *De Malo* q. 4, a. 4 resp. et ad 3; *De
Anima* a. 12 resp. et ad 15.

[57] Ad septimum dicendum, quod ipsae potentiae rationales derivantur ab
essentia animae in quantum est agens naturae; et ideo esse susceptivum peccati derivatur ad potentias ab essentia animae (*De Malo* q. 4, a. 4 ad 7).

[58] *In Post. Anal.* I, lect. 10, numbers 7, 8 (Leonine edition vol. 1,
p. 178 a-b); cf. lect. 13, no. 3; lect. 14, no. 2.

instance of the emanation of proper accidents from their subject. Moreover, both in the particular treatment of the soul and its potencies and in the general discussion of subject and proper accident, the causality which we have been attempting to determine is efficient causality. Finally, we may note that the evidence of the texts themselves is confirmed by the interpretations of representative commentators [59].

It is hardly necessary to observe that when we speak of the « clearest texts » in this matter the adjective is relative. The whole question of the emanation of the potencies from the essence of the soul remains obscure. St. Thomas seems hesitant with his « *quodammodo activa* » and his commentators have labored to elucidate his teaching without great success. Cajetan explains that there is question of a special kind of efficient causality, without any intervening *actio* [60].

John of St. Thomas, admitting that there is something

---

[59] Cf. *Cajetan, In S.T.* I, q. 54, a. 3, no. 16 of the commentary (Leonine ed. vol. 5, p. 49 b); q. 77, a. 1, no. 8 (p. 239 b); q. 77, a. 6, no. 8 (p. 247 b). JOHN OF ST. THOMAS, *Cursus Philosophicus Thomisticus* (ed. Reiser, Romae, 1933) vol. II, *Naturalis Philosophia*, P. I, q. XII, Appendix « De Dimanatione », pp. 267b-270b; vol. III, *Nat. Phil.* P. IV, q. 2, a. 2, pp. 65b-67b. Cf. also among the modern authors E. HUGON, O. P., *Philosophia Naturalis* (Paris, *imprimatur* 1922) 523-524; JOSEPH DE FINANCE, S. J., *Être et agir* (Paris, 1945) 212.

[60] ... Et ad primam instantiam, de causatione accidentis a substantia, dicitur quod nullum accidens causatur a substantia immediate *per operationem mediam*. Cum hoc tamen stat quod multa accidentia consequuntur substantiam et in genere *causae effectivae,* et materialis, *per modum naturalis sequelae.* Et hoc modo substantia est causa suarum passionum et potentiarum (*In S.T.* I, q. 54, a. 3, no. 16).

... Similiter non obstat (i. e. it does not conflict with the principle that potency and act are in the same genus) quod anima sit principium suarum passionum, quas ponimus accidentia: quia nec activum nec passivum earum est principium essentialiter ad eas ordinatum: sed habet modum activi *per naturalem quandam resultantiam,* et rationem passivi in hoc quod sustentat eas inhaerentes sibi (*Ibid.* q. 77, a. 1, no. 8).

Responsionem ad tertium diligentissime notato, quoniam ex ea solvuntur multae difficultates: scilicet et quomodo substantia est immediate causa effectiva; et quomodo causa effectiva non potest impediri: et quomodo aliquid agit in seipsum: et alia huiusmodi, quae in suis locis solvimus (the Leonine editors refer to the passages which I have quoted above); utendo hac distinctione de causa activa per actionem mediam, et sine aliqua media actione per solam naturalem resultationem; hoc enim modo activa multa habet quae aliis impossibile est convenire (*Ibid.* q. 77, a. 6, no. 8).

of formal causality in the emanation of the potencies from
the soul [61], in addition to the final and material causality which
are obvious, struggles to solve the real difficulty concerning
the efficient causality.   There is no real efficient causality
without *efficientia* and *actio*.   Nor does it do any good to say
that they result or flow (from the essence), for this is playing
with words.   We are trying to find out what that resulting
and that emanation is if it is not efficiency, and how the nature
is said to produce and cause its properties if it does not reach
them by efficient causality [62].   Rejecting Suarez' explanation
that the emanation is a true and proper action of the nature,
distinct from the action of the *generans* by which the substance
is produced, he holds that the emanation is the very action of
the *generans,* which reaches both the substance and the properties, and which is called emanation with respect to the essence because the latter is the reason why the action of the
agent does not cease in the substance, but passes farther on
to the properties.   It is called *naturalis resultantia,* that is:
a passage of the action to a farther term because of its connection with that term, and hence it is said to be somehow
active [63].

Since we are not concerned here with evaluating the interpretations of later writers, nor with attempting to make a
further development of the theology of St. Thomas, we may

---

[61] ... Imo aliquid habet de causa formali, quatenus ipsa essentia est ratio
formalis, propter quam connectuntur et conveniunt ipsi tales passiones; ratio
autem formalis ad causalitatem formalem pertinet (*op. cit.,* vol. 3, p. 65 b).

[62] *Ibid.* p. 66 a.

[63] Itaque emanatio entitative est ipsa actio generantis, quae substantiam
et proprietates attingit, denominative vero inducit formalitatem dimanationis
respectu essentiae, quia est medium seu ratio ipsa essentia, ut actio agentis
non in substantia sistat, sed ulterius ad proprietatem transeat. Et dicitur
ab ea dimanare propria passio, quia se habet ut ratio et medium, a quo
generatio habet attingere ipsam propriam passionem, et non sistere in substantia. Et vocatur naturalis resultantia id est transitus actionis ad ulterio-
rem terminum propter connexionem cum illo, et ideo dicitur quodammodo
activa. Iste modus probabilior est, quia salvat veram et propriam efficientiam
respectu propriarum passionum, sed non distinctam ab actione generantis,
ne cogamur ponere duplicem actionem respectu propriae passionis, alteram
ab essentia, alteram a generante, vel negare quod generans influat et attingat ipsas passiones (*op. cit.* vol. 3, p. 67 ab).

be content to conclude that there is some indication of efficient causality of the soul in the origin of the potencies, but that the teaching remains very obscure. When we seek to apply this theory to grace and the virtues, according to the analogy which we have noted, the difficulties and the obscurity increase, for the basic argument for the causality of the soul with respect to its potencies no longer holds strictly. There is no longer question of substantial and accidental form, nor, properly speaking of subject and proper accidents. Grace is not a substantial form, nor is it the subject of the virtues. It is difficult enough to make the necessary adjustments in an analogy in which the teaching on one analogate is clear. Even that minimum clarity is wanting here, and there is little to be gained by advancing farther into the gathering darkness.

2. *Form and Disposition*

At the outset we may say that the teaching on form and ultimate disposition casts little additional light on our subject. In fact, the theological texts regarding the ultimate disposition are generally clearer than the purely philosophical discussions. As Father Hoenen has pointed out, the philosophical texts do not present a clear and consistent teaching, and there is need of a thorough study of the matter [64]. In our present consideration it will be sufficient to examine the theological texts which are concerned directly with our question, to see whether the comparison of grace and the act of free will in the instant of justification with the substantial form and ultimate disposition in natural generation calls for some revision of our notion of the causality of grace with respect to the virtues.

Briefly the problem is this. We have seen that an act of free will in the instant of justification is required as a disposition for the infusion of grace, in order that man be moved in accordance with the freedom of a rational creature. This act of free will is related to grace as the ultimate disposition is related to the substantial form. It would seem to be implicit

---

[64] P. HOENEN, S. J., *Cosmologia* (ed. 4, Romae, 1949) 561-563.

in this teaching that the infused virtues which are the immediate principles of that act are also required as dispositions. What, then, is the causal relationship between the form and the dispositions which are simultaneous with it? Some have held that it is formal causality [65], and there seems to be some textual foundation. If this is the case, we must revise somewhat our description of the causality of grace with respect to the virtues, which to this point has appeared to be somehow efficient or active. On the other hand, those who follow the interpretation of John of St. Thomas would find no difficulty here, since he holds that the ultimate disposition is a proper accident of the new subject [66]. The causality of the form with respect to the disposition is the same as in all cases of proper accidents, somehow efficient or active [67].

We shall confine our discussion to the texts on justification in the Commentary on the *Sentences,* the *De Veritate,* and the *Summa Theologiae.* Moreover, we are concerned only with the texts which treat the act of free will in the instant of justification. The question of the remission of sins is different: though the expulsion of the old form is somehow reduced to a disposition of the matter, it is effected immediately by formal causality and it does not involve the problems connected with the ultimate disposition in the strict sense.

In the Commentary St. Thomas rejects three proposed explanations: we cannot say that the acts of free will precede the infusion of grace and the remission of sins as unformed acts, because there is question not of preparatory acts but of those which enter into the substance of the justification; nor that they are midway between the infusion and the remission, since nothing intervenes between the infusion of grace and the

---

[65] On these grounds Father VOLLERT has criticized Bittremieux's explanation of the mutual causality involved in grace and original justice as he conceives it: BITTREMIEUX speaks of an efficient cause and its disposition, citing *De Ver.* q. 28, a. 8; Vollert maintains that the text is fatal to Bittremieux's theory, since it has to do with formal, not efficient causality (*op. cit.,* p. 382, note 61).

[66] JOHN OF ST. THOMAS, *op. cit.,* vol. 2, pp. 588-599; esp. pp. 590-591.

[67] E. HUGON, O. P., *op. cit.,* pp. 165-167.

remission of sin; nor that they follow both, for they would not be required for justification if they did not have some causality with respect to it. Accordingly it must be said that in some way the infusion of grace and the remission of sin precede, and in some way the act of free will. This is clear from the similar case in natural generation, which is the term of alteration. In the same instant alteration terminates in the disposition which is necessity, and generation terminates in the form. Yet in the order of nature each somehow precedes the other: the disposition which is necessity precedes the form in the order of material cause; but the form is prior in the order of formal cause. In this way that perfect quality is also the formal effect of the substantial form, according as the substantial form is the cause of accidents.

Consequently since those acts in the very justification of the sinner are in their own way as the ultimate disposition for the reception of grace, they precede in the way of material cause, but follow in the way of formal cause. Hence nothing prevents their being formed, since this pertains to the nature and perfection of formal being, just as qualities which are introduced simultaneously with the substantial form are somehow formed by the substantial form. Just as that quality before its consummation and the introduction of the form was not formed, but unformed; so it is also with the act of free will, but if it is continued, it is perfected through the infusion of grace.

There is no difficulty here, for though it is in some way the same according to its natural genus, it is not the same according to the moral genus. It happens that the same act according to natural genus is an act of virtue, and an act of vice according to the moral genus, as is clear in the case of one who on his way to church changes his intention from evil to good [68].

---

[68] ... Et ideo dicendum est quod aliquo modo gratiae infusio et culpae remissio praecedunt; aliquo autem modo praedicti motus: quod patet ex simili in generatione naturali quae est terminus alterationis. In eodem enim instanti terminatur alteratio ad dispositionem quae est necessitas et generatio ad formam. Et tamen secundum ordinem naturae utrumque est prius altero

Prescinding from all other considerations which would be of importance in a study of the teaching on ultimate disposition, let us observe what is said here of the causality of the form with respect to the disposition. At first sight it would seem that the causality is formal. By now, however, the sense of « formal » and « formation » involved in this text is familiar : it is the same as in the early texts on charity and grace as the form of the virtues, a causality which seems to be somehow formal because there is a communication of perfection, but which in the parallel series of texts on charity and grace comes to be recognized as being rather efficient causality.

It is one thing to say that the form is prior in the order of the formal cause, and another thing to say that it is the formal cause of the disposition. The order of the formal cause is also the order of the efficient and final cause [69] : the three coincide, and hence this priority is absolute : it is the order of excellence and dependence in being. From the identity of the order of formal and efficient causes one could argue equally well that the form is the efficient cause of the disposition, if this form of argument were well founded. Actually it is not. Grace is formal with respect to the free act as a substantial form is formal with respect to the quality which it causes :

---

aliquo modo; quia dispositio quae est necessitas, praecedit formam secundum ordinem causae materialis; sed forma est prior secundum ordinem causae formalis. Et secundum hunc modum illa qualitas consummata est etiam formalis effectus formae substantialis, secundum quod forma substantialis est causa accidentalium.

Et ideo cum isti motus qui sunt in ipsa justificatione impii, sint quasi dispositio ultima ad gratiae susceptionem suo modo, praecedunt quidem in via causae materialis, sed sequuntur in via causae formalis. Et ideo nihil prohibet eos esse formatos, quia hoc ad rationem et perfectiónem esse formalis pertinet : sicut qualitates quae introducuntur simul cum forma substantiali, quodammodo formantur per formam substantialem. Et sicut qualitas praedicta ante sui consummationem et formae introductionem non erat formata, sed informis; ita etiam est de motu liberi arbitrii, si tamen continuatus in fine perficiatur per gratiae infusionem.

Nec est inconveniens; quia etsi sit aliquo modo idem secundum genus naturae, non tamen est idem secundum genus moris. Contingit enim unum motum secundum genus naturae esse virtutis et vitii secundum genus moris, sicut patet de illo qui eundo ad Ecclesiam mutat intentionem de malo in bonum (*In IV Sent.* d. 17, q. 1, a. 4 sol. 2).

[69] *Ibid.* sol. 1; cf. *De Ver.* q. 28, a. 7 resp.

the analogy carries us back again to the causality of subject
with regard to proper accident, which we have seen to be
efficient in some sense.   And the description of what grace
does for the act, giving it a new form according to a moral
genus without changing its natural genus, takes us back again
to the texts on charity and grace as form of the virtues.   There
is no strict formal causality here.

The same is true in the text of the *De Veritate*, which
we have analyzed in the series of texts on the causality of grace
earlier in this chapter [70].   The body of the article is much more
restrained than that of the Commentary: especially notable is
the disappearance of the term *formalis effectus formae substantialis*, which was applied to the disposition in the earlier text.
Moreover the replies to two objections indicate in what sense
formalis is to be understood in the whole discussion.   Contrition is said to be from grace as from that which informs it,
and thus it follows that with regard to the formal cause grace
is prior [71].   The answer to the fourth *in contrarium* is remark-
able.   The objection is that the effect of an efficient cause is
never a disposition to the efficient cause, which it follows *in via
motus,* for in the same order a disposition precedes that to
which it disposes.   Since grace, as a habit, is an efficient cause
of the act of contrition, the act cannot be a disposition for grace.
The answer is doubly interesting: first, because it is an example
of an evasion which seems to leave the difficulty intact; secondly, because it brings out clearly the sense of « *formalis* ».
St. Thomas says that just as the act formally perfects the
potency, so that which is left in the act from the habit is formal
with respect to the substance of the act, which is afforded by
the potency.   Thus the habit is the formal principle of the
formed act, although with respect to the formation it has the
character of efficient cause [72].   Here in the *De Veritate* we are

---

[70] *De Ver*. q. 28, a. 8 resp.

[71] Ad primum quod in contrarium obiicitur, dicendum, quod contritio
est a gratia sicut ab informante: et ita sequitur quod in ratione causae
formalis gratia sit prior (*Ibid.* ad 1 in contr.).

[72] Sed Contra: «...4. Praeterea, effectus causae efficientis nunquam est
dispositio ad causam efficientem, quia in via motus sequitur efficientem; cum
tamen in eadem via dispositio praecedat id ad quod disponit. Sed contritio

still moving in the atmosphere of texts in which « *formalis* » is being used improperly of a cause which is rather efficient than formal. I believe that the relation of these texts to the series on charity and grace as form of the virtues is obvious.

We have already called attention to a difficulty in this article of the *De Veritate*. St. Thomas rejects the opinion that grace effected the remission of sin through the formed meritorious acts involved in justification: his reason is that an efficient cause must exist in order to operate, and if grace expelled sin by operating, the operation would intervene between the infusion of grace and the remission of sin. There seems to be a similar objection to his own position: acts of which grace is the efficient cause cannot be a disposition for grace, since grace must be regarded as existing first, then operating; and thus the operation of grace intervenes between its infusion and the disposition required for its existence. It is substantially the same objection which St. Thomas evades in the reply which we have just considered.

Significantly, then, it would seem, he approaches the whole question from a different point of view in the *Summa Theologiae*. With regard to the other elements which we have been observing, we have already seen how in the *Summa Theologiae* the term « *forma virtutum* » is not used in connection with grace, and when it is applied to charity it designates properly efficient causality. With regard to the problem of priority among the elements of justification, the point of view consistently is that of God, the efficient cause of justification.

---

se habet ad gratiam sicut effectus causae efficientis ad suam causam efficientem. Ergo contritio non est dispositio ad gratiam; et sic idem quod prius. *Probatio mediae.* Habitus et potentia ad idem genus causae reducuntur, cum habitus suppleat quod potentiae deest. Sed potentia est causa actus in genere causae efficientis. Ergo et habitus. Sed gratia comparatur ad contritionem sicut habitus ad actum. Ergo contritio comparatur ad gratiam sicut effectus ad causam efficientem.

Ad quartum dicendum, quod sicut actus formaliter perficit potentiam; ita id quod ex habitu relinquitur in actu, est formale respectu substantiae actus, quam potentia ministrat: et sic habitus est *formale principium* actus formati, *quamvis respectu formationis habeat rationem causae efficientis* (*Ibid. Sed Contra,* fourth objection and reply).

Though there is question of a disposition for the infusion of grace [73], there is not a single mention of « ultimate disposition » as such, nor is there any wrestling with the mutual causality in terms of formal and material cause. In the one case in which there is question of a priority of disposition, it is considered not so much in relation to the form, as to the action of the agent [74].

Thus the particular inquiry which we have made into the texts on the act of free will as the disposition in the instant of justification reveals nothing which would necessitate a revision of earlier conclusions concerning the causality of grace with respect to the virtues. Directly these texts concern not the virtues, but the acts formed by the virtues. Difficulties in the earlier texts with regard to an operation intervening between the infusion of grace and the act which is its disposition would not apply to the unique efficient causality by which the virtues emanate from grace, a causality which does not involve a *motus* or *operatio*. In answer to the question with which we undertook this inquiry, then, we may say that there is no evidence from the texts on the disposition for grace which would indicate a true formal causality of grace with respect to the virtues. As far as there is any indication of the nature of that causality, we must say that it is somehow efficient or active.

We may conclude, therefore, as follows concerning the threefold causality of grace. In so far as it perfects the essence of the soul its causality is strictly formal. As the principle from which the virtues proceed it is somehow active or efficient. As the first principle of meritorious operation it exercises a strictly efficient causality.

---

[73] *S.T.* I-II, q. 112, a. 2 resp.

[74] Ad secundum dicendum quod dispositio subiecti praecedit susceptionem formae ordine naturae: sequitur tamen actionem agentis, per quam etiam ipsum subiectum disponitur. Et ideo motus liberi arbitrii naturae ordine praecedit consecutionem gratiae, sequitur autem gratiae infusionem (*Ibid.* q. 113, a. 8 ad 2). Cf. *Ibid.* q. 20, a. 1 ad 3.

CHAPTER FOUR

THE NATURE, UNITY, AND CAUSES
OF ORIGINAL JUSTICE

A. THE NATURE OF ORIGINAL JUSTICE

As we have observed earlier, one cannot settle the question concerning the causality of grace in original justice simply by proving that grace was part of original justice and therefore was its formal cause. It is necessary to consider what kind of whole is involved and in what sense one may speak of the formal and material elements which constitute it.

Original justice was the perfect rectitude of human nature, the complete subjection of the body and the lower powers of the soul to reason, and of the reason to God. It was the perfect health, the harmony of a nature whose parts were in perfect order, a habit properly disposing a nature composed of many elements. Thus St. Thomas describes it as a gift of grace whose power was not confined to the higher part of the soul. It was diffused to the lower parts of the soul, which by virtue of that gift were kept completely subject to reason; and it extended even to the body, in which nothing could happen to oppose the union of body and soul as long as that gift remained [1].

---

[1] Quia vero per peccatum gratiae donum privatur, oportet idem considerare in peccato quod consideratur in dono gratiae, quod tollitur per peccatum. Fuit autem in principio conditionis humanae quoddam donum gratuitum primo homini divinitus datum non ratione personae suae tantum, sed ratione totius naturae humanae ab eo derivandae, quod donum fuit originalis iustitia. Huius etiam doni virtus non solum residebat in superiori parte animae, quae est intellectiva, sed diffundebatur ad inferiores animae partes, quae continebantur virtute doni praedicti totaliter sub ratione; et ulterius usque

Original justice, then, was not a simple perfection. It was a perfection, a rectitude, which was diffused through the whole of human nature, participated diversely by the elements of that nature. Like original sin, the disorder of the whole nature, original justice had a unity. It was, however, a unity not of nature but of order. To understand how it was constituted we must understand this kind of unity.

B. The Unity of Order

Since the unity of order is a common and extremely important aspect of human action, St. Thomas takes care to explain its nature. « One » is said in the way in which « being » is said. Being simply is substance, but being in some respect (*secundum quid*) is an accident or being of reason. Hence those things which are one in substance are one simply, and many in a certain respect. Thus a whole in the genus of substance, composed of its integral or essential parts, is one simply : for the whole is being and substance simply, but the parts are beings and substances in the whole. Those things, however, which are diverse in substance and one accidentally are simply diverse, and one in a certain respect : as many men are one people, and many stones one heap. This is the unity of composition or order. Similarly also many individuals, which are one in genus or species, are simply many, and one in a certain respect : for to be one in genus or species is to be one according to reason.

As in the genus of natural things some whole is composed of matter and form, as man is composed of soul and body, and is one natural being though he have a multitude of parts, so also in human acts, the act of an inferior potency is material

---

ad corpus, in quo nihil poterat accidere, dono praedicto manente, quod contrariaretur unioni ipsius ad animam. Et ideo rationabiliter hoc donum fuisset ad posteros propagatum, propter duo : primo quidem, quia consequebatur naturam ex Dei munere, licet non ex ordine naturae ; secundo, quia pertingebat usque ad corpus, quod per generationem traducitur ... (*De Malo* q. 4, a. 8 resp.).

with respect to the act of a higher, in so far as the inferior
potency acts in virtue of the higher which is moving it: for
thus the act of the first moving principle is formal with respect
to the act of the instrument. Hence it is clear that the command and the commanded act are one human act, just as a
certain whole is one, but is many according to its parts [2].

This unity of order is characteristic of human action.
Though man would seem to have several specifically different
actions, according to his different potencies and habits, still
there is a unity of action in any one man, since all his operations proceed from the first action of the will [3]. There is a
unity of interior and exterior acts: in so far as the moral
goodness or evil of the latter depends on the former, they
form one act, with a single perfection or deformity [4]. The

---

[2] *S.T.* I-II, q. 17, a. 4 resp. Cf. *C. G.* II, c. 58 (« Praeterea »): «... Esse
unum secundum ordinem non est esse unum simpliciter; cum unitas ordinis
sit minima unitas. *Ibid.* IV, c. 35: Fit autem unum ex multis, uno quidem
modo, secundum ordinem tantum: sicut ex multis domibus fit civitas, et ex
multis militibus fit exercitus. Alio modo, ordine et compositione: sicut ex
partibus domus coniunctis et parietum colligatione fit domus. Sed hi duo
modi non competunt ad constitutionem unius naturae ex pluribus. Ea enim
quorum forma est ordo vel compositio, non sunt res naturales, ut sic eorum
unitas possit dici unitas naturae.

[3] Respondeo dicendum quod unitas et pluralitas actionis potest ex duo-
bus considerari. Uno modo, ex parte subiecti agentis: et ex hoc consideratur
unitas seu pluralitas actionis secundum numerum. Sicut et quodlibet aliud
accidens habet numeralem unitatem vel pluralitatem ex parte subiecti ... Alio
modo, potest considerari unitas vel pluralitas actionis ex parte principii quo
agens operatur; et ex hoc actio dicitur esse una vel plures secundum speciem ... Considerandum tamen quod, si virtus quae est actionis principium,
ab alia superiori virtute moveatur, operatio ab ipsa procedens non solum est
actio, sed etiam passio; in quantum scilicet procedit a virtute quae a superiori movetur. In homine autem omnes virtutes sensitivae partis moventur
quodammodo a voluntate sicut a quodam primo principio. Et ideo et audire
et videre et imaginari et concupiscere et irasci non tantum sunt actiones,
sed etiam quaedam passiones procedentes a motione voluntatis: in quantum
scilicet homo ex propria voluntate ad praedicta progreditur. Et ideo, licet
in uno homine secundum diversas potentias et habitus videantur esse plures
actiones specie differentes; tamen, quia omnes procedunt ab una prima actione voluntatis, dicitur esse una actio unius hominis. Sicut si unus artifex
per multa instrumenta operaretur, una eius operatio diceretur (*De Unione
Verbi Incarn.* a. 5 resp.).

[4] *De Malo* q. 2, a. 2 ad 11, 12; *S.T.* I-II, q. 18, a. 6. Cf. *ibid.* q. 20,
a. 3 ad 3: Ad tertium dicendum quod, quando aliquid ex uno derivatur

most interesting example for us at present is the formation of the virtues by charity, which we have studied at length. The principle involved is the relation of ordered movers: the first mover is formal with respect to all the others. As we have seen, there is a blend of two kinds of causality, because there is a diffusion of a single perfection which is found essentially in one power and is participated analogously by all the lower powers. In the will alone do we find the virtue of charity, and here charity is strictly a formal cause. But in so far as charity moves the other virtues as an analogous cause impressing its order on each according to its mode, and thus in a sense informing them, giving them a further determination in their moral genus, it exercises a causality which we have seen to be efficient.

There is, then, an order in the potencies and virtues which are the principles of human action. Basically there is a natural order in the potencies themselves. In the order of nature, in which the perfect precedes the imperfect, the intellective potencies are prior to the sensitive, which they direct and command [5]. The higher potencies proceed first from the essence of the soul, and they are somehow the cause of the emanation of the others [6]. Proportionately, as we have observed in the texts on charity as the form of the virtues, there is an order of the virtues which perfect the potencies.

This theory of order plays an important part in the discussion of the essence of original sin. The formal and material elements of that sin are determined on the basis of two anal-

---

in alterum sicut *ex causa agente univoca,* tunc aliud est quod est in utroque: sicut cum calidum calefacit, alius numero est calor calefacientis, et calor calefacti, licet idem specie. Sed quando aliquid derivatur ab uno in alterum *secundum analogiam vel proportionem,* tunc est tantum unum numero: sicut a sano quod est in corpore animalis derivatur sanum ad medicinam et urinam; nec alia sanitas est medicinae et urinae, quam sanitas animalis, quam medicina facit, et urina significat. Et hoc modo a bonitate voluntatis derivatur bonitas actus exterioris, et e converso, scilicet secundum ordinem unius ad alterum.

For a study of the unity of human action see the article of Father KLUBERTANZ already cited.

[5] *S.T.,* I, q. 77, a. 4 resp.
[6] *Ibid.* a. 7 resp.

ogies. In one, the substance of the act is material and the
lack of order is formal. In the other, the disorder of the
highest power is formal, and the disorder of the lower powers
is material. This second analogy prevails in the description of
original sin. Since the will is the highest power, moving all
others, its rectitude was the cause of the rectitude of all the
other powers, and in original sin its deformity is the cause
of the deformity of the others. In this theory, the relation
of formal to material is that of *movens* to *motum*.

The unity of original sin, the unity of a disorder of the
whole nature, can be understood only by contrast with its positive counterpart, the order and harmony of original justice.
Original justice involved many elements, many particular perfections : grace in the essence of the soul, charity in the will,
temperance in the concupiscible power, and a certain disposition
in the body. Yet it was not merely an aggregation of many un-
related perfections. These many perfections, each in its own
way a kind of rectitude, were somehow one with the unity
of order, for the highest moved all the others to its end, and
all were united in the participation of that order with respect
to the last end.

C. Formal and Efficient Causality in Original Justice.

Since this is the kind of unity which was proper to original justice, what kind of formal and material principles must
be said to have constituted it? It seems that we can determine
the formal element of original justice at two levels, according
as we consider the first mover relatively or absolutely.

Within the realm of the potencies, the formal element
was the rectitude of the will. As we have seen, St. Thomas
makes a very limited application of this terminology to original
justice, but in so far as he does, it is the rectitude of the will
which is called formal. The rectitude impressed upon the lower
powers was material. Here, as in the analysis of original sin,
it is analogy of the ordered movers which prevails. We have

here the same blend of causalities which we have noted in the theory of the formation of the virtues by charity, for this is merely an application of that theory. Charity as a formal cause perfected the will, constituted its rectitude, a union with God and a constant orientation to God as the last end. Beyond this, in the diffusion of its command through the lower powers, impressing upon them a participation of its own order with respect to the end, charity was rather an efficient cause. Within the realm of the powers of the soul, then, the rectitude of the will, constituted by charity, was formal in original justice.

Can we go beyond this and say that absolutely speaking grace was the formal element? As far as the actual use of the term is concerned, certainly St. Thomas did not say this. If we regard the reality rather than the words, however, we can say that it is implicit in his teaching and that it would be a reasonable extension of his terminology. The principles are clear. It is the first mover which is formal, and among the created movers in the series of ordered causes sanctifying grace was the absolute first. Original justice was first of all in the essence of the soul: grace was the root and principle of the whole rectitude, the first source of the constant inclination to God as the last end, the source of charity itself and all the infused virtues, the first principle of the meritorious acts of all the virtues. Thus grace can be said to be formal as an absolute first mover among the created causes of original justice.

Having said, then, that grace was formal in original justice, what must we say of the kind of causality which it exercised? The answer has been provided by the texts on the causality of grace. In so far as it constituted the supernatural life, elevating the essence of the soul to a share in the Divine nature, grace was a formal cause in the strict sense. Here in the essence of the soul the perfection of grace is found in its fullness, a potential whole whose perfection is diffused through all the powers which can participate it. In that diffusion grace was an efficient cause: somehow an active cause of the procession of the infused virtues, strictly an efficient or moving cause in all meritorious operation.

We may turn back now to the question which served as the occasion for this study: Is grace the formal or efficient cause of original justice? In the sense in which the question was asked, perhaps one should say it was neither. It was both formal and efficient cause, with the distinctions and limitations we have noted. Saying, then, that grace was formal in original justice, we must limit its strict formal causality to the essence of the soul. Grace did not produce the whole of original justice by formal causality, for the diffusion of its perfection through the powers was the effect rather of efficient causality. It was not the efficient cause of the whole of original justice, but only of the rectitude of the powers of the soul. Saying that it was an efficient cause in this manner, we do not mean that grace was completely distinct from original justice as efficient cause from effect. We are concerned with the unity of order, in which all the ordered elements are related as cause and effect. The efficient causality of grace, then, does not impede its being part of that justice. If it did, the same would be true of the efficient causality of the will perfected by charity. We should have to say that since efficient cause and effect are completely distinct, original justice was either exclusively in the will or exclusively in the lower powers moved by the will, and in either case we should have to burn half of the texts.

Thus we may conclude our study of St. Thomas' theology of original justice, a theology which to be sure has its share of subtleties and obscurity. But patience with subtleties is indispensable for the man who would do any serious work in theology. And patience with the obscurity of a teaching which did not receive in all its details a final and complete clarification should seem reasonable to all who recall that even St. Thomas Aquinas was a man descended from Adam.

LAUS DEO SEMPER

BIBLIOGRAPHY

I. SOURCES.

S. Thomae Aquinatis, *Opera Omnia,* ed. E. Fretté et P. Maré. Paris, Vivès, 1872-1880. 34 vols.

—, *Opera Omnia* jussu impensaque Leonis XIII, P. M. edita. Romae, Typis R. Garroni, 1882-.

Tome: I: *Comm. in Arist. Peri Hermeneias et Post. Analyt.,* 1882.

IV-XII: *Summa Theologiae cum Comment. Thomae de Vio, Card. Caietani,* 1896-1906.

XIII-XV: *Summa contra Gentiles cum Comment. Sylvestris Ferrariensis,* 1920-1930.

—, *Opuscula Theologica,* Volumen I, De re dogmatica et morali, cura et studio R. A. Verardo, O. P., Taurini-Romae, Marietti, 1954. (I have cited the *Compendium theologiae ad fratrem Reginaldum*... according to this edition, pp. 13-138).

—, *Quaestiones Disputatae,* ed. R. Spiazzi, O. P. ... Romae, Marietti, 1949.

—, *Quaestiones Quodlibetales,* ed. R. Spiazzi, O. P., Romae, Marietti, 1949.

—, *Scriptum super Libros Sententiarum Magistri Petri Lombardi,* ed. P. Mandonnet, O. P. et M. F. Moos, O. P., Paris, Lethielleux, 1929-1947. 4 vols. (Moos edited vols. 3 and 4).

II. STUDIES.

D'Alès, A., « Justice primitive et péché originel, d'après un livre récent », *Nouvelle Revue Théologique* 50 (1923) 416-427.

Bittremieux, J., « La distinction entre la justice originelle et la grâce sanctifiante d'après Saint Thomas d'Aquin », *Revue Thomiste* 26 (1921) 121-150.

—, « Het geestelijk leven en de oorspronkelijke gerechtigheid », *Ons Geloof* 8 (1922) 112-121.

—, « De instanti collationis Adamo justitiae originalis et gratiae, Doctrina S. Bonaventurae », *Ephemerides Theologicae Lovanienses* 1 (1924) 168-173.

—, « De materiali peccati originalis juxta S. Thomam », *Divus Thomas* (Piacenza) 31 (1928) 573-606.

—, « Justitia originalis et gratia sanctificans. Doctrina Cajetani », *Ephemerides Theologicae Lovanienses* 6 (1929) 633-654.

Bouillard, H., S. J., *Conversion et grâce chez saint Thomas d'Aquin,* Paris, 1944 (Appendice: Date du Commentaire de saint Thomas sur l'épître aux Romains, pp. 225-241).

Boyer, C., S. J., *De Deo Creante et Elevante*[4], Romae, 1948.

BROGLIE, de, Guy, S. J., review of Gilleman, *Le primat de la charité ...*, *Gregorianum* 34 (1953) 538-540.

CAJETAN: see S. Thomas Aquinas, *Opera Omnia* (Leonine edition).

CARPENTIER, R., S. J., « Vers une morale de la charité », *Gregorianum* 34 (1953) 32-55.

CHENU, M.-D., O. P., « La surnaturalisation des vertus », *Bulletin Thomiste* 3 (1931-1932) 93*-96*.

—, « L'amour dans la foi », *Ibid.*, 97*-99*.

COPPENS, J., « Une controverse récente sur la nature du péché originel », *Ephemerides Theologicae Lovanienses* 1 (1924) 185-191.

CROMBRUGGHE, van, C., « De relatione quae existit inter iustitiam originalem et gratiam sanctificantem », *Collationes Gandavenses* 13 (1926) 110-114.

DEMAN, Th., O. P., « Eudémonisme et charité en théologie morale », *Ephemerides Theologicae Lovanienses* 29 (1953) 41-57.

—, review of Gaudel, « Péché originel », *Bulletin Thomiste* (1936) 625-632.

ESCHMANN, I. Th., O. P., « Studies on the Notion of Society in St. Thomas Aquinas. I. St. Thomas and the Decretal of Innocent IV, *Romana Ecclesia: Ceterum.* II. Thomistic Social Philosophy and the Theology of Original Sin ». *Mediaeval Studies* 8 (1946) 1-42; 9 (1947) 19-55.

FALANGA, A. J., *Charity the Form of the Virtues according to Saint Thomas* (Catholic University of America, Studies in Sacred Theology, Series II, 18) Washington, 1948.

FERNÁNDEZ, A., O. P., « Justitia originalis et gratia sanctificans juxta D. Thomam et Cajetanum », *Divus Thomas* (Piacenza) 34 (1931) 129-146; 241-260.

FERRARIENSIS, SILVESTER: see S. Thomas Aquinas, *Opera Omnia* (Leonine edition).

FINANCE, de, J., S. J., *Être et agir,* Paris, 1945.

FITZPATRICK, E. J., *The Sin of Adam in the Writings of St. Thomas Aquinas,* Mundelein, St. Mary of the Lake Seminary, 1950.

FLICK, M., S. J., *L'attimo della giustificazione secondo S. Tommaso* (Analecta Gregoriana 40) Romae, 1947.

GAGNEBET, M.-R., O. P., « L'amour naturel de Dieu chez saint Thomas et ses contemporains », *Revue Thomiste* 48 (1948) 394-446; 49 (1949) 31-102.

GARRIGOU-LAGRANGE, R., O. P., « Utrum gratia sanctificans fuerit in Adamo dos naturae an donum personae tantum », *Angelicum* 2 (1925) 133-144.

—, *De Deo Trino et Creatore,* Taurini-Romae, 1944.

GAUDEL, A., « Péché originel », *Dictionnaire de Théologie Catholique* XII¹, cols. 275-606.

GILLEMAN, G., S. J., *Le primat de la charité en théologie morale, Essai méthodologique,* (Musaeum Lessianum) Louvain-Paris, 1952.

—, « Théologie morale et charité », *Nouvelle Revue Théologique* 74 (1952) 806-820.

GILLON, L.-B., O. P., « Primacía del apetito universal de Dios según Santo Tomás », *Ciencia Tomista* 63 (1942) 328-342.

GLORIEUX, P., « Essai sur les Commentaires scripturaires de saint Thomas et leur chronologie », *Recherches de Théologie Ancienne et Médiévale* 17 (1950) 237-266.

HÉRIS, V., O. P., « L'amour naturel de Dieu d'après saint Thomas », *Mé-*

langes Thomistes (Bibliothèque Thomiste 3) Le Saulchoir, Kain, 1923:
pp. 289-310.

HOENEN, P., S. J., *Cosmologia*[4], Romae, 1949.

HOVE, van, A., « Heiligmakene gratie en oorspronkelijke gerechtigheid »,
Collectanea Mechliniensia 4 (1930) 423-435.

—, *De Erfzonde,* Brussels, 1936.

—, *Tractatus de Deo Creante et Elevante,* Mechliniae, 1944.

HUARTE, G., S. J., « De distinctione inter justitiam originalem et gratiam
sanctificantem », *Gregorianum* 5 (1924) 183-207.

HUGON, E., O. P., *Philosophia Naturalis,* Paris, 1922.

—, « De gratia primi hominis », *Angelicum* 4 (1927) 361-381.

—, « Utrum primus homo habuerit scientiam omnium », *Divus Thomas* (Piacenza) 30 (1927) 445-453.

IOANNIS A SANCTO THOMA, O. P., *Cursus Philosophicus Thomisticus,* nova
editio a B. Reiser, O. S. B., 3 vols., Romae, 1929-1936.

KLUBERTANZ, G., S. J., « The Unity of Human Activity », *The Modern
Schoolman* 27 (1950) 75-103.

KORS, J. B., O. P., *La justice primitive et le péché originel d'après S. Thomas* (Bibliothèque Thomiste 2) Le Saulchoir, Kain, 1922.

LABOURDETTE, M.-M., O. P., *Le péché originel et les origines de l'homme,*
Paris, 1953.

LOTTIN, O., O. S. B., « Les éléments de la moralité des actes chez Saint
Thomas d'Aquin », *Revue Néo-scolastique de Philosophie* 24 (1922) 281-
313; 389-429; 25 (1923) 20-56.

—, « La connexion des vertus avant saint Thomas d'Aquin », *Recherches
de Théologie Ancienne et Médiévale* 2 (1930) 21-53.

—, « Les théories du péché originel au XIIᵉ siècle », *ibid.* 11 (1939) 17-32;
12 (1940) 78-103; 236-274.

—, « Le traité du péché originel chez les premiers maîtres dominicains
de Paris », *Ephemerides Theologicae Lovanienses* 17 (1940) 27-57.

—, « Le péché originel chez Albert le Grand, Bonaventure et Thomas d'A-
quin », *Rech. Théol. Anc. Méd.* 12 (1940) 275-328.

—, « Le traité du péché originel chez les premiers maîtres franciscains de
Paris », *Eph. Th. Lov.* 18 (1941) 26-64.

—, *Principes de Morale,* 2 vols., Louvain, 1947.

—, *Psychologie et morale aux XIIᵉ et XIIIᵉ siècles,* Tome IV, *Problèmes
de morale,* troisième partie, I, Louvain, 1954.

LUMBRERAS, P., O. P., « Notes on the Connection of the Virtues », *The
Thomist* 11 (1948) 218-240.

MARTIN, R., O. P., « Les idées de Robert de Melun sur le péché originel »,
Revue des sciences philosophiques et théologiques 7 (1913) 700-725; 8
(1914) 439-466; 9 (1920) 103-120.

—, « Le péché originel d'après Gilbert de la Porrée († 1154) et son école »,
Revue d'Histoire Ecclésiastique 13 (1912) 674-691.

—, « La doctrina sobre el Pecado Original en la Summa contra Gentiles »,
Ciencia Tomista 10 (1914-1915) 389-400.

—, « Bulletin de théologie spéculative », *Revue des sciences philosophiques
et théologiques* 10 (1921) 646; 11 (1922) 705.

—, *La controverse sur le péché originel au début du XIVᵉ siècle. Textes
inédits* (Spicilegium Sacrum Lovaniense 10) Louvain, 1930.

MEERSCH, van der, J., « Het geestelijk leven en de oorspronkelijke gerechtigheid », *Ons Geloof* 8 (1922) 455-466.

—, « De distinctione inter justitiam originalem et gratiam sanctificantem », *Collationes Brugenses* 22 (1922) 424-431; 506-517.

MELCHIOR DE SE MARIE, O. C. D., « La justice originelle selon les Salmanticenses et saint Thomas d'Aquin », *Ephemerides Carmeliticae* 2 (1948) 265-304.

MICHEL, A., « La grâce sanctifiante et la justice originelle », *Revue Thomiste* 26 (1921) 424-430.

—, « Justice originelle », *Dictionnaire de Théologie Catholique* VIII², cols. 2038-2042.

NAULAERTS, J., « Quid est justitia originalis? » *Vie Diocésaine* 12 (1923) 550-554.

PARENTE, P., « Il primato dell'amore e San Tommaso d'Aquino », *Acta Pont. Acad. Rom. S. Th. Aq.* . . . 10 (1945) 197-211.

ROEY, van, E. Card., « De Caritate forma virtutum », *Eph. Théol. Lov.* 1 (1924) 43-65.

—, *De virtute charitatis quaestiones selectae*, Malines, 1929.

ROUSSELOT, P., S. J., *Pour l'histoire du problème de l'amour au moyen âge*, Paris, 1933 (also in *Beiträge zur Geschichte der Philosophie des Mittelalters*, Band VI. Heft 6. Münster, 1908).

SANDERS, N., O. F. M., « De oorspronkelijke gerechtigheid en de erfzonde volgens S. Thomas », *De Katholiek* (1923) 400-410.

SCHULTES, R. M., O. P., « De caritate ut forma virtutum », *Divus Thomas* (Piacenza) 31 (1928) 5-28.

SIMONIN, H. D., O. P., « La primauté de l'amour dans la doctrine de saint Thomas d'Aquin », *La Vie Spirituelle*, Suppl. t. 53 (1937) [129] - [143].

STUFLER, J., S. J., « La justice primitive et le péché originel d'après S. Thomas... Par J. B. Kors, O. P. » (review) *Zeitschrift für katholische Theologie* 47 (1923) 77-82.

TEIXIDOR, L., S. J., « Una cuestión lexicográfica. El uso de la palabra JUSTICIA ORIGINAL, en Santo Tomás de Aquino », *Estudios Eclesiásticos* 6 (1927) 337-376; 8 (1929) 23-41.

—, « Algo acerca del pecado original y de la concupiscencia según santo Tomás », *ibid.* 10 (1931) 364-384.

—. « Suárez y S. Tomás », *ibid.* 15 (1936) 67-82.

TESSON, E., review of Gilleman, *Le primat de la charité en théologie*, in *Recherches de science religieuse* 42 (1954) 151-153.

URMANOWICZ, V., *De formatione virtutum a caritate seu de caritate qua forma virtutum secundum doctrinam sancti Thomae Aquinatis*, Vilnae, Libraria S. Adalberti, 1931.

VOLLERT, C. O., S. J., « Saint Thomas on Sanctifying Grace and Original Justice », *Theological Studies* 2 (1941) 369-387.

—, « The Two Senses of Original Justice in Medieval Theology », *Theological Studies* 5 (1944) 3-23.

—, *The Doctrine of Hervaeus Natalis on Primitive Justice and Original Sin*. . . (Analecta Gregoriana 42, Series fac. theol. B, n. 18) Rome, 1947.

INDEX OF TEXTS

INDEX OF AUTHORS

" ANALECTA GREGORIANA „

cura Pontificiae Universitatis Gregorianae edita

I. - Schwamm, H.: Magistri Ioannis de Ripa doctrina de praescientia divina. — 1930, in-8°, p. XII-228.

II. - Adamczyk, Stanislaus: De obiecto formali intellectus nostri secundum doctrinam S. Thomae Aquinatis. — editio altera correcta, 1955, in-8°, p. XVI-152.

III. - Druwé, Eugenius S. J.: Prima forma inedita operis S. Anselmi « Cur Deus homo ». — Textus, cum Introductione et notis criticis — 1933, in-8°, p. XII-150.

IV. - Bidagor Ramon, S. I.: La « Iglesia Propria » en España. Estudio historico-canonico. — 1933, in-8°, p. XXII-176.

V. - Madoz, José S. I.: El concepto de la Tradición en S. Vincente de Lerins. — 1933, in-8°, p. 214.

VI. - Keeler Leo W. S. I., The Problem of Error from Plato to Kant. — 1934, in-8°, p. 284.

VII. - De Aldama J. A., S. J.: El Simbolo Toledano. — 1934, in-8°, pag. 167.

VIII. - Miscellanea iuridica Iustiniani et Gregorii IX legibus commemorandis, cura Pont. Univ. Gregorianae edita. — 1935, in-8°, p. 185.

IX et X. - Miscellanea Vermeersch — Scritti pubblicati in onore del R. P. Arturo Vermeersch, S. I. — 2 vol., 1935, in-8° — I vol. p. XXIX-454; II vol. p. 406.

XI. - Bévenot M., S. J.: St. Cyprian's de Unitate. Chap. IV. — 1938, in-8°, p. LXXXV-79 et 6 tab.

XII. - Gómez Helin, L.: Praedestinatio apud Ioannem Cardinalem de Lugo. — 1938, in-8°, p. XII-191.

XIII. - Daniele, Ireneo: I documenti Costantiniani della « Vita Constantini » di Eusebio di Cesarea. — 1938, in-8°, p. 219.

XIV. - Villoslada, Riccardo G., S. I., Dr. Hist. Eccl.: La Universidad de París durante los estudios de Francisco de Vitoria O. P. (1507-1522). — 1938, in-8°, p. XXVIII-468.

XV. - Villiger, Iohann, Dr. Hist. Eccl., Prof. in Fac. Theol. ad Lucernam: Das Bistum Basel zur Zeit Iohanns XXII., Benedikts XII, und Klemens VI. (1316-1352). — 1939, in-8°, pag. XXVIII-370.

XVI. - Schnitzler Th.: Im Kampfe um Chalcedon. Geschichte und Inhalt des Codex Encyclius von 458. — 1938, p. IX-132, in 8°.

XXXIV. - Muñoz P., S. I.: Introducción a la síntesis de San Augustín. 1945, in-8°, p. 351.

XXXV. - Galtier P., S. I.: Le Saint Esprit en nous d'après les Pères Grecs. 1945, p. 290, in-8°.

XXXVI. - Faller O., S. I.: De Priorum saeculorum silentio circa Assumptionem B. Mariae Virginis. p. XII-135, 1946, in-8°.

XXXVII. - D'Elia P. M., S. I.: Galileo in Cina. Relazioni attraverso il Collegio Romano tra Galileo e i gesuiti scienziati missionari in Cina (1612-1640) — p. XII-127; 1947, in-8°.

XXXVIII. - Alszeghy Z., S. I.: Grundformen der Liebe. Die Theorie der Gottesliebe bei dem hl. Bonaventura. — 1946, p. 300. in-8°.

XXXIX. - Hoenen P., S. I.: La théorie du jugement d'après St. Thomas d'Aquin. — Editio altera, recognita et aucta, 1953, p. XII-384, in-8°

XL. - Flick M., S. I.: L'attimo della giustificazione secondo San Tommaso. — 1947, p. 206, in-8°.

XLI. - Monachino V., S. I.: La cura pastorale a Milano, Cartagine e Roma nel sec. IV. — 1947, in-8°, p. XX-442.

XLII. - Vollert C., S. I.: The Doctrine of Hervaeus Natalis on Primitive Justice and Original Sin. — 1947, p. 335, in-8°.

XLIII. - Hoenen P., S. I.: Recherches de logique formelle. La structure du système des syllogismes et de celui des sorites. La logique des notions « au moins » et « tout au plus ». — p. 384, 1947, in-8°.

XLIV. - Selvaggi Fil., S. I.: Dalla filosofia alla Tecnica. — La logica del potenziamento. — 1947, p. XII-278, in-8°.

XLV. - Klotzner Iosef., Dr. Hist. Eccl.: Kardinal Dominikus Jacobazzi und sein Konzilswerk. — 1948, p. 300, in-8°.

XLVI. - Federici Giul. Ces., S. I.: Il principio animatore della Filosofia Vichiana. — 1948, in-8°, pag. 220.

XLVII. - Nanni Luigi: La Parrocchia studiata nei documenti lucchesi dei secoli VIII-XIII — 1948, pp. XVI-234, in-8°.

XLVIII. - Asensio Felix, S. I.: « Misericordia et Veritas » — El hesed y'émet divinos: su influjo religioso-social en la historia de Israel. — 1948, pp. 344.

XLIX. - Ogiermann Helm. Aloysius, S. I.: Hegels Gottesbeweise. — 1948, pp. 230.

L. - Orban Ladislas: Theologia Güntheriana et Concilium Vaticanum. — Vol. II, 1949, in-8°, pag. 218.

LI. - Beck, G. J. Henry: The Pastoral Care of Souls in South-East France, during the Sixth Century. - 1950, in-8°, pag. LXXII-415.